More Praise for
Your Customer Rules!

"As Price and Jaffe cover so well in *Your Customer Rules!*, the concept of 'the customer is in charge' requires alignment throughout the entire organization, including support partners. They share many great stories that you can apply to make it easy for customers to work with you, positively surprise them, and address their other critical needs."

—Bert Quintana, chairman and CEO, Sitel

"Price and Jaffe bring to light a much needed and modern view of service strategy in a world where customers have unprecedented power and employee engagement is more important than ever. In the Me2B world, service flaws become magnified, viral, and destructive. Leaders and organizations can't hide. *Your Customer Rules!* will enable the delivery of a service experience that customers demand and employees will embrace using new mediums, technologies, and strategies."

—Scott Tweedy, vice president, customer service, T-Mobile

"Placing the guest at the center has always been Hyatt's focus, removing the roadblocks for our customers and for our associates. With *Your Customer Rules!*, Price and Jaffe capture seven critical customer needs to make this work. Their stories and frameworks will become the building blocks for other companies to sustain great customer experiences and increase customer loyalty."

—Sara Kearney, senior vice president, operations, Asia Pacific, Hyatt Hotel Corporation

"As Price and Jaffe so clearly describe in *Your Customer Rules!*, many businesses have forgotten who pays the bills. While the customer is not always right, the goal is to ensure that each customer is valued and provided with a great experience that makes them believe they are the central focus of the company. Price and Jaffe demonstrate the importance of the customer-centric focus with well-presented examples. They help provide ideas, tools, and measures that will help businesses of all sizes begin, sustain, and deliver on the benefits of a customer-centric focus."

—Jeff Robison, COO, WorldPay

"*The Best Service Is No Service* became a brilliant icon for leading and guiding the consumer customer experience community. In *Your Customer Rules!*, Price and Jaffe address the customer side of businesses, flipping the old B2B model with fresh insights from global customer experience leaders. Open at any place and you'll come away with solid ideas to improve how your company operates—a new icon in the making!"

—**Gary Hagel, chief commercial officer, Vodacom South Africa**

"Price and Jaffe continue to challenge business thinking on how to interact with customers. *Your Customer Rules!* is essential reading for the changes in business today."

—**Jane S. Hemstritch, board member, Commonwealth Bank Australia, Santos, and Lend Lease**

"Building on the success of *The Best Service Is No Service*, Price and Jaffe have come up with an equally challenging concept in *Your Customer Rules!*: why and how to reorient the entire company to recognize that the customer is (and always was) in charge. Using fun cartoons, good (and bad!) stories, and clearly laid-out steps, they give hope that the successful company types outlined in this book can create great customer experiences."

—**Jardon Bouska, chief operations officer, SafeGuard**

"The service industry needs to learn the clear guidance and inspiration in Price and Jaffe's new book, *Your Customer Rules!*, especially now in the era of mobility and integrated, interconnected platforms. The explosion of multichannel contacts and the change of customer behavior and expectations in this multi-contact channel, mobile, and social network world must be managed in totally different ways. The management of customer expectations will have a new meaning and importance for companies in the future. Service is what customers want to talk about, and they now choose their preferred channel and provide the requirements of their needs based on service."

—**Vicky Giourga, senior vice president, customer service, Home Shopping Europe**

YOUR **CUSTOMER** RULES!

Delivering the **Me2B** Experiences That Today's Customers Demand

BILL PRICE
DAVID JAFFE

JB JOSSEY-BASS™
A Wiley Brand

Cover design by Wiley
Cover image: © iStock.com/letty17

Published by Jossey-Bass
A Wiley Brand
One Montgomery Street, Suite 1200, San Francisco, CA 94104-4594 www.josseybass.com

Jossey-Bass books and products are available through most bookstores. To contact Jossey-Bass directly call our Customer Care Department within the U.S. at 800-956-7739, outside the U.S. at 317-572-3986, or fax 317-572-4002.

Wiley publishes in a variety of print and electronic formats and by print-on-demand. Some material included with standard print versions of this book may not be included in e-books or in print-on-demand. If this book refers to media such as a CD or DVD that is not included in the version you purchased, you may download this material at http://booksupport.wiley.com. For more information about Wiley products, visit www.wiley.com.

Library of Congress Cataloging-in-Publication Data

Price, Bill, 1950-
  Your customer rules! : delivering the Me2B experiences that today's customers demand / Bill Price, David Jaffe. — First edition.
    1 online resource.
  Includes bibliographical references and index.
  Description based on print version record and CIP data provided by publisher; resource not viewed.
  ISBN 978-1-118-95481-2 (pdf)—ISBN 978-1-118-95482-9 (epub)—ISBN 978-1-118-95477-5 (cloth)
1. Customer relations. 2. Customer services. 3. Consumer satisfaction. I. Jaffe, David, 1963- II. Title.
  HF5415.5
  658.8'12—dc23

                                                                        2014032520

Printed in the United States of America
FIRST EDITION
HB Printing   10 9 8 7 6 5 4 3 2 1

To Erika and Rachel
Rebecca and Patrick

CONTENTS

Preface

The past ten years have seen a profound change in business: The balance of power has shifted back to the customer; businesses are no longer in control—now your customer rules! When we wrote our first book, *The Best Service Is No Service*, in 2007 and '08, sites such as Facebook and Twitter were just emerging. No one understood the profound implications of social media, the Internet, mobile access, and other explosive new trends. No one predicted the profound shift in information and power in customers' hands.

Today it is critical to respond to this new world, or to anticipate it and get ahead of the pack. We decided it was time to write our next book. We no longer believe that *B2C* or *B2B* are accurate terms to describe the way companies and customers relate to each other. We now see only a *Me2B* model: The customer directs the relationship, and businesses need to think first and foremost from the customer's point of view.

At the same time, we've seen a trend toward poor consulting in the customer experience space, creating the risk that important insights that could help companies adapt and grow would be improperly dismissed as a flawed or trumped-up fad. The average customer experience consultant seems to be focused on repeated research around detailed change journey mapping and an obsession with measurement and monitoring. Others home in on culture or measurement and feedback systems to the exclusion of everything else.

We have nothing against customer feedback surveys, research groups, or analysis of the customer experience. Yet our observation is that the industry of customer experience is starting to be dominated by those with a vested interest in only one or two solutions. We believe that meeting customer needs in this new era where your

GLADYS LOVED SEEING HOW MANY CALL CENTRES SHE COULD PUT ON HOLD AT THE SAME TIME...

customer rules requires a holistic and integrated approach, and that companies can save time and money by not making this a "research and customer feedback" problem. We suspected that there were some underlying principles to the customer experience that had never been clearly articulated but whose guidance was needed. So we set out to prove that companies could put these new principles into practice.

Our first book focused on simplifying, automating, and eliminating customer interactions, and at the end offered ways for organizations to maximize the positive effect of interactions when they occurred. This time we wanted to dig a lot deeper into what was required to deliver a great experience at every point of contact from pre-sales through using the products or services. Both of us run cross-industry forums where members seek out customer best practices and bring them into discussions as case studies. We knew that few organizations, even those with great reputations, rarely do everything well for the customer. Our goal was to bring all those stories together to define what the ultimate customer experience—and the theoretical company behind it—might look like. With help from our global LimeBridge partners, we interviewed organizations that seemed to be doing things well and tried to distill out their "secret sauce." The more we researched, the more we observed dominant patterns, which we ultimately boiled down to the seven key customer needs we describe in this book.

We present both good and bad stories that illustrate these seven needs. We have no hesitation in naming the good companies or good stories. However, we have deliberately not named the protagonists in what we have called the bad stories. This is because some of them have been clients of ours and therefore we are restricted by contracts and confidentiality. Rather than name some and not others, we thought it fairer to leave them all unnamed and we hope you enjoy trying to work out who they are.

Our Unique Process

This remains a very unusual collaboration. We live on different continents and are usually sixteen hours apart: David in Melbourne, Australia, and Bill outside Seattle in Bellevue, Washington, in the United States. (David always tells Bill what his next day will be like!) We only got together once in the same room during the writing of this book. Everything else was done using Skype, shared Dropbox files, and other tools. The fact that we're able to work this way reinforces that, as in global business, incredible partnerships no longer need to be local.

We hope you enjoy exploring how your customer rules and the seven Me2B needs with us, learning from the many examples both good and bad that we've assembled here so that you can then build your own path to greatness.

October 2014   Bill Price
                                                                  David Jaffe

YOUR **CUSTOMER** RULES!

CHAPTER ONE

FROM B2C TO ME2B

Customer service today gets slammed by customers right and left. While technology offers the promise of highly customized, seamless customer experiences at limitless scale, few companies have fulfilled on that promise. Consumers seem to share the impression that service and sales interactions are getting worse, not better. In many industries, customers are complaining more, with Internet-enabled breadth and speed. To pull a few recent headlines:

> "Complaint-to-Compliment Ratio of MBTA Tweets Remains High."[1]
> "Npower Ranks Top for Moans: Customer Complaints Against Energy Giant Soar 25%."[2]
> "70% of Companies Ignore Customer Complaints on Twitter."[3]

In the utilities industry in Australia, for example, the volume of complaints to the central complaints body (the Ombudsman) has risen dramatically despite no significant change in customer numbers—doubling in five years, four times the rate of population growth. Similar complaint bodies in other countries such as the Office of Communications in the United Kingdom show complaint rates rising over the same period.

Despite billions spent to win customers' affection, we are only just exceeding the levels of customer satisfaction reported in the early 1990s. In addition, customer switching between providers is on the rise, often prompted by a poor customer service experience.[4] The companies that are lagging in customer experience perform poorly compared to customer experience leaders across a variety financial data points. For example, a Watermark Consulting study compared the six-year stock performance of customer experience leaders and laggards against the S&P 500, and found that leaders exceeded the S&P by 28 percentage points while laggards registered a 33 percent decline in stock value.[5]

As we all wait endlessly on hold with customer call centers across the world, only to keep repeating information to agents that we've given elsewhere in the purchase process, who can resist yearning for the good old days when mom-and-pop stores offered personalized and knowledgeable service? Perhaps selection and store hours were more limited, but at least business owners knew their customers as well as they did their products and were excited by both. Perhaps you can still remember going into the corner grocery store with Mom, watching with delight as the owner pulled out something special that he had ordered for her, along with a treat for you. Reconciling past and present creates a kind of cognitive dissonance that recalls a scene from the iconic '80s film *Back to the Future*, in which Michael J. Fox, transported via a plutonium-powered DeLorean back to 1955, stops dead in his skateboard tracks as he watches customers being waited on at the old full-service gas station.

What Used to Work, Doesn't Work Anymore

So what happened? Have our needs changed over the years, bringing customers and businesses out of sync? Or are companies today simply failing to deliver on the needs customers have always had?

Certainly, the landscape has changed. Today's businesses are bigger and incredibly more complex. Scale may have produced efficiency and economy, but it has distanced executives and management from their customers and from their frontline employees. Not only are businesses now headquartered in cities many miles from their customers, in an era of global operations the top executives may be in another country and speak another language. Senior management rarely spends time talking with customers, listening to their calls, or asking customer-facing staff for their take on what customers are saying. The bottom line is that scale has dissolved intimacy, and many organizations have forgotten the importance of moments of truth that required one-to-one interaction and connection.

Adding even more complexity, today's customer service operations have many moving parts that don't communicate with each other. The range of interaction channels, such as contact centers, SMS, co-browsing, the Internet, and social media, has proliferated. The net result is the omni-channel dilemma. While customers have clamored for new ways to deal with organizations, for example, via text messaging to take advantage of their always-at-hand smart phone, and while organizations have pressed ahead to open new channels, few of these channels have been integrated. This only increases customer frustration—and on top of that, support costs—a lose-lose scenario.

The Accenture Global Pulse, a study of customer attitude and behaviors across the world, reveals how frustrating this disconnect is for consumers.[6] On a scale from 1 ("not frustrating at all") to 5 ("extremely frustrating"), 23 percent of customers choose 4 and an incredible 66 percent choose 5 to describe their reaction to having to repeat the same information to multiple employees of a company or through multiple channels.

Customer relationship management (CRM), widely in practice today, is a flawed methodology that isn't working. Those who promoted it pushed technology solutions to control the relationship with customers. The very name *customer relationship management* reveals the heart of the problem. The organization should *manage* the relationship, the theory went. But customers were never asked if they wanted to be managed by organizations. And who would have asked to be managed? We'd argue that no one should *manage* a relationship; relationships are *shared* rather than managed. CRM has been flawed from the start, but is even more at odds with today's business climate.

The outcome of all this? Businesses continue to do stupid things that upset customers, like the ones captured in a U.K. survey: "Sending standard letters when I write an individual enquiry about something specific," "They make everything so complicated," and "Offering you the world when you're a potential customer and then treating you like crap when you're an existing customer."[7] Sound familiar?

Welcome to the Me2B World: Now Your Customer Rules!

Unsatisfying, clunky customer service experiences pose an even more serious threat to businesses' survival than they would have ten years ago. Today's customers have significantly more power. The Internet, social media, mobile access, and all the other recent dynamic changes have moved us far beyond the command-and-control era, when organizations could tell their customers what was best for them—while really aiming to increase short-term profits.

For many years, people have largely categorized businesses in two models, B2B and B2C. B2B organizations sell to other businesses; B2C organizations sell to mass-market consumers. (There's also the more complicated third model, B2B2C, where an intermediate business such as a reseller or broker sells to the consumer.) These models suggest that the business controls and directs the relationship: They go *to* the other business, or *to* the consumer. They hold the power and direct the relationship.

Meanwhile, in the past decades, we've seen these sweeping global changes:

1. Social networks via the Internet have forever changed the way organizations operate. Customers, whether individuals or businesses, have access to limitless information about competing goods and services. And for the first time customers now have the opportunity to influence thousands, or even millions, of other customers; they are helping each other, often trusting their peers instead of the companies themselves. We call this C2C communication.

2. We have entered the mobile age, where information travels with us and is at our fingertips. Customers can be anywhere and access Internet-sourced information, impacting decisions straight up to the point of sale.

3. Internet-enabled transactions, the cloud, Big Data, and other technologies are transforming business models. Whole industries are being disrupted, in many cases significantly lowering the barrier to entry. The handful of upstart companies that have created new ways to operate and are successfully delivering scaled, personalized omni-channel customer experience have raised the bar for legacy businesses saddled with old and expensive ways to operate.

4. The powerful Millennial generation is emerging as a customer base and has vastly different expectations of the buying experience. This generation has been raised on Amazon and Apple, as well as on the flexibility and power of rapidly growing C2C peer-to-peer sharing networks such as AirBnb, Uber, and Facebook. When they do act as consumers, they have higher standards for customer experience than their older siblings or parents and are less patient—and more willing to switch fast if treated marginally. That said, they are willing to remain brand or service loyal if treated well.[8]

All these trends add up to a new reality: Customers, not businesses, hold the power. The only business model today, therefore, is not B2C or B2B but Me2B. Customers own the relationships and determine how they want to interact with the business. Businesses must shift their thinking to drive decision making from the consumer's point of view. Repeat after us: *Me2B because the customer rules!*

There are some major implications of this reversal, threatening to some organizations but exhilarating and business defining to others.

- *Customers have significantly greater choice.* There is now so much information out there for consumers—online and offline, from their homes or when walking past stores—that this choice is now much wider than any one provider or company.
- *Customer feedback, wants, and desires are broadcast loud and clear.* No longer do organizations have to conduct outbound consumer tastes surveys, mall intercepts asking customers to answer questions while strolling around shopping centers, or other forms of expensive research. Customers are using a plethora of electronic mechanisms to tell their friends actively what they like and dislike, and to tell organizations what they think about them.
- *Companies can no longer hide poor products or service.* Third-party customer feedback sites encourage open postings and comments on others' experiences, and general social sites have proliferated as well. Any customer who encounters poor service can tell thousands of people in seconds, and since customers tend to trust other customers, even those they do not know, more than the companies themselves, the viral effect is amazing![9] YouTube views (and likes or dislikes) and other video options intensify these customer reactions, to the peril of organizations asleep at the wheel or in denial about their product or service performance.
- *Pricing is transparent without leaving home or having to visit multiple stores.* From their smart phones or tablets, thanks to comparison engines, customers know more about their choices than many sales clerks or product managers. Moreover, customers rebel when they encounter variable pricing by time of day or by customer segment. They seek the lowest possible price and have bots and applications to tell them when their

desired flight is cheaper or when they win a bid for a hotel stay at their preferred price.

This much more is clear: Businesses that fail to find ways to satisfy customer needs at scale—using all of today's channels and providing the sort of experiences we remember from the mom-and-pop days—will not survive.

Back to Fundamentals in the Me2B Era

Not all is lost. Some businesses today *are* thriving at delivering the experience that customers need. We call these customer experience heroes Me2B Leaders. They understand that the customer rules. They are outpacing their competition in sales growth, profitability, customer and employee retention, and other key metrics. Companies like Amazon, Apple, Disney, IKEA, John Lewis, Lego, Nordstrom, Southwest Airlines, USAA, and Virgin are household names and often appear in published rankings of best customer experience.[10]

However, some of the Me2B Leaders are younger, rapidly expanding companies like Shoes of Prey or companies well known in their own countries such as Vente-Privee in France or Yamato Transport in Japan, but less known outside their home markets.

We were motivated to write this book as a way to find out how these companies are succeeding while others struggle, and to help both new and legacy businesses adapt. We sought out many of these Me2B Leaders, interviewing managers, customers, and vendors and suppliers, adding secondary analyses including social chatter and what we call WOCAS, data showing "what our customers are saying."

The more we learned, the more our original hunch was confirmed: Me2B customers are still looking for the same things they always have. Fundamental customer service needs haven't changed. What has changed is businesses' ability to recognize and deliver on these needs. Now that your customer rules, delivering to the needs is more important and more complex since customers have more information and more choice for interaction methods.

Me2B Leaders, we've found, are creating experiences that don't just deliver a product but fulfill relationship needs that are fundamental and predate even the mom-and-pop era. They are by no means radical innovations. The innovation the Me2B Leaders have brought is in figuring out how to deliver these fundamentals in today's world of scale and channel complexity and to connect to the customer even with the tyranny of scale and distance that separates head offices from the front line and the consumer.

Customers today still want to be recognized and served as they would have been in their local corner store—but in a digital world, the shape of this service is entirely different. For example, customers who shop an online grocery store expect the website to remember their standard weekly order in the same way that the local butcher could reel off a customer's regular order. The medium is changed; the need has not.

As we studied these Me2B Leaders we saw a pattern emerge in the ways that these companies are recognizing and satisfying customer needs and building lasting relationships. We have called these the Seven Customer Needs for Me2B success. The language we use to describe them takes the customer's point of view:

1. You know me, you remember me.
2. You give me choices.
3. You make it easy for me.
4. You value me.
5. You trust me.
6. You surprise me with stuff I can't imagine.
7. You help me be better and do more.

The challenge of meeting these needs will guide the vital strategies that businesses need to adopt in order to sell and serve in the Me2B world. Over the course of this book we show you what they are and how they connect to fundamental *relationship* needs. We demonstrate how the Me2B Leaders are satisfying these needs. We also clearly illustrate via examples what success and failure look like and outline the obstacles to success.

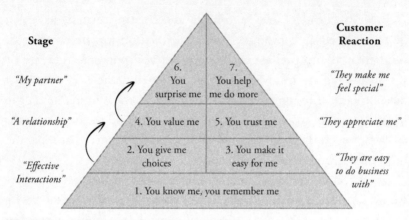

Figure 1.1   The Hierarchy of Customer Needs.

The seven customer needs are not created equal. Not unlike Maslow's famous hierarchy, they form a pyramid (see Figure 1.1). The first three (Know Me; Give Me Choices; Make It Easy) are fundamental to most interactions and form the bedrock for all Me2B relationships to deliver great customer experiences.

Companies that fulfill the next two needs (Value Me; Trust Me) are more mature in becoming Me2B Leaders; they truly see themselves in a two-way, meaningful relationship with customers, and they have recognized that customers do, and should, have more control. Those companies delivering the final two needs show greater maturity still. They need not deliver on these needs all the time, just in carefully chosen moments that make a powerful and meaningful impact on the customer and demonstrate a willingness to invest in relationships for the long term.

What Drives Me2B Leaders

As we analyzed the Me2B Leaders we asked why they were different from other organizations. Why did they seem more focused on these seven customer needs than other businesses? We started to look for common strategies driving the Me2B Leaders and began to classify these strategies and the companies into common groups.

Our conclusion was that there are four types of organizations that take different paths to become customer-focused:

- The Naturals
- The Challengers
- The Rebounders
- The Defending Dominators

All the Me2B Leaders had one or more of these types. In Chapter Nine, we describe each of the groups, giving examples of the organizations that fall into the groups and of the strategies that they are pursuing.

The Foundations of Me2B Success

Many of the Me2B Leaders we analyzed have had the luxury of building their organizations from scratch, making it much easier to incorporate customer-centricity into their DNA. However, the vast majority of companies need to transform their organizations from within to respond to the challenge of meeting today's customer needs. Throughout the book, we look at obstacles that existing companies will have to overcome if they wish to change. We also describe some of the foundations that need to be put into place if organizations are to deliver the seven customer needs at scale:

- Streamlined processes.
- Integrated channels.
- Customer-oriented culture that recognizes business is personal.
- Energized, empowered people.

Those companies at the pinnacle of Me2B leadership seek a common bond with customers, the hallmark of true relationships. Me2B companies value customer relationships above all, and recognize financial success and stability is best achieved by rethinking business through the lens of the customer's experience.

Perhaps that's why we've found that recent research into the success factors for *personal* relationships, even marriages, applies surprisingly well to the business environment. We have built on some of that work in this book. To succeed in the Me2B era, big business is once again becoming personal, and it turns out that all those things that support quality customer relationships matter to *employee* relationships, too.

Now it's time to start the journey to Me2B success!

CHAPTER TWO

YOU KNOW ME, YOU REMEMBER ME

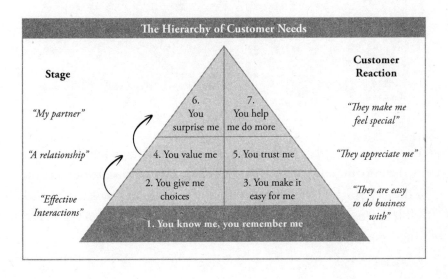

The Hierarchy of Customer Needs

Stage

"My partner"

"A relationship"

"Effective Interactions"

6. You surprise me

7. You help me do more

4. You value me

5. You trust me

2. You give me choices

3. You make it easy for me

1. You know me, you remember me

Customer Reaction

"They make me feel special"

"They appreciate me"

"They are easy to do business with"

HE WAS A STICKLER FOR THE SECURITY TEST

Customers today demand to be recognized and known by the companies they do business with, throughout every interaction and every stage in the relationship. Companies that meet this need fulfill the first customer need for Me2B success, which makes all the others possible: *You know me and you remember me.*

Amazon, a customer experience pioneer, is without a doubt the most high-profile, end-to-end example of a company that knows and remembers its customers—and we don't only think that because Bill was Amazon's first global VP of customer service; the company's track record speaks for itself. Beyond fast shipping, low prices, and incredible selection, Amazon is famous for delivering great experiences. For example, unlike many other online retailers today, Amazon has always employed customer cookies (data stored in users' web browsers) to speed sign-in and enable customers to access their accounts with ease.

Unfortunately, despite all the progress in centralized customer databases, repositories, and interaction histories, most organizations today keep their information in separate silos and are unable to recognize their customers across all interactions or channels. In the good old days, the best of the local merchants or bankers or candlestick makers either knew all their customers by sight and by name or found a way to make it seem so. Customers rewarded these merchants with repeat business and favorable mentions to friends and family. Intimacy and personal memory allowed small companies to retain this knowledge of the customer. Even today, many local companies operate this way.

But for the majority of businesses, small has turned into giant, local into global, and personal into unknown, and companies have largely lost the ability to know and remember the customer. As organizations have grown, they have built and maintained customer data in separate repositories, sometimes with different markers that don't let them connect the dots. For example, they might show Clifford Smith in one database, Cliff Smith in another, and C. G. Smith in yet another. It's true that some companies do manage to cleanse their data so as to combine all three examples as one customer, but many don't know how to do it or don't even bother. Some companies even count these three variations as three different customers!

In the good old days of small and intimate organizations, there was less specialization into departments. People played multiple roles and therefore retained customer knowledge between interactions. Today, specialization has resulted in different employees knowing only certain details about the customer. Organizations today may not even remember the customer from interaction to interaction. They lack short-term memory, let alone long-term connections.

Success with "You Know Me, You Remember Me" goes beyond collecting data. Some organizations have been particularly smart in finding ways to use those data to serve customer needs. Even back in the good old days, not all shopkeepers remembered their customers well or exploited that knowledge. The same is true today.

Me2B Leaders—by no means just Amazon—are finding ways to cut across their departmental and product silos to deliver the consistent experiences that today's customers want. The Know Me, Remember Me need has many different facets, presenting many opportunities to embrace and satisfy your customer, as we'll explore in this chapter. In Table 2.1 we summarize examples when the need is met well and when it is not met.

For an intuitive understanding of why this first customer need is fundamental to quality business relationships, simply look to personal relationships. "You Know Me, You Remember Me" is fundamental to life partners, parents and children, and friends. When partners share a mutual understanding of prior commitments, needs, desires, and history, it is much easier for them to connect and support each other in the relationship. Each of us wants to be appreciated, as well, and be able to say, "Thanks, you did what I asked you to do" or "I'm so glad that you remembered X (be that an anniversary or shared story)." In their 1996 research on long-term satisfying marriages, Kablow and Robinson determined that expressions of appreciation and communication were two of the seven crucial drivers of marriage success. Those processes both require knowledge of the partner and the things they are doing. The relationship research shows that knowing one's partner well enough to communicate with them and show

Table 2.1 The Customer's Experience of Success and Failure

You Know Me, You Remember Me Success	You Know Me, You Remember Me Failure
You know me everywhere and all the time.	You don't recognize me when I return or switch channels.
You never ask me something twice.	You force me to repeat myself.
You know my preferences.	Can't you remember that I've already told you what I like and dislike?
You predict my needs intelligently.	You keep suggesting things I don't want and can't even use!
You know me and mine.	But we're the same household!
You know when I don't want to be known.	Leave me alone!

appreciation of them is critical to success in relationships, and all these ingredients are needed to sustain customer relationships in the business world, too.

You Know Me Everywhere and All the Time

Whenever and wherever a customer interacts with an organization, Me2B Leaders understand and apply the history of the relationship to each interaction. They know which products and services the customer has today and has purchased in the past. They know the history of touch points with that customer across all channels—retail stores, online, customer care centers, social media, in-person meetings, and any other point of communication.

Tracking customer-initiated interactions is important, but the company equally needs to track its own outreach. Wherever possible, it's also useful to know not just when something happened but the details of the interaction. For example, it's *somewhat* helpful to know that a customer called yesterday. It's *very* helpful to know that they called to complain and then declined the agent's proposed solution. It's also important to know if they left a comment online or in a forum or at the hotel concierge desk, and then sent e-mail message about the same unresolved issue.

All of these *dots*, to use the industry term, should reside in a central information database, but most important is that they are current, relevant, and available during all other touch points along the way. For example, someone who has just spent twenty minutes brooding over an online purchase and then calls the sales center loves it when the sales agent greets them by name and says, "Looks like you've been exploring our new product; how can I help you?" For once, it isn't necessary to start from scratch.

Bad Stories: Fractured Communication

The age of CRM software in the cloud makes it readily accomplishable to "know me everywhere and all the time," yet many companies aren't set up for it. For example, a leading travel retailer in the United States, United Kingdom, and Australia has grown dramatically in recent years through great service and competitive pricing. Despite that success, it has a giant hole in its ability to know the customer: Each store still runs an independent booking and customer database. Change stores and the relationship starts from scratch. This can get awkward since customers can't check on bookings at other stores and each store only knows about its own transactions with this customer. As a result, this model runs the risk of delivering less-than-perfect customer experiences. The disconnected system may be working for the company now, but leaves it vulnerable to a competitor that provides great travel service *and* knows its customers wherever they choose to connect.

We could list many organizations where the branch, contact center, and Internet channels have limited or even no visibility to each other. For example, when David went into a retail store with the intention of purchasing a phone, he was told that no special offers were available for him. Within twenty-four hours, the same company called him offering special deals on new phones if he renewed his contract. David explored this with company management, who admitted that the offers were not shared across the channels and that the call center had no way to see branch conversations and vice versa. In this company, the channels were so separate that products and discounts weren't available consistently. We have seen examples in utilities, banks, insurers, and health insurers where the offers were different by channel and no one could tell what offers were available elsewhere.

Good Stories: The 360-Degree View

Banks such as JP Morgan Chase and USAA, a financial services institution supporting current and former military, have been leaders in implementing the technology needed to know customers everywhere, all the time. They were among the first companies to invest in 360-degree view software to bridge their multitude of channels and products, so they can see their customers in every channel and every interaction. Thanks in large part to this capability, they are both ranked at the top of their industry by a number of measures. USAA has a Net Promoter Score (NPS) in several of its product areas approaching 80 (meaning that in response to "would you recommend us to a friend?" 80 percent of its customers would provide a 10 or 9 score versus those giving a score from 6 through zero, which in the insurance sector is market-leading), and it has won the JD Power Chairman's Award, which is given only once every three to four years "to individuals who have distinguished themselves through outstanding achievement, or to organizations that demonstrate exemplary performance and innovation in quality, customer satisfaction or employee relations."[1] Chase posted the biggest NPS gains in 2013 of any national bank, moving from the third quartile to the second quartile and opening a lead over other national banks.[2]

In a well-organized bank, contact center agents and retail branch bankers can see every interaction that a customer has completed, identifying the products and services used as well as the comments the customer has made and the channels involved. They can see that a customer withdrew from an ATM or logged onto Internet banking to make a transfer or reset a warning limit to get notified when a key balance breached a threshold.

The Internet banking revolution has also meant that banks can now provide this complete view to their customers via Internet and mobile phone banking, a huge boon. In the early days of Internet banking, customers had to opt in to make each of their accounts visible over the web. Now customers expect any new product to be visible.

Bill recently checked in at a hotel and he heard the clerk ask another guest beside him, "Is this the first time you are staying with us?" If this were a Me2B-focused hotel, the clerk would have instead said either, "Enjoy your first stay with us!" or "Welcome back, Ms. X!" The hotel should have known whether this was the first, third, or tenth time the guest had stayed with the chain. Being recognized while on a visit, particularly to a new city, makes guests feel happy and at home, and perhaps rubs off on others checking in next to them—"Gee, I'd like to be treated that way, too."

Compare that experience to Bill's situation when he stays with his wife at the hotel chain Joie de Vivre. Regardless of location, they are always delighted to find a half-bottle of California Chardonnay in a bucket of ice when they check into the room. He requested this as an in-room amenity the first time he stayed with the chain, and the system remembers that preference. Joie de Vivre is an example of an entrepreneur-led company that set out to provide a differentiated experience. Other opportunities to bring Me2B needs into the customer experience for a hotel visit include confirming prior-stated preferences that the guest wants to see the *New York Times* in the morning, and to have a king-size bed facing away from the street in a nonsmoking room.

You Never Ask What You Already Know

If an organization has succeeded with "know me and remember me," then it already has a lot of information stored about the customer. Given that, it should use this information to save the customer effort, never asking anyone to input or repeat data they've given in the past.

Retaining memory of partially completed processes is also valuable. Smart websites let companies retain information from half-completed applications even though the user may not yet be a customer. Leaders in this space extend this across channels so that forms are pre-filled at the counter or in any other sales channel when the customer does decide to make a purchase.

Bad Stories: Putting the Customer to Work

One burdensome failure about "Never ask what you already know" is found in U.S. hospitals and doctor's offices that persist in asking patients to complete a health history form, again, every time they show up for an office appointment. Instead of asking for any changes from the last visit, which might have been only two months ago, the original five-page form is presented.

Similarly, information a customer has supplied to a business in an interactive voice response system (IVR), on a web form, or anywhere else should carry through the process. We've all experienced giving information to an IVR only to have to repeat it two minutes later to a live agent. (At Bill's bank, where he's been a customer for fifteen years, his complaints about this experience with contact center agents always produce the same response, *"We tell the IT group but they don't listen to us!"*)

Poorly integrated computer systems are often to blame here. When customers are transferred across a company and switch systems, they may have already identified themselves in system A, but the agent they are talking to in a new department is on system B. It's difficult to get this level of integration, but that doesn't excuse the effort it creates for customers.

Of course, companies do have ways to confirm customer identity without excessive questioning, but the lowest-effort solutions use expensive new technologies such as voice biometrics (recognizing your voice) and retina scanning. Even if such systems aren't practical in a given instance, however, companies can make the ID process as painless as possible.

Landline telephone companies have good forms of identity in their systems but seem to ignore them. They often ask at the outset of a customer call, "What is your account number?" eliciting a "huh?" in response. In many cases the customer's phone number *is* their account number. If a customer uses that number to call the telephone company, technologies like ANI or CLI can associate the customer's number with a database, and use it to ID the customer. Still, these companies often require further proof questions, even for calls when sensitive data doesn't come into play. It would be a lot easier for both parties if the agent simply asked, "I see that you're using the phone number associated with an account we have, is this Joe Smith?"

Good Stories: Personalized Experiences

Me2B Leaders are simplifying customers' lives by reusing data intelligently and consistently. American Express, for example, recently updated its card payment sign-in page, which now pre-populates the data fields for user name and password, thus moving members more quickly into their account. This is a great example of using browser cookies to avoid asking the member for information already on hand.

The company prides itself that "Membership Matters," and even in just this one small change, it shows.

Amazon CEO Jeff Bezos has long spoken of his vision to have Amazon deliver personalized pages for each customer, and the company is well on its way. When someone visits Amazon, the company's home page immediately appears with four to seven personalized features based on its knowledge of that customer's shopping history. That data enables Amazon to display recommendations particular to this customer, along with account details, video streaming service, wish list, and previously viewed items.

You Know My Preferences

An important part of knowing customers is mining their previously expressed preferences for things like billing statement frequencies and delivery mechanisms, such as mail or e-mail. Customers may also have a preference for how they wish to be contacted, for example, by text or e-mail. Whenever a customer provides feedback or makes a suggestion, it's important and is often an explicit expression of a preference. Nothing should be considered too small for the organization to keep in mind—even the newspaper preference of a hotel guest.

Satisfying this need not only means saving preferences and putting them to use but proactively asking customers what they want. Me2B Leaders are looking for these preferences in ways others do not (as we discuss further in Chapter Three, You Give Me Choices).

Bad Stories: Forced Conversations

A full-service airline once tried to offer its highest-category frequent flyers improved service by making sure they dealt with a live telephone representative. These customers were given a special call number that bypassed the normal IVR system and went straight to a trained human agent. The airline made sure calls were answered quickly and agents were hand-picked—but the results were not uniformly happy.

The problem stemmed from the assumption that all customers prefer speaking to an agent. The airline never asked; it simply acted as though it understood the preferences of this customer group. It didn't offer choices—and thus entirely missed the fact that some in the group actually preferred self-service. It could have captured details from these high-value customers as to the type of service they preferred and then used this information to route their calls. Knowing preferences isn't about assuming them in this way.

Good Stories: Fast Transactions

The National Australia Bank, meanwhile, has done an excellent job of putting customer preferences to work by adding a "remember me" feature in its ATMs. When completing transactions, customers can store what the system calls a "favorite transaction"—for example, a $100 withdrawal with a printed receipt. After that point, the favorite always appears first in the list of available transactions, thereby saving the customer time. (Bill remembers asking Bank of America circa 1997 for this exact ATM feature and being told, "Sorry, but that's not good for your privacy." Bank of America still doesn't offer it today.)

Amazon also led the practice of knowing—and implementing—customers' check-out preferences so that they can make purchases with as few clicks as possible—for some customers, just one (called, appropriately, "1-Click Ordering"). Later, by listening to customer requests for additional features, Amazon pioneered what's become known as "drop-down 1-click." The company collected all combinations of shipping preferences, credit cards, and addresses, and then automatically placed them in a drop-down on the purchase page. For customers, being known at the point of sale, and indeed throughout the shopping process, takes all the friction out of online ordering, and makes Amazon the preferred destination for them.

You Predict My Needs Intelligently

What we find amazing these days is how few companies use the data they have to help the customer. The Me2B Leaders learn, for example, what channels customers prefer, without ever asking. They analyze behavior, and, if they're really smart, inform the customers of the preferences they are intuiting. A smart airline will spot the seat selections that a customer chooses, and in the future, default to that option. The goal here is to pay attention to what customers are doing and put that information to good use.

Bad Stories: Slow Learners

Earlier we celebrated National Australia Bank's "favorite transaction" feature—but even it could be improved with more intelligent predictions. While some customers have a preference, others don't. The way the software worked, once the bank rolled out the "store a favorite transaction" feature, it kept prompting customers after every transaction to see if they wanted it to be stored as a favorite. Even after fifty instances of saying *no*, the customer was still prompted. An intelligent program would have prompted five to ten times, and then shut down the feature with a message explaining how to set it up if desired in the future. The bank's mistake was assuming all customers would want to store a favorite.

An Australian newspaper company got intelligent prediction half right. It e-mailed customers whose debit cards had upcoming expiration dates asking them to update their information. On the surface, this looks like a helpful action; no one wants a service interruption because their card has expired. However, the newspaper e-mailed customers three months prior to expiration. Meanwhile, banks only issue new cards *one month* prior to expiration. The result was that customers didn't know the new details when they got this letter, and therefore couldn't do anything about it. In fact, many cards reissue in a standard way; the account number remains unchanged and the expiration date rolls on a standard period (say three years). The new details are completely predictable. That being the case, why didn't the newspaper company find out and send a letter stating the following? *"Dear customer, we know your ABC card expires in a month. We assume that the new details are YYY and ZZZ, so please call us if that is not the case."*

Good Stories: Winning Entertainment

Contrast the frustration of a useless notification with Bill's recent experience at Netflix. One of his credit cards was about to expire, and of all the online places where he had stored it (for repeat purchases or subscriptions), Netflix was one of the only ones that reminded him to update the expiration date before losing out on ongoing access to DVDs or streaming video. Unlike the bank in the preceding section, Netflix advised him in the same month when the credit card was about to expire. Obviously this is good business for Netflix—no interruption in revenues—but it's equally good for Netflix's busy customers, who—like Bill—had forgotten where they had stored that particular credit card.

Australian ticketing company Ticketmaster tries to predict its customers' intentions intelligently. The company stores your purchase history for concerts and events and allows customers to opt in to receiving future offers based on prior purchase history. Ticketmaster ignores the demographics of the buyer and instead concentrates on buying behavior. This is intelligent since it recognizes that the customer may be purchasing gifts—for example, a parent buying concert tickets for a daughter—and then provides recommendations that help with future gift purchases.

One of Bill's clients recently cited her experience with Ticketmaster as an example of intelligent prediction. The Ticketmaster IVR phone system simply prompted her with a series of questions to enable her to place her order in the IVR, instead of waiting for a busy agent to assist with the transaction. The questions went like this (with disguised information), using stored data from her earlier transactions:

> "Is this Nancy Jones?"
> "Yes."
> "Are you using your credit card ending in 2345?"
> "Yes."
> "Do you want your tickets shipped to the address we show as 123 Main Street?"
> "Yes."

This was what our LimeBridge U.K. partner Peter Massey calls "being Fast + Simple for the customer," an interaction employing intelligent prediction.

You Know Me and Mine

An organization needs to understand the person it is dealing with in a broader context. Is this customer related to someone else who is also a customer? Does the customer hold a significant role in an organization that might have a corporate relationship? Treating a customer badly as an individual is never good business—but when that person is also CEO of a major corporate customer it is particularly foolish. Working from a broad understanding also means understanding relationships and roles across different products and parts of the organization—admittedly hard to do without being intrusive.

Bad Stories: Limited Recognition

One of Melbourne's leading dentists has a network of practices. He also runs a dental consultancy firm. All these businesses work with one bank, where he also has his personal accounts. A couple of years ago, he let one of his account balances decline. Despite the millions of dollars in his other accounts, the bank bounced a check off that account, embarrassing him. He withdrew all his business and moved elsewhere—a classic example of a business losing out because it lacked the systems and processes to understand and exploit the broader relationship.

While all customers should receive quality service, the potential damage of failing with an influential customer is much greater, so Me2B Leaders find ways to identify them. In Australia in 2011, the premier of Queensland (comparable to a U.S. state governor) received his utility bill and found it contained errors. That very night, he was on television, waving his bill and warning everyone in the state to check their own bills and make sure they weren't being overcharged. The utility's contact center went into meltdown and the volume of Ombudsman complaints rose dramatically. It was a very expensive mistake and also damaged the company's reputation. The company's marketing campaigns were far less effective in winning new customers after this event. Of course, the real issue was the error on the bill, but failure to manage customers with significant influence magnified its impact. The company reacted after the fact by setting up a special unit to manage all its high-profile customers such as politicians and business leaders.

If that seems like too extreme an example, consider this one. One of Bill's clients asked his team to figure out ways to increase customer satisfaction in their small Seattle-based contact center. The team went out to listen in on customer calls. (No better way!) During one of these calls, in the late afternoon, a customer with a British accent asked if the company could speed up an order because "my people need to use it tomorrow."

The contact center agent went through all the standard processes and wound up telling him, "Sorry, but we can't get it to you before the end of the week," at which point the customer said, "Very well, I understand, I'll have to get it from another company." The call ended. When Bill and his team shared the story with his client's marketing vice president later that week, he stirred in his chair and asked his contact center director to find out who had called. He was very unhappy to learn that the British caller was his second biggest account whose CEO himself had made the call. Lost business, and maybe a lost account.

Good Stories: VIP Treatment

Many companies are working hard to understand the broader context of a customer relationship. The Commonwealth Bank in Australia has mechanisms to flag what it calls "special customers." This can include prominent politicians or large account holders and the members of their families. However, the trick is not merely flagging them but following through to make sure that certain systems and processes are managed differently for these special cases. Rather than sending a threatening collection letter for a credit card debt, for example, the bank would handle a flagged customer more discreetly.

Other companies, notably satellite TV provider DIRECTV and others with extensive integrated customer databases, recognize important customers when they are online or when they come through the IVR phone system and immediately divert them to their best agents for support. Sometimes this VIP treatment is well known to the customer, as with the airlines or hotel chains whose frequent customers get a different phone number to call, and possibly a different URL to use to access their account online. But sometimes VIP treatment has the most impact when it takes the customer by surprise, often leading to "wow!" reactions that kick off great customer experiences.

You Know When I Don't Want to Be Known

As an extension of "You Know My Preferences," customers sometimes prefer to remain anonymous, or at least do not want to be treated in a personalized manner or receive promotions simply based on expressed preferences for certain goods or services. This helps explain why many customers insist that companies do not share their data or transactions with other organizations, and why they get so upset when they receive unsolicited suggestions or offers. Customers want to feel that they are in control; they want to manage their own relationship with the company, and not be managed or controlled.

Bad Stories: Privacy Breach

In 2012, Target Stores in the United States made headlines by pushing too hard to predict customer life situations based on purchase history.[3] A father opened a mailing from the store full of coupons for baby items. He immediately called the local store to complain vigorously. It turned out that his teenage daughter had used his credit card to purchase items that triggered the store's "pregnancy score," which led to coupons being sent to the prospective mother who, unsurprisingly, hadn't told her parents about her purchases. The retailer made two mistakes: First, marketing based on an assumption about what might be a sensitive subject for the customer, and second, failing to recognize multiple customers in the same family and respect their privacy.

Companies should always thoroughly consider privacy implications when looking for ways to use data, even—or especially—when the intent is purely to improve the customer's experience. A few years ago, an Australian bank rolled out its first system that allowed staff to search for customers and all their accounts by name. One unfortunate consequence was that in the first week of use, more than ten thousand staff members accessed the account details and balances of the prime minister of Australia. Word had spread across the branch network that you could check the PM's bank accounts, so of course lots of curious staff did just that.

Good Stories: Opting Out

Rampant unwanted telemarketing has prompted many national authorities to invoke "Do Not Call" lists that cover landline and mobile phone numbers, and by and large telemarketers have respected these restrictions (partly to avoid large fines and public humiliation). Online retailers have followed a similar route, aiming to make sure that their promotions are tailored to their customers' needs and don't irritate them. For example, just because you purchase one kid's book for a nephew doesn't mean you're interested in a slew of e-mail messages promoting more kid books. Maybe you are, but maybe you'd rather opt out of that type of message while still receiving promotions for crime novels, action-packed DVDs, and kitchen tools. Amazon and others have figured this out and offer precise messaging options, similar to Do Not Call, allowing their customers to shape the communications that they want to receive.

Me2B Leaders recognize that customers don't want e-mail or brochures that don't interest them. Online travel site Wotif asks members, *"Would you like to hear about more offers?"* but defaults the response to the "off" setting so that no one accidentally opts in. It knows that customers who want such information will sign up, a classic case of trusting customers to manage the relationship.

Why "You Know Me, You Remember Me" Is So Important

If customers do not feel that they are recognized, there is no way they can feel appreciated. This is the critical basis to deliver great

Table 2.2 The Benefits of Knowing and Remembering the Customer

Customer Need Met	Potential to Increase Revenue	Potential to Reduce Cost
You know me everywhere and all the time.	More steady revenue across more channels	Shorter handling and processing time
You never ask me for something you already know.	Retain sales otherwise lost when customer hangs up or walks out	Shorter handling and processing time
You know my preferences.	Higher attachment rate for cross-sales or related products and services	Less waste and fewer returns
You predict intelligently.	Additional sales not otherwise obtained, leading to more repeat purchases and positive word of mouth	Lower product development costs Less marketing expense
You know me and mine.	More sales Greater customer loyalty, less churn	Lower advertising and marketing costs
You know when I don't want to be known.	Greater loyalty	Lower costs, for example, in direct mail

experiences: Me2B customers want to be remembered, they want and need to be known across all the touch points and interactions they've had with you and with any partner organizations. If you don't know who they are and what they have done, how can you have an effective relationship? Without fulfilling this basic need, it is very challenging to deliver the other six customer needs for effective Me2B relationships. Table 2.2 summarizes the basic benefits.

Meet the Challenge: You Know Me, You Remember Me

If the customer's need to be known and remembered is so logical and so fundamental, then why is it so hard for organizations to make it work? We have documented five key paths to take to prevent disabling an effective Me2B customer experience by failing to remember across relationships, across channels, and across time.

Integrate Technology

In most medium-to-large organizations, "You Know Me, You Remember Me" requires technology integration across products and channels. Many institutions developed separate systems for different product types and have subsequently added new layers of technology for channels such as Internet or mobile phones. They may have different technologies in face-to-face retail branches, contact centers, and back offices.

In the late 1990s CRM software emerged to provide a common view of all this complexity. However, implementing CRM is just one way to achieve the goal. Another way is to have a single enterprise system that everyone uses, or a layer of software that acts as the glue between systems, of which CRM is an example. But to be effective, the software has to be well designed. Provide too much information and it overwhelms the end users; too little, and it loses its value. The only way we know to get this result is to involve end users in both the design and testing of these applications so that those who encounter common customer interactions can recommend what will work.

Integrate Processes

Unfortunately knowing the customer effectively is not just a software problem—it's also (and more often) a process and motivational problem. While frontline staff may have access to lots of recent interaction history, that doesn't mean they know when to look, where to look, or how to use the information. You must develop training and effective processes that tell the front line what to do so that knowing the customer is a priority, and so that measures and incentives align to these behaviors. For example, though branch personnel might be able to reuse data that a customer completed in online application, they may choose not to do so if the measurement system only provides an incentive on their own sales.

Integrate Across the Organization

Another barrier to "You Know Me, You Remember Me" behaviors is organizational history. Often channels are owned by different executives whose teams have different targets and goals, and are set up almost in competition with one another. This doesn't encourage data sharing and the creation of processes that span channels. Similarly, product silos can pose obstacles to sharing of data and process. To overcome this tendency to subdivide organizational goals, the leadership needs to set out a broader agenda and realign measures to encourage the sorts of sharing behavior that customers expect.

Make Sure Knowledge Travels Across Channels and Tools

It is challenging for those in the front line of the business to understand and support all these mechanisms and interaction types across all the channels and ways customers have of interacting with a business. Companies must rethink the organizational model and roles of frontline staff so that knowledge of other channels beyond a given frontline employee's specialty is accessible. Many organizations now have tiered service and sales models that enable some staff to support a range of products and channels while those in a second tier become more specialized. Companies must also develop knowledge-sharing tools that provide frontline staff with information on more of these products and services without needing everyone to be an expert.

Develop a Design Philosophy

The minimization of customer effort through pre-population is an important design philosophy. It's relatively easy and cheap to design forms and processes where the customer starts from scratch. It's much harder to identify a customer, retrieve the appropriate data, and populate the form intelligently, but it is essential that companies make this a central part of their design philosophy. Pre-population needs to be embedded in design methodologies for systems and processes. It's a classic short-term versus long-term investment trade-off: On one hand, it's far quicker to design an online form that the customer completes, but on the other hand, the long-term paybacks of pre-populating are manyfold. In addition to customer loyalty and satisfaction, pre-populating avoids data duplication issues and avoidable errors that creep into a database.

The design philosophy extends beyond IT to product design and marketing. For example, an organization needs to capture and use preferences. A leading customer service organization will always give customers a way to ask for marketing and other material—letting them opt in rather than waiting for them to opt out. That choice is a hard one for a marketing and sales team trying to maximize lead generation, but customers will opt in if the benefits are sold correctly and if the marketing is intelligent and relevant. In that case, both customers and companies will benefit enormously.

CHAPTER THREE

YOU GIVE ME CHOICES

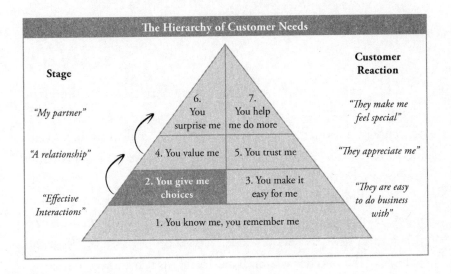

The Hierarchy of Customer Needs

Stage

Customer Reaction

"My partner"

6. You surprise me | 7. You help me do more

"They make me feel special"

"A relationship"

4. You value me | 5. You trust me

"They appreciate me"

"Effective Interactions"

2. You give me choices | 3. You make it easy for me

1. You know me, you remember me

"They are easy to do business with"

THE GROUNDHOG DAY HOTLINE

At first glance, it would seem that the modern era far outshines the past in its ability to give consumers choices, thanks to the Internet, endless product development, shopping malls, big-box retail, and so much more. On the other hand, maybe we are exhausted, in some ways, by that volume of choice.

The good old days offered a different kind of choice in the form of personalization enabled by the intimate relationship between customer and provider. Tailors made suits to order based on style and materials. The butcher was on hand to cut your meat to your liking. Candy stores had a mouthwatering array of jars and trays, all full of sweets that could be bought in any weight or mix, and other specialized shops offered similarly focused selections. As well, many stores offered channel choices like home delivery.

Today, customers are thrilled to see their customization choices expanding once again thanks to technology, the Internet, and the intrepid businesses that are embracing these trends. For example, the home delivery of milk products is staging a resurgence in the United States, thanks to companies such as Smith Brothers Farms. Milk deliveries were common in many countries up to the 1970s but had largely ceased as supermarkets prevailed. This Seattle-area family business was established in 1920, but by providing home milk delivery in the new millennium, it is capitalizing on one of the most important Me2B customer desires: Expanding customer choice. Its website's "Who We Are" page captures the Me2B zeitgeist by assuring customers in boldface, "You're in charge."

Customers are now looking for expanded choice via home delivery in many areas. This trend is mirrored in Australia with the re-emergence of fresh food delivered to the door via Aussie Farmers Direct, which has been on the top five fastest-growing companies list in the last five years, and in Singapore with RedMart, delivering efficiently through the highways and narrows streets of this small country.[1]

Customers have always liked to be given choices. Choice satisfies our need to feel in control. Today, choice—not so much among products, but in our relationships with individual vendors—is again becoming an expectation, thanks to our Internet- and mobile-driven commercial playground. With so many companies aggressively fighting for their attention, customers are particularly quick to reward those who cater to their need for control.

Companies serious about having true relationships with customers—as are all the Me2B Leaders—know they can't dominate the relationship. Imagine being in a personal relationship where your partner dictated everything: What you ate and when, where you went, the topics of conversation you shared. No one would like having so little involvement. Choices create the opposite experience, providing the give-and-take that marks quality relationships, both personal and professional. And so businesses that reap every opportunity to provide customers with choices show them that their time, wishes, and needs are valued.

Of course, some very successful organizations do compete successfully on parameters other than choice or on limited selection and service. For example, the Aldi supermarket chain stocks only its house brands, allowing it to offer customers extremely low prices. However, it makes the resulting value proposition—what the customer gets in return for the restricted choice—exceedingly clear. In fact, Aldi's strategy is based on giving customers a relatively novel choice in the marketplace: Rather than navigate through a traditional multibrand, multiprice supermarket, customers can now shop at no-frills Aldi, swapping abundant product choice for a much lower grocery bill and a simplified shopping experience. In a similar way, the U.S.-based Costco, which operates in ten countries, earns $100 billion in annual revenue by offering a limited selection of high-quality produce, meat, and wine, and a wide range of other products, many of them sold in bulk. Costco has a popular house brand called Kirkland but also stocks brands that consumers recognize and trust, and of course you can get large quantities at Costco!

Me2B companies are highly sensitive to the customer's desire to feel in control. That means providing choices, but it also means taking care to explain those times when choices are limited. For example, if a process can only be performed in one channel because of regulations or security issues, then the company needs to explain that constraint. Customers are far more likely to push back or feel slighted if the restrictions seem arbitrary or designed to serve the company's needs, not theirs.

Me2B companies are satisfying customers' desires for choices in six key ways, just as many other companies are failing them. The rest of this chapter focuses on the six underlying needs summarized in Table 3.1.

You Let Me Choose "What" and "How Much"

Me2B Leaders allow customers to set the meter on what choices will be offered and how much choice they'll have. The very best companies use personalization to create "segments of one," to use a term coined by Don Peppers and Martha Rogers in their seminal book *The One to One Future* in 1996.[2] This allows the customer to tailor the choices for products and services completely. Incorrect ways to serve this need include offering only bundled product selections that limit the customer's ability to mix and match or to choose from among volume options—at least without offering some kind of bonus as a trade-off for limited choices.

Table 3.1 The Customer's Experience of Success and Failure

You Give Me Choices Success	You Give Me Choices Failure
You let me choose "what" and "how much."	You restrict my purchase range or volume for no good reason and without providing an incentive for me.
You let me decide how and where I do things.	You only offer one purchase channel or require me to return to same channel (or location, even worse) where I made the purchase.
I can do it on my time.	You restrict me to hours of operation that don't fit my schedule or time zone.
You give me the advice that I need, when I need it.	Your product information is clearly promotional, limited, or overly filtered, introducing doubt or confusion.
I get to control with whom I work.	You force me to work with someone who doesn't appreciate me or doesn't speak the same language as I do. (For example, I keep meeting a new salesperson when I've been a very frequent shopper.)
You let me design it.	Your way doesn't always fit my needs, and you won't let me help.

Bad Stories: Limited Information and the Danger of Spam

Offering clear and thorough explanations of the choices available is one way of helping customers make choices. Online ticketing sites are an example of an industry that's gone only halfway. The outlets appear to offer choices; you can go online and choose the type of ticket (Level, Row, and so on) and pick between delivery methods. But the information provided isn't nearly as sophisticated as it needs to be to provide a true choice of "what." For example, when selecting tickets for a sports stadium, customers can choose a price bracket and often a general area of the stadium. However, the sites lack venue-specific information; if you've never been to the stadium, it's impossible to know how high up or far from the court or stage you'll be, or which side will house the home team. You'd have to speak to a contact center agent to get that information, a frustrating experience when you're trying to make a convenient and fast web transaction.

Letting customers choose "what" and "how much" also applies to marketing and service communications. Customers can opt in and request e-mail alerts from a menu of options or limit service calls to before 10 P.M. or only between 2 and 4 P.M. Companies that ignore their customers' choices, sending messages to customers or prospects based on flimsy connections, and not at all from customer preferences, very quickly become spammers in the customer's mind and are utterly rejected, if not mocked in the next blog or forum posting.

Good Stories: Guided Selection

The Nationwide Building Society in the United Kingdom, one of the country's few remaining mutual financial institutions, is always looking to find easier and better ways for its customers to do business with it. In the late 1990s—before the era of general web access—it experimented with a range of self-service technologies. Seeking to help customers select and purchase products, the company tried a computer-based solution in which customers were asked series of questions, after which—*presto!*—the system made an appropriate product recommendation. This seemed like a great technology, in theory—but clients rejected it. They didn't trust the machine to present them with the one perfect solution. They wanted a role in the selection process.

The Building Society later tried the idea again in a new prototype. This time the system recommended three products that met the customer's criteria, with one called out as the best option, and the customers were asked to choose which one they preferred. The results were very different. Customers invariably accepted the best option. Furthermore, even where branch staff talked to them later and recommended something different, they were very hard to move from their original decision; they trusted the choice they'd already made. Letting them compare and contrast similar products made all the difference.

One of Amazon's many renowned personalization examples is its recommendations engine, the feature that suggests, "Customers like you bought this item and you might also like it." This engine has produced significant incremental revenues for the company, but what's behind it is even more impressive: Customers can select which recommendations they want to see, and which ones they no longer are interested getting; for example, when you buy newborn toys but don't intend to buy other baby items, you can turn off those recommendations while keeping ones for music or books. Therefore the choice engine itself is built on choice.

You Let Me Decide How and Where I Do Things

Me2B Leaders provide a wide range of communication channels and interaction methods, some experimental and others suited to niche audiences. They understand that opening the spigot of choice across channels benefits customers and the organization.

Meanwhile, customer experience laggards restrict the ways they interact with customers, perhaps in a penny-pinching effort to reduce costs. Most telecommunication companies have been guilty of this as they moved customers from paper to e-mail billing and communication. Rather than offering the choice to go to paperless statements or a discount for doing so, these companies informed customers that they would be charged for the privilege of paper bills—not a customer-friendly tactic at all.

The trouble for companies that haven't embraced new channels or deny customers the choice is that customers are now able to compare across industries and within industries. We've heard many phone calls where customers say, *My insurance company (or shipper or other organization) lets me do that on the phone or on the web, so why can't you?* Once *one* company finds a way to increase channel choice—or indeed, choice in general—customers discover it, share it with their friends, and then demand it everywhere. In our first book we called this "last contact benchmarking"—and it still applies even more today as the range of channel options increases.

Bad Stories: Unintended Consequences

Sometimes, in the attempt to provide specialized superior service, companies restrict choice and unintentionally inconvenience the very customers they hope to impress. Use of customer account managers is a great example. The idea is that specialized personnel provide the best customers with the best support, but time and time again in practice we've seen these account-managed relationships limit choice. In one of our utility clients, business customers were assigned account managers. When they called the customer contact center, the agents on staff (who weren't account managers) were not allowed to handle the call, regardless of how simple it was. Customers were often forced to leave messages for their account managers. The result was that typical customers got things done on the spot, while business customers (who had larger and more valuable accounts) had to wait up to a day for a response. Preferential treatment restricted choice and produced worse experiences. We have seen the same issues and the same diminished experiences in banking where account-managed customers had to wait until their account manager was available rather than deal with the general call center, even on a simple call.

Sometimes companies arbitrarily restrict the "where" of transactions in an effort to protect privacy—a valuable goal, but customers can rightfully question the efficacy of the restrictions. Take the experience of David's business partner Graham Howard, who called his bank and initially failed one of the ID questions about his birthday. Quickly he realized that the bank had transposed the month and day of his birthday and changed his answer, thus passing the security check. Once he finished his other business, he asked the agent to update his date of birth. "You'll have to visit a branch," he was told. After requesting a supervisor, he protested that if he had been identified sufficiently to complete financial transactions, why couldn't he update his birthday as well? Again he was told, "That's a branch-only transaction." Ultimately, the call ran for a total of fifty-seven minutes and became legendary in David's company as a result, but the bank staff was unwilling to budge from the rule. "Where" was not an option for this customer.

We found the story so bizarre that it generated the cartoon on this page.

Good Stories: Service on the Customers' Terms

The Paris-based flash-sales site creator Vente-Privee epitomizes giving its customers choices in how they shop for fashion and apparel, with the tagline "we give products a second life." The site takes end-of-season clothing lines and other attractive merchandise and totally revitalizes it through careful marketing and savvy positioning. Customers first get to choose what types of products or offers they will receive rather than be bombarded with offers that don't interest them.

Aside from offering a wide array of alluring products, Vente-Privee has also been obsessive in its willingness to open channels of communication—social media, phone, e-mail, and more. Its service strategy is to offer the customers support and help by whichever channel they choose. The primary goal is to help the customers, rather than restrict them to one medium of communication.

Customer service agents also keep track of what customers want and then notify them in person when certain new offers will occur. Other flash-sales companies have tried to copy Vente-Privee's business model, but the company's success continues thanks to its abiding passion for customer service, as seen in its perennial awards for providing the best customer service of any French-based online company and its determination to provide choices.

Australia's largest health insurer, Medibank Private, offers an example of how to influence customer behavior by offering *more* choice rather than less. The company was frustrated that customers continued to perform simple, low-value transactions such as claims in the retail network rather than online. It invested in a new branch configuration in which meeter-greeters became the first stop for all customers arriving in the branch. If a transaction could be completed online, the concierge took the customer to an Internet terminal in the branch and demonstrated how to complete the transaction. The company recognized that an investment in education would open up customers to new choices in the "how and where" of their transactions. This style of "do it with me" education enables customers rather than restricting them.

I Can Do It on My Time

"Do it on my time" recognizes the need of customers to control the timing of interactions relative to other activities or priorities in their lives. Traditionally companies have presented standardized options for when customers are allowed to interact, based more on the company's needs than the habits of the customers. These restrictions include offering limited customer service hours, but also transaction schedules such as billing periods. For example, many customers would prefer to pay all their bills on the same day each month. Yet the companies they transact with each have their own unbending schedules for bill payment, often requiring customers trying to streamline their accounting to check and make sure they're aligned with the company's payment cycle. Why not let the customer drive the payment schedule, so long as the period and amount are agreed upon?

Bad Stories: Phony Support

Accommodating customers on *their* schedule is especially important when a business has experienced product or service problems. One telecommunication supplier provides a classic negative example. After a range of operational failures, call demand was high and people faced long waits for agents. The increased call volume meant that customers were often transferred to contact centers in other locations. Unfortunately, the company didn't sync up the hours of operation at these remote locations; when a call was transferred, customers often got a message that the center was closed. This was one of many reasons that eighteen months later, this operation had lost 20 percent of its customers.

Many organizations make outbound calls to customers without asking the customer first whether these calls are welcome. Each call represents an intrusion into the customer's time and therefore it needs to start with the question, "Would you be able to spare me ten minutes now?" Many don't ask this question, yet basic civility and courtesy suggests that if you'd like some of a customer's time, you should at least ask when it is convenient to talk.

Good Stories: 24/7 Convenience

One of the most innovative examples of expanding the customer's choice in "when" that we know of is automated dry cleaning. Typically, dry cleaners require clerks and therefore have standard business hours that make it difficult for customers who also work the same standard business hours to get their dry cleaning done when they need it. Some dry cleaners have tackled this problem by making partners of other businesses whose model has them open 24/7, such as convenience stores. However, one dry cleaner in Melbourne, called Distinctive Dry Cleaners Australia, has found an even better answer—a 24/7 self-service system. Customers deposit clothes in a secure drop area and register the drop using a credit card. When it's time to collect, they swipe their card and the system identifies the items in question. Behind the scenes it locates the items on a movable rack and rotates them to be collected by the customer. It's an amazing blend of automation and intelligent self-service design.

The Northern California–based paving materials producer Graniterock provides another example of expanding business 24/7. Customers had been requesting round-the-clock access to its road paving materials depots. Rather than take on the burden of full-time staff, the company moved to a trust-based system by providing keycard access with weigh in, weigh out billing that enabled its customers' drivers to get exactly what they needed, day or night—extremely important, as a lot of road repair is done at night these days.[3] The program was a big hit with customers, and in 1992 Graniterock won the Malcolm Baldrige National Quality Award, a highly prestigious program given to only a handful of winners each year, oftentimes to household names such as Xerox or Ritz-Carlton.

Companies would do well to find and mine even small opportunities to adapt to their customers' schedules. For example, Bupa, a $16 billion health insurance group in Australia, the United Kingdom, and other countries, has adopted a phone service protocol that saves customers time. An agent who has to tackle complex problems or investigations has the freedom to take the case offline. Rather than keep customers on the phone while they research an issue or get hold of another department, experienced Bupa agents offer the customer a call back later that day or even the next day, if it suits their schedules and the problem is not urgent. Customers are often thrilled that their time is treated with such respect, and Bupa agents recognize that they must follow through on this commitment and return calls when they say they will. Planning and managing these cases becomes an important obligation for the contact center but also allows the agents to spread work more evenly over the day.

You Give Me the Advice That I Need, When I Need It

Supporting choice also means adapting the depth of advice or support different customers require in different situations. Many organizations don't customize this aspect of their customer service, yet it is an important trait in building relationships with all customers. Some customers are novices; some are experts. Some are analytical and like lots of detail while others are outcome driven and just want to know what works. It's similar to the tried-and-true situational leadership principle: leaders need to change their style to suit the needs of the folks who work for them.

Sophisticated organizations recognize that customers of different types need different levels of information during different types of interaction. For example, a sophisticated financial planner in the investment and savings industry will not only perform a proper needs analysis for each client but will also assess the information needs of that customer and match the responses accordingly. Some customers will want to know lots of detail about their investment choices. Others may be only interested in the returns or the risks.

Bad Stories: Hidden Availability, Limited Info

One of the biggest mistakes companies make is using generic error or availability messages that don't explain the full context of the situation. We've all had experience trying to book something like a show, a hotel room, or an airline ticket online, only to be told that nothing is available. Unfortunately many of us have come to mistrust what that really means. Error messages should explain if a hotel or train or plane is really full or the tickets or booking quotas just haven't been released. For example, during the run-up to one of the Olympic games, the booking website stated that tickets for an event were sold out. Yet four weeks later a customer was able to book tickets for that event. What the site should have explained was that the current quota was exhausted, and customers should check back later to see if more tickets had been released. (Or even better, let them know *when* more tickets would be released!)

Similarly, when David once tried to use a European train online booking site to book an overnight trip from Germany to the Czech Republic, the system claimed that the train was sold out. Since it was months before the journey this seemed unlikely. He called the German train service and found out that, in fact, all the seats were available—the Czech train company simply had yet to release those trips. Too bad the website's error message didn't make that clear.

Airlines have tremendous opportunity to improve their support in the moment of customers' greatest inconvenience: flight delays or cancellations. This is a moment in which customers need to know the exact cause of the delay and the likely options so they can remake plans, adjust schedules, or consider alternative transport. Rarely do airlines provide their frontline staff with that kind of information. Of course, some things, such as weather delays, the airline can't control—but even then knowing that O'Hare Airport has been closed for two hours helps customers gauge the extent of the issue and its implication for them. The other irony here is that airlines experience these situations over and over again. Wouldn't it be great if they learned from those experiences and informed customers of the likely outcomes? For example, they could at least say, "The last time Kennedy had a storm two years ago, it was three hours before it could reopen."

Good Stories: Virtual Guides

One of the biggest barriers to buying something these days is apt to be too much choice. Trusted retailers who do the best job of helping sort through those choices are at the head of the pack. U.S. outdoors retailer Moosejaw has made it easy to buy online, in stores, or with a call to its sales and customer service line by taking customers through questions—the ones the best sales associates would ask—to narrow the field of possible products leading to a best-fit solution.

Here's how it works, with tent shopping as an example. Using special software, customers or sales representatives go through a series of logical questions such as "will you be hiking or car camping?" and "how many people will be using the tent?" and "will you need to stand inside the tent?" reducing several dozen possible tents to two to four possibilities that fit the customer's needs—all shown side by side with pricing, customer reviews, specifications, and accessories. If this is done in the Moosejaw store it might be that some of the best-fit tents aren't in stock, but the retail sales rep can show the customer online photos and a simple way to place the order online. The solution is fast and simple for the customer and surely increases Moosejaw's sales conversion rates.

Other companies have been creative in making support feel more personal. Alaska Airlines and IKEA were two early adopters of online "virtual agents," avatars that portray a brand image and provide just the right amount of answers that consumers need. In Alaska's case, that avatar is named Jenn. The airline has devoted a full webpage to its Ask Jenn service to explain exactly what she can do for you. For example, Jenn can respond to customer questions and link the customer to the most appropriate parts of the website for their needs.

The National Australia Bank has offered help for its electronic kiosk customers via a cartoon character based on the "i" information symbol. In the late 1990s, the cartoon helped reduce customer fear using its first self-service kiosks. If a user appeared stuck or confused, the character would offer to help. It was programmed to offer different levels of support depending on where the user was in the program and what they were doing—a great example of allowing the customer to choose how much help they needed and when.

I Get to Control with Whom I Work

Customers sometimes need the ability to delegate their business relationship to someone else in their family or organization. In this they are choosing who the "Me" is in Me2B. The company should understand the relationship sufficiently to enable this to happen. Reasons vary from wanting to share responsibility for an account or service to needing to delegate because of age or health issues.

Bad Stories: Failure to Delegate

For years we've heard talk about the need to create better house-holding data—data that identifies each of the members of a household—to permit richer interactions and connections. All too many companies, with the excuse that they need to "protect your privacy," insist on speaking only with the account or policy holder. This is compounded in households where the spouses do not share the same last name. Some have to carry their marriage certificate to prove to retail sales or airline gate agents that, indeed, they are living together.

The ability to delegate becomes especially important in situations such as those that involve children, the elderly, or the sick, or when people are traveling or working with an assistant, just to name a few. We've observed customer service calls in which someone rings on behalf of a customer who is sick in a hospital but their proxy is still denied access to an account. We've also seen mobile companies insist on dealing with a teenager for a phone even though it was purchased and funded by the parents. These ridiculous situations represent a misinterpretation of privacy legislation and make no sense to customers. Privacy legislation is meant to protect private information, not to prevent friends and family from helping each other pay bills or manage their personal affairs.

Good Stories: Caring by Sharing

Some companies are getting it right helping their customers decide who works with whom. The retailer Energy Australia has recognized that customers are in relationships and offered shared accountability for energy accounts. The company has three account structures that offer customers a range of choices for how other family members interact with the account. Spouses or partners can be involved at three different levels of control. This allows the company to deal with a variety of different relationship types—for example, roommates leasing a property together or an individual supporting an elderly relative by transacting on an account but not owning it.

The USAA financial services company also does an excellent job of recognizing family needs. Given its military customer pool, its members may be deployed or away from their loved ones, needing to move the relationship to spouse or family. USAA has an extensive member database that keeps track of all members' spouses, kids, and other relatives so that they can get direct support. The insurer doesn't share confidential data about the policies, respecting privacy, but offers claims help. For example, if an officer is in Afghanistan and his daughter has a collision driving to school, she is able to call and make a claim on the policy.

You Let Me Design It

The ultimate experience to offer the Me2B customer is to let them design the product or service just as they want it. What that looks like can range from offering choices of options and features to building products that uniquely conform to a customer's specifications. It takes a broad-thinking organization to collect the requests and then act upon them in a cost-effective way, and to have the flexibility of design and technology to enable cost-effective production and delivery. It's not a fit for all businesses, but those who can offer product customization are rewarded by customer loyalty and heightened word of mouth.

Bad Stories: Cutting the Customer Out

Some companies resist collaborating with customers by reflex, because they're used to doing things the old way, their way. Bill experienced that working with a client in the precision steel business. His team visited company customers across the globe to figure out how it could better serve its demanding customers. They heard one constant refrain: "We love the quality of their steel but when we have new requirements down the road, we'd love to work with them to design next-generation products." Bill and his team endorsed this idea, but the client executives immediately dismissed it. "Why would we let them into our R&D lab?" they said, arguing that they already had their best engineers on the job. Instead of sharing control with their customers they embarked on a cost-cutting program. Shortly thereafter, they wound up getting acquired by their biggest competitor in a hostile takeover.

Good Stories: DIY Everything

Many other companies have been excited to bring customers into their process, or have even built entire businesses around customized products. Online these days you can build your own watch with Boccia (face, hands, straps, and more), design your own T-shirts, mugs, stickers, and magnets with many companies, and produce customized signs with Build-a-Sign. The niche car companies MINI Cooper and Tesla have built their reputations in part by giving customers custom design and feature options.

Some businesses offer both standard and self-design options. You can add custom messages to M&M candies through the Mars website—and order special colors as well. Sportswear companies Reebok and Nike both now offer custom design options for sneakers online such as the popular Nike Flyknit Racer. The online hamper sales company Your Hamper lets customers choose either hampers designed by the company or a custom-built one. It lets the customer decide on the size and style and then provides a great system of feedback to let a customer know how much room they have as they add selected goods into the hamper. Customers can decorate their finished hampers with photos and text. Your Hamper allows for the low-time, low-touch option of a preconfigured hamper but also satisfies customers who want to build their own.

The online company Shoes of Prey may represent the ultimate example of "You let me design it." Founder Jodie Fox set up the company when she couldn't find shoes that she liked on the Internet. The whole premise of the company is that customers can design their own shoes. Occasions such as weddings or other special events create a huge market for unique shoes. According to Fox, women buy up to thirteen pairs of shoes each year. Customers literally design every aspect of their pair, from style to color to materials, and each is made to that unique order. The company has a fanatical following. It does smart things like letting the customers return the shoes if they aren't happy (even if it's their own design that failed) and sending them a picture of the manufactured shoes as they ship them to increase the excitement. Customer reviews show that many customers love the process and the way they can experiment as they design. It has even spawned a new industry of shoe stylists who help others design the perfect shoe.[4]

Why "You Give Me Choices" Is So Important

Offering choices gives customers a sense of control, increasing their perception that they are in a relationship with the company, not at its behest. When companies offer customers options, tailoring the experience to suit not just anybody but *them* specifically (or so it feels), the relationship becomes much more personal, building upon the first need: "You Know Me, You Remember Me." Many companies experience higher average order size when customers are presented with choices rather than default solutions, for example, by presenting different colors or configurations in response to searches for a product. Most consumers want to be in control, and they understand the trade-offs involved, such as slightly longer shipment times or higher prices. Table 3.2 summarizes the benefits.

Meet the Challenge: You Give Me Choices

Me2B customers are demanding increasing levels of control, so why aren't companies adapting? We believe that four forces are at work here that prevent companies offering increased choice, but each can be met by intrepid organizations that take the proper steps in response.

Table 3.2 The Benefits of Delivering Choice

Customer Need Met	Potential to Increase Revenue	Potential to Reduce Cost
You let me choose "what" and "how much."	Higher average order size More spend over time, greater loyalty	Fewer returns, less reverse-logistics expense Lower self-service costs than assisted support
You let me decide how and where I do things.	Higher spend More cross-selling Higher spend with lower need for support	Less cost in assisted channels Fewer returns Easier to process sales
I can do it on my time.	More ad hoc or unplanned spend	Load spread throughout the day rather than peaks requiring extra staffing Greater use of self-service, saving cost and time
You give me the advice that I need, when I need it.	Improved customer retention, satisfaction levels, and loyalty More positive word-of-mouth marketing to others	Fewer returns More self-service use
I get to control with whom I work.	More positive word-of-mouth marketing to others	Fewer repeat contacts and complaints
You let me design it.	More avid purchases plus positive word of mouth Increased share of wallet	Lower R&D and product development costs

Pay Attention to Changes in Customer Behaviors and Needs

Some companies seem to believe that they're the experts—that they know more than the customer—but this is a delusion. If companies keep striving to perfect the last generation's products or way of doing things they inevitably ignore changes in customer behaviors and needs. The business world is littered with companies that perished or shrank because the world outpaced them. For example, former handset leaders Blackberry, Motorola, and Nokia all struggled as smart phones changed customer demand because they didn't pick up on the trends fast enough. They all are examples of companies whose product development processes became internally focused and got out of touch with customer needs. Other handset manufacturers have leaped to the top of the stack, for example, Apple and Samsung, both known for their innovation and their willingness to try new things, over and over again.

Leave Customer Feedback Open-Ended

Many companies don't believe their customers have anything to contribute, and see only the risk in sharing their plans for the future. These companies close their doors on options not already in their master plan, even when customers are asking for them. In essence, they are not trusting their customers (or their customer support staff), hiding instead behind a wall of silence. Companies must learn to monitor customer feedback and leave it sufficiently open-ended to allow new ideas to flow into the business. Open-source leaders like Android, RedHat, and Samsung (again!) show that offering design options to customers and development partners can produce stunning results.

Add Options

Short-term financial thinking that restricts options ignores the wide collection of revenue enhancements and cost reductions from providing greater choice. Adding channels or options does come at a cost, but if options displace high-cost mechanisms or have become customer expectations, you can't ignore them. Sometimes this does mean having a willingness to experiment with new channels and choices to see how customers react. Customers cannot always express their needs without seeing or experiencing a new channel product or service; therefore, a willingness to experiment and fail fast is important. Even Apple demonstrated this with early efforts to introduce a tablet called Newton, only to perfect the idea years later with the amazing iPad. Amazon constantly offers choices while it experiments with online testing, not merely A/B testing but more like A/B/C … /Z testing!

Make Choice Work

"We can't make choice work" is a fear-based reaction, and it kills innovation. The many examples in this book show that company after company *has* made it work by finding clever ways to design choice into the products and services on offer. Shoes of Prey, for example, did not accept the accepted practice that all shoes had to be mass-produced; instead, it found ways to build standardization into parts of the shoe while leaving the customer free to design the rest.

Chapter Four

YOU MAKE IT EASY FOR ME

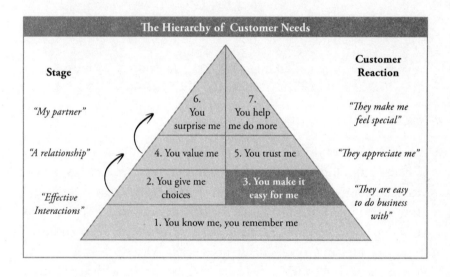

The Hierarchy of Customer Needs

Stage			Customer Reaction
"My partner"	6. You surprise me	7. You help me do more	*"They make me feel special"*
"A relationship"	4. You value me	5. You trust me	*"They appreciate me"*
"Effective Interactions"	2. You give me choices	3. You make it easy for me	*"They are easy to do business with"*
	1. You know me, you remember me		

DAVE WAS STARTING TO THINK THE REFUND PROCESS WASN'T WORTH THE FIVE DOLLARS.

In the good old days, companies made it easy for customers in many ways. Just like in the movie *Back to the Future*, the gas station attendants not only filled your tank but also cleaned your windshield and topped up your tires. Butchers, bakers, and others delivered to your door. Grocery store clerks packed your bags and carried heavy items to your car. Doctors made house calls. Often sales reps or service providers hid complexity by helping customers with application forms or researching alternatives. Part of good service was reducing effort for the customer, and the directness of the relationship and smaller scale of operations offered companies many opportunities to do so.

As organizations and the regulations that govern them have grown in complexity, it's also become harder to deal with them. Waves of centralization and cost reduction over the past thirty to forty years have often added work for the customer and made life harder rather than easier. Some processes have been designed to reduce internal costs at the customer's expense, or so it appears. Customers can experience frustrating complexity in every aspect of their experience with a company, from figuring out which product fits their needs to using or upgrading products or services to replacing them when it's time for something new. Figure 4.1 shows the challenges customers face through this life cycle.

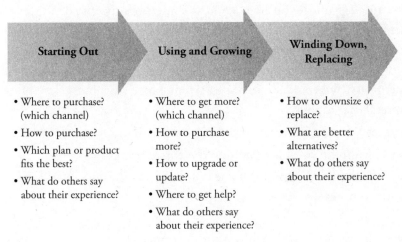

Figure 4.1 Customer Life Cycle—Vexing Questions.

In today's relationship-focused Me2B world, asking the customer to do the heavy lifting is becoming an ever-riskier proposition. Once again, hints to sustaining quality customer relationships can be gleaned from research on quality personal relationships. The Open University's Enduring Love research, in examining common factors among long-lasting relationships, demonstrated that reducing the effort for one's partner by sharing work and household chores is one of the key drivers of relationship success.[1] In personal relationships, doing your best to make things easier for your partner shows care and respect; ignoring your partner's needs or making their life more difficult quickly throws the relationship out of balance.

The same is true with customer relationships for organizations: When the business puts the customer to work and makes things hard, the customer feels exploited or disrespected, and the relationship doesn't endure. The Customer Research Council in 2009 identified that customer effort, namely the amount of work customers had to do (or the lack of it), was the best predictor of customer loyalty. Customers were more loyal when companies did not make them do unnecessary work.[2]

After the sale the relationship analogy breaks down a little because *easy* in the business context sometimes means spending less time together, not more. After all, not needing to interact at all requires no effort from the customer.

When interaction between the customer and the company is necessary, it should be low effort. For most customers, low-effort interaction means:

- It should be quick (valuing the customer's time).
- It should be straightforward (not putting the customer through unnecessary steps—or hoops; hence the cartoon at the start of the chapter).
- It should directly address the customer's need.
- It must feel simple and logical to the customer.
- It needs to fit with the way the customer likes doing things.

For some, going to a branch is hard, while for others going online is stressful. Providing choices is also part of being easy, because you can't assume you know what will work best for everyone.

While low effort sounds simple, it's actually very hard to do it well, because it requires organizations to understand their customers' expectations and skills, as well as how business processes affect these customers. And yet, thanks to the Me2B Leaders, customers' lives are getting easier once again. The best companies have found a number of ways to make doing business with them simple and low effort, across all stages of the customer life cycle. Table 4.1

Table 4.1   The Customer's Experience of Success and Failure

You Make It Easy for Me Success	You Make It Easy for Me Failure
You make it easy for me to buy from you.	You delay me or confuse me when I want to buy something from you.
You allow me to use your product or service without contacting you.	You insist on phone conversation or other personal contact when self-service would work better. (The same principle applies in reverse when the customer *does* want to make contact.)
You let me make the process easy for me.	You make me jump through your hoops, repeating known information or following tortuous paths.
You don't make me have to learn to navigate your organization.	I would require an org chart to find the right department when I don't even know, or want to know, how you're organized.
You get it right for me the first time—or if not, you fix it once and for all.	I keep running into the same blocks; I get no resolution from my previous request for help; it's like being stuck in the movie *Groundhog Day*.
You don't ask me about my effort.	You send me a survey asking how hard it is when I already wasted thirty minutes trying to figure out what to do.

shows the six underlying needs that we focus on in the rest of this chapter.

You Make It Easy for Me to Buy from You

Customer-business relationships start with some kind of purchase experience. That may begin with product research and comparison, a sales discussion, or a series of negotiations in the case of business-to-business transactions where sales cycles can be long and complex. You would think that every organization would look long and hard at its sales process and focus it around the customer's experience, but there are long, complex, or hard sales and purchase experiences in every channel:

- Check stands with long lines in supermarkets or empty check-out desks in department stores
- Online buying processes that ask for too much information or break down at key stages
- Long and complex application forms that request information the organization knows or that doesn't seem relevant to this purchase
- Sales discussions on the phone that are long and drawn out
- Complex quotations and pricing information
- Very complex terms and conditions statements
- Difficult payment processes

Bad Stories: Keep Me Grounded on Every Ticket

In a typical example of a broken online purchase process, a major airline had to upgrade its booking and reservation system and abandon the custom self-service platform it had developed, which had been very popular with customers. The new system had one major flaw: When frequent flyers identified themselves, the airline no longer pre-populated the online booking form with the customer's stored information. Having to enter their information for each new booking added two minutes to the process for most customers—extremely irritating for the most important customers, the frequent flyers, who knew how well the system worked before. You might think that this was just the inevitable wrinkle of installing a new system, but a year later the problem still hadn't been addressed. Why do companies forgo opportunities to make their customers' lives easier when that is the very point that can make or break a fledgling relationship?

Even worse was our LimeBridge U.K. business partner Pete Massey's experience getting a property insurance quote from a local insurance company. He went through many screens of questions, which collected information for Marketing rather than just what was needed for a quote. After nearly twenty minutes of effort, he reached the final screen, where he was asked to input the overall value of the property. When he did so, he was told it was above a threshold value, so he could not complete the process online and would have to talk to someone. Infuriated, he did not pursue the offer.

You might have thought that such a crucial question would have been the first one asked, not the last one. But the company was so focused on marketing and generating leads that it completely failed to think about the customer's experience, and as a result, lost many potential high-value sales. Peter had the same experience on other insurance websites, where the process was designed from the company's and not the customer's perspective.

Good Stories: Simpler Is Better

Me2B Leaders make both shopping and buying easy. Amazon, a leader in simplifying the point of sale, even makes it easy to cancel an order after it's been placed. Amazon understands that making things easy for the customer and protecting the relationship is always more important than making any given sale. One holiday season, the company faced a rare backlog in its distribution centers. Realizing that some orders were not going to make it to customers before the big day, the company sent an e-mail message for all at-risk orders, apologizing and offering two simple alternatives: (1) click here to cancel your order or (2) hang on and we'll get the order to you as soon as possible. While some customers did cancel, the vast majority thanked Amazon for the alert and opted for #2—saying either "I can't find it anywhere else" [so I trust Amazon to find it for me] or "it's not for the holiday season so I can wait."

RACV, one of the leading insurance companies in Australia, has been working hard to make the sales process easier. The old sales quotation process took more than ten minutes of customer effort. That was ten minutes just to get to a first quotation. Worse, it was designed to produce a quotation including all possible features that customers might want. Mostly this produced very expensive results and many prospects walked away, not realizing that some of these options could be removed to make the product more affordable, thus diminishing the sales center's conversion rate.

In rethinking the process RACV turned everything inside out, setting things up to present the lowest possible quotation as quickly as possible. Additional features that the customer needed for proper coverage were explored afterward. Reversing the process got people what they wanted—a baseline number for comparison shopping—quickly. Once they had an attractive starting point, customers were more interested in hearing about other aspects of the product. The conversion rate for prospects went up dramatically, so the company was delighted. But prospects and customers also won because the process required hardly any of their time, up until the point that they were likely to buy.

The Swedish retail furniture and home store IKEA is a global phenomenon and offers a unique customer experience. Inside the store, IKEA is a giant exercise in self-service, but designed in a way that makes it easy to buy. The store showroom designs are standard all over the world and deliberately maze-like (but at least offer clearly marked shortcuts) and take customers past all the products on offer before they reach the marketplace section, where smaller goods and knickknacks are sold, and then finally the warehouse where the flat-packed products are stored.

IKEA has also thought carefully about how to make a long visit with many bulky purchases easy for guests. Catalogs and order forms are everywhere, along with free pencils, so customers can figure out what they need and write down the items they want before they get to the warehouse. Customers have access to shoulder bags, carts, and dollies, and there's never a shortage. Knowing many customers have families, IKEA provides play areas and a cheap cafeteria with kid-friendly food. Support staff are everywhere, and at checkout, both manned registers and self-serve checkouts are available.

A visit to IKEA can still be an exhausting experience, but customers are rewarded with inexpensive, well-designed goods. They can readily see that IKEA has exploited every opportunity to make the buying experience easy and fun.

You Allow Me to Use Your Product or Service Without Contacting You

In our first book, *The Best Service Is No Service*, we emphasized that customers are happiest when organizations get things right in the first place—in other words, when they don't need to contact the company at all. In some way we consider this the ultimate in "making it easy." Companies that deliver on "Make it unnecessary to contact you" ask themselves relentlessly, across all functions and across the customer journey, "Why did our customers have to bother themselves to ask us for support or help?" They don't just manage the supply end of service—they try to reduce demand. They may also ask the same type of question in the sales areas, such as "Why aren't customers using our self-service sales systems?"

In *The Best Service Is No Service*, we also presented the concept of the "Value-Irritant" matrix, which asks, "Was this issue valuable for your customer, or an irritation to them?" and "Was the same issue valuable for your company, or an irritation?" Over the past six years we have run across strikingly similar results that tell us that more than 60 percent of the current effort in support centers should either be eliminated or automated since it is valuable for neither customers nor companies. Despite this compelling data many sales and marketing executives continue to argue, "Let's not remove these contacts! They're opportunities to sell more!" This is an old argument based on an obsession with cross-selling or up-selling. In our studies the success rate to cross-sell and up-sell is about 15 percent or lower, and so the vast majority of customers aren't happy with the process. Companies that continue to offer accessories, warranty plans, or other features on all contacts through cross-selling fail 85 percent of the time, so it's no wonder that customers are frustrated and say that it's hard to do business with them.

Others accept the "recovery theory," which says customers who have a problem that gets fixed have a higher loyalty rate than those with no problem in the first place. Despite data in numerous case studies to the contrary, these recovery theoreticians abound—but there are signs that they too agree that not having to contact companies for help is the preferred solution.

Bad Stories: Software Bumps and Backlog Bumps

Many software companies today operate around a beta-launch mindset, putting lightly tested products into the market and then using customers' failure reports to improve them. One of Bill's former clients, a prominent U.S.-based company, has even said, "Quality is v2," meaning that it will release products with a modicum of testing and await customer feedback to fix what needs fixing.

This may speed up the development process and make it easier to bring new products to market, but it certainly doesn't help make things easy for customers. Companies that do not perform sufficient usability testing before release suffer the consequences of making it hard for their customers to use their products in the first place. Frustrated customers may leave for good rather than provide the feedback required to improve the product quality.

For most companies, scrimping on testing and refinement is almost a sure way to alienate or lose customers. In Australia the four largest utilities implemented new billing systems over a five-year period, one after the other. In all four, software went live with major flaws: Bills were wrong, bills were late, discounts weren't applied, customer details were missing, and so forth. The contact volumes in these companies increased between 20 percent and 50 percent at various times. In one tracked period, the "irritating to customer" calls exceeded 50 percent. Inevitably these issues led to a loss of customers, reduced revenue, and increased complaints.

None of the three companies who had the chance learned from the experience of its predecessor, and the net result in all cases was that a flawed system went live, leading to massive amounts of work for customers and staff afterward. Another three months of testing and refinement might have reduced months of backlogs and avoided the armies of extra staff that the companies needed to handle things like increased complaint volumes. They also hit cash flow issues (if bills go out late, the money comes in later), had to manage a blowout in their debt books, and lost brand value.

Cross-functional backlogs are another common source of customer strife that unnecessarily burdens contact centers. Most businesses are complex, dynamic models of interconnected parts. If one part is broken, others also struggle. For example, in one health insurance business the claims area was a week behind with its work, leading to 20 percent more callers than usual, all demanding "where is my claim?" Unfortunately all the contact center agents could say was the claims were "in a queue" since no one had told them to reset customer expectations for claim duration. While the company thought it needed more staff in the contact center, what it really needed were more people on the claims team!

This kind of cross-functional backlog leading to irritating interactions is very common. Anytime a process goes slower than customers expect, call volume goes up. For example, we've seen backlogs in home loan applications, utility transfers, in-home installations, and life insurance claims drive exactly the same outcomes. If service levels on these kinds of processes fail to meet customers' expectations, then people will call—and increasingly they will complain online.

Good Stories: Solving Problems Before They Happen

In the last decade telecommunication companies including mobile carriers such as Telefonica O_2, Swisscom, British Telecom, and T-Mobile have embraced these principles of best service and as a result have reduced subscriber contacts dramatically. In 2002 British Telecom first assessed the volume of repeat calls, finding it to be over 30 percent in billing and faults. As a first step to solving the problem, BT focused on resolving customer issues on the first call, which got rid of 15 percent of all calls. Then they started looking at the demand side and asked, "Why was the call needed in the first place?"

The results were quite dramatic: Over a four-year period the volume of calls decreased from 2.3 million per day to 1.0 million per day, removing 60 percent of manned interactions. Some of these contacts did migrate to self-service, but it's still a remarkable reduction. BT also measured customers' reaction to these sorts of change. The number of customers who would recommend BT increased by 40 percent and the company attained savings of over $300 million per year.

Payments company CheckFree also embraced the idea of reducing customer contact and has produced impressive results. In 2002 and 2003, it sought to understand the causes of calls so that categories or types of calls could be reduced. The reduction initiatives included

- Having a single customer service representative handle a customer's call, rather than transferring it to a central research team
- Educating customers at the end of each call so that they could use self-service functions the next time
- Applying rigorous Six Sigma analysis to eliminate several broken processes that were causing delays in meeting customer commitments for payments
- Greatly simplifying the IVR system and website to provide engaging self-service solutions that worked, preventing customers from having to contact customer service in the first place

As a result of these and other initiatives, CheckFree went through the next eight years with the same customer support headcount even as the company grew the top line by more than six times. Customer satisfaction soared, as did employee satisfaction. The overall results have been very impressive, with contacts per active subscriber plummeting 20 percent year over year while customer satisfaction scores kept rising steadily.[3]

You Let Me Make the Process Easy for Me

It's easy for us to say that companies should make it easy for the customer. What makes this goal hard to achieve is that individuals and groups have different needs and therefore different definitions of what makes things easy for them. Saying that organizations need to find ways of making it easy for customers with different needs may sound like inviting in expensive complexity. The solution actually lies in outstanding design principles when building websites, product manuals, business processes, and the customer experience itself.

Good design creates services and channels that everyone can use, while outstanding design builds in flexibility for different needs; for example, a website with outstanding design allows for the learner as well as the power user.

Making the customers regard processes as responsive to their needs requires understanding what people are prepared to do, when they need help, and how to support and anticipate their way of working. It may also include education so that a customer becomes aware of options or methods to get help.

Bad Stories: Tuned to the Wrong Channel

Sometimes companies let customers make the process harder for themselves by sticking with a specific channel even when it doesn't suit the work that needs to be done. E-mail processing teams seem to be the worst offenders for this. We saw a team in a health insurance business that had no process at all to offer alternative channels even when it was clear that some customer requests couldn't be handled via e-mail. They also refused to look forward in the process, often spreading their information requests from inquiring customers over up to ten e-mail messages rather than thinking carefully about what would be needed and asking for it all upfront.

Supporting the customer's way of working also means being flexible around language, always prepared to use terminology that's natural to the customer. We spent some time with a prominent computer manufacturer that insisted on calling its portable computers "notebooks" instead of "laptops" or other generally used terms in an attempt to differentiate the brand. It even constrained its speech IVR system to recognize only the word *notebook*; using any other expression bounced the customer to a technical service representative. Clearly making customers' lives easy wasn't the top priority!

Other organizations fall into the trap of company-speak: they use internal jargon or expressions that make no sense to their customers and sometimes make no sense to their own employees but are viewed as the common language. You see this on software company websites that are almost impossible to navigate. They might use version numbers or internal code names that baffle customers, forcing them to pick up the phone to speak to someone—or, in an increasing number of cases, complain online in forums or community sites.

Good Stories: Intelligent Design

Honda Motor Company's Quick Start Guide is a great example of design that carefully considers the user's needs. Typically car companies saddle new owners with 300-plus-page manuals that offer so much detail no one wants to bother with them. Honda's Quick Start Guide is seventeen-page summary of the most important information in the manual to start and operate your car, making it easy to access the key points, including simple diagrams of the most frequently used features and components, such as the car's instrument panel. It has the added advantage of being plastic-coated so that it can survive heavy usage, spills, and being stepped on or crammed into the glove compartment.

Health insurer Bupa designed a friendly solution to encourage customers to shift out of e-mail for interactions that weren't suited to that channel. After identifying the issues that were complex enough to be better handled by a phone call, it sent customers who e-mailed with any of those issues a message with the option to either phone in or receive a call to address the problem. This allowed the customers to help decide their easiest path to resolution.

The net result of this added upfront communication was a win for the company and for the customer. Customers got faster resolution of complex issues and invested less effort. Bupa also won through reduced interaction volumes and faster handle times on these calls compared to addressing the same problems via e-mail.

You Don't Make Me Have to Learn How to Navigate Your Organization

Making it easy also extends to how well companies have organized themselves to meet customer needs. Many companies today have developed their customer-facing organization structures for internal reasons. Some structures reflect the growth of products and services, while others attempt to build skill-based specialization. While that may seem to work for the organization, it can make life much harder for the customer, who then has to negotiate complex IVR systems and speech engines to reach the desired department or make contact multiple times to get things done. There's nothing more frustrating than when, at the end of a long conversation, the customer service agent tells the customer, *"Sorry, I can't help you here. Hang up and call our other number and someone there will take care of you."*

Even website designs—ostensibly built with the customer in mind—often reflect product and functional silos rather than customer needs. For example, banks typically organize their websites according to their internal department structure. Meanwhile, a customer who goes on the site preparing to buy a car might find it more convenient to find related services like personal loans and insurance in one place.

Bad Stories: Customer-Facing Complexity

We've seen numerous examples of layers of IVR systems that achieve no purpose for the customer. For example, one asked customers to identify themselves as retail or business, but all calls went to the same agents. Some companies do this for reporting but it's lazy and unnecessary; they are saying, *"We can't find a way to count our stuff so please do it for us!"*

The worst case of complexity we saw was a large telco with sixty-seven different skill sets. The irony here was that it spent $1 billion on a new CRM system to provide a common view of company across its product and system silos, but it still left the sixty-seven specializations in place. Therefore, while the agents now knew and understood more about your whole relationship with the company because of the new system, they couldn't act on it. If your query related to a product or service that wasn't in their narrow skill set, they had to transfer you.

Good Stories: Putting the Customer First

Me2B Leaders find ways to make themselves easier to deal with by simplifying their structures and the associated processes, putting the customer's experience front and center. Amazon jolted the tech support world by offering the Mayday Button in the Amazon Fire HDX tablet, and more recently on the Amazon Fire smart-phone, a free built-in video link to an Amazon technical support representative—an impressive example of saving customers from the trouble of navigating a support system when they most need help. Blizzard Entertainment has offered something similar for its multi-player gamers: free in-game support that allows players to continue finding orcs or gathering gold coins while getting help.

With standards being set by companies like Amazon and Blizzard, increasingly customers are demanding what we call "first contact resolution," with minimal call transfers and no requirement to navigate the organization's complexity. But companies face some tricky choices here. It's hard in a complex business to train agents to do everything for everybody and to create super generalists or universal agents. These models can also cause problems because the training time is so long and many staff often still need to seek help and support to solve problems because they lack the required depth of knowledge.

Bankwest, based in Perth, Western Australia, found a great way to balance the customers' need for simplicity with the real practical issues of complex service problems. The bank learned that customers were very unhappy with their contact center experiences, and it sought to improve them. The bank's business strategy was to sell customers multiple products, but the contact center wasn't built to support that. It was organized around product silos like retail accounts, Internet banking, and mortgages. Customers often got lost, and nearly 20 percent of calls were transferred. Repeat call rates were also very high as some agents tried to help customers without the skill to do so. Customers also had to negotiate a speech system just to get to these agents.

To fix these issues, the bank redesigned the contact center from product-based to complexity-based, creating a two-tier structure. The first person the customer spoke to was trained to be able to handle 70 percent of inquiries for all products. But the bank took an additional step: Agents were trained to identify calls too complex for them to handle within sixty to ninety seconds, so that the customer got to a capable expert quickly.

The net result of the new contact center approach was a customer experience that was 25 percent shorter, with repeat calls slashed in half. Additionally, the new structure created a shorter training period for new staff and a well-structured career path. Customers found the new process easier, and they never had to navigate complexity on their own.

You Get It Right for Me the First Time—or If Not, You Fix It Once and for All

As we've already described, solving customers' problems on first contact isn't easy, even for intelligently designed customer service organizations. Aside from the challenge of mastering complexity, mistakes do happen and organizations can put the customer through annoying experiences like repeat contacts or correction of mistakes. If they do that, it is essential that the problem gets fixed on the next contact. If a customer is forced to perform this extra effort, the repair and recovery needs to be perfect.

Bad Stories: Twenty-Seven Contacts

In one of our forums, a leading U.S. financial services provider told us about a business customer of theirs who contacted the company twenty-seven times to get the same problem fixed. Can you imagine this customer's frustration? If nothing else, you have to admire his persistence. Because of the balkanization of its customer data, the firm found it very hard to figure out that this was the same customer who had contacted it so many times. Once this became clear, and the customer contact systems were better aligned, "twenty-seven contacts" became a prominent case study to make sure that going forward, problems would be solved at first contact.

In our client work with high-tech companies, we find that many of them require 2.75 contacts to solve the same issue. That's far fewer than this disastrous example—but still 1.75 too many.

Good Stories: Melting Snowballs and Handling Complexity

While the best practice is to prevent problems in the first place, it is also critical to fix them once and for all if they do occur. Any issue that is not solved the first time becomes a repeat contact. At Amazon, Bill and his team used to call these repeat contacts "snowballs": When a snowball continues to roll downhill unobstructed or unabated, it grows in size and power and can become deadly.

Bill and his customer service group put in place a simple concept that tracked which customer service agents, which teams, which centers, and which outsourcing partners caused repeat contacts, as opposed to which ones resolved repeat contacts, or "melted the snowballs." This became very important when Amazon contracted with its first outsourcing partner to provide e-mail support. That company was made well aware of all the financial implications and customer experience impact of causing repeat contacts, and therefore developed new ways to prevent repeats and melt any repeat contacts it encountered. This contributed to Amazon's stellar American Customer Satisfaction Index (ACSI), among other highly regarded customer satisfaction ratings.

Amazon's rate of repeat contacts dropped quickly to well under 10 percent. In our studies of more than a hundred organizations since, we have never found another organization with less than 9 percent repeat contacts, and the average we have seen is 13 percent, setting Amazon well ahead of the pack.

Elsewhere, complexity-split models, those that get complex queries to experienced staff like the one employed at Bankwest in Perth, have proved very effective in increasing first contact resolution and reducing repeat contacts. But matching complex problems to the most experienced agents is much harder to do than it sounds. Customers don't know if their issue is complex—and nor does the technology. David's company solves this problem by redesigning call-handling processes to quickly identify complex problems and get customers to an experienced agent. Once companies get this right, they can offer the second tier, the complex problem team, increased authority and empowerment to solve problems. This is the group who are expected to sort out any repeat contacts.

Bupa International is a great example of a company that redesigned its customer support system to match agent expertise with the customer's specific complaint. Bupa sells health insurance to individuals working offshore all over the world. With so many situations and a complex claims process, the potential for repeat contacts was high. In one observation sample, over 40 percent of calls were repeats.

The company redesigned the system to align complexity with experience and raised the authority level of the experienced agents. In the new model, 70 percent of callers got first-point resolution and 30 percent were transferred to the expert team. But these experts resolved nearly all these contacts, with the intent of 100 percent first-contact resolution. Interestingly, many customers don't perceive the shift to an expert as a transfer. Instead of feeling lost, they feel they've been escalated to someone more important. That can be a game-changer in terms of perception of first-point resolution. Workload in the new model (a combination of call volumes and the number of contacts) fell by 40 percent. Nearly 20 percent of call volume disappeared, and the time that agents spent on the contact also fell by nearly two minutes a call. This also meant that every contact was answered faster. Wait times all but disappeared. Clearly, the customer was the real winner.

You Don't Ask Me About My Effort

Many organizations have embarked on a strategy "to reduce customer effort" ever since a *Harvard Business Review* article first promoted this concept in July 2010.[4] This article urged organizations to measure customer effort by surveying customers about how hard it was for them to sign up, change details, and conduct other interactions with the organization. The irony has been that companies have started putting the customers through extra effort to ask them about their effort!

Bad Stories: Surveys of Doom

Two separate airlines in Australia are offenders. Both survey their customers by sending e-mail after their flights, starting with the statement, "This will take 12–15 minutes of your time." That alone is a significant effort for a customer, but it gets worse. In both cases the first parts of the survey ask things the airline already knows like "how did you book and how did you check in?" The airline expects the customer to recycle all this information that the airline already knows because the survey process has not hooked into the core systems and data. When a customer indicates a serious problem by giving a low score, no follow-up questions ask for more information. Not only are the surveys long, they are also frustrating. It's hard to say whether this frightful survey experience is better or worse than the old method used by one of the airlines: Customers on long-haul flights received a paper survey that was so long, almost a meter, that David used to unfurl it at conferences to show people how *not* to do it. On the other hand, since the forms were offered during the longest flights, at least passengers had plenty of empty time to complete them.

Good Stories: Letting Data Speak

Like most U.S. businesses, the regional cable and entertainment company Suddenlink asks its customers for their satisfaction levels, and whether they'd recommend the company to a friend after interacting with the company (the NPS). Recently, Suddenlink has augmented this practice with its Customer Insights initiative, which mines recorded calls and agent notes to determine how easy it is to do business with the company. The approach has yielded numerous insights that have reduced customer demand for support and replaced the quality monitoring function that used to sample contacts in favor of the ability to analyze 100 percent of customer contacts. Nuggets of extracted information have helped Engineering to pinpoint problem areas and Marketing to simplify offers and promotions.

But as perhaps its greatest achievement, Suddenlink's Customer Insights has relieved the customer from having to say again, in a sealed survey, what it's like to work with the company. Instead, the company can analyze the customer's conversation verbatim and link it with other information sources, producing a sharp analytical tool to improve every aspect of the business. The company's focus on customer ease can be seen in its internal values statement that includes cultural goals such as "I make easy easier" and "I am hassle free."

Australian utility AGL has also rethought every customer interaction process. This included investing more time in setting up the customers for success when they moved into a property or transferred to AGL so that they didn't have to call when the first bill wasn't what they expected. Other changes included giving experienced agents more authority to solve problems and enabling staff to send more information to customers in real time via e-mail. The reduction in customer-effort measures in the 2012 annual report demonstrated that effort had been reduced by over 15 percent and the rate of complaints to the central Ombudsman had been halved.

Why "You Make It Easy for Me" Is So Important

Organizations that have made business easy for their customers have reaped huge harvests. They have lower operating costs, higher customer propensity to purchase and to repurchase, and lower customer and staff attrition (with the related advantage of lower replacement costs).

Moreover, operating on a simpler scale creates an operation that can be more agile and able to capitalize on opportunities. These organizations are outward looking, instead of constantly focused on managing failure demand—reactively fixing things that are broken. Because they have folded ease and simplicity into process design thinking, their profits increase compared to old models and their customers are happier.

The strategic and relationship benefits of making things easy for the customer are clear: Fewer contacts, shorter contacts, and above all, less customer frustration. Table 4.2 summarizes the benefits. In many of these instances, once the experiences are easier, customers are far more willing to contemplate other products and offers. After a major simplification program, one of Bill's U.S. telecommunications clients raised its take-up of cross-sold products by over 30 percent because the staff had the time to make the offers and customers were far more willing to listen.

Meet the Challenge: You Make It Easy for Me

Many factors have led organizations away from being easy to work with as they have become bigger and more complex. Companies often just don't realize how hard to deal with they have become, but several straightforward steps will help cut through the hassle.

Put Customer Goals Before Marketing Goals in the Sales Process

Plenty of companies throw large amounts of time and effort into their sales force and their marketing spend, only to fall short at the stage when the customer actually wants to buy something. Marketing is one of the culprits making the sales and purchase experience unduly burdensome. For example, the Marketing Department is usually very keen to obtain lots of information from what it sees as the "prospect" or "new customer" to enable follow-up or future promotions, but customers don't want to give up information unless they get something back. They walk away from websites that ask for information that isn't related to the product or service at hand. Companies must design sales processes from the customer's perspective, not the company's, which may mean capturing less information even though Marketing really wants it.

Table 4.2 The Benefits of Making It Easy

Customer Need Met	Potential to Increase Revenue	Potential to Reduce Cost
You make it easy for me to buy from you.	Higher sales conversion rates, larger average order size, greater amounts of cross-sales and up-sales More frequent purchases Greater retention and higher lifetime value	Reduced cost per sale Fewer returns, less reverse logistics expense Less capital for sales support operations
I don't want to have to contact you.	More time for marketing Increased cross-sell propensity Positive word-of-mouth marketing	Less capital for care and tech support operations, and less operating costs for both areas
You let me make the process easy for me.	Faster sales (order to cash) Higher levels of sales Positive word of mouth influencing others to buy	Less time and cost to rework Lower customer retention and win-back expenses
You don't make me have to learn how to navigate your organization.	Higher spend Greater cross-sell propensity and time to cross-sell	Less time with distractions and multiple handling of same issues
You get it right for me the first time—or if not, you fix it once and for all.	Customer retention and loyalty Positive word of mouth	Less time and cost to rework Much less demand for support because it works!
You don't ask me about effort that you already know.	Higher spend More purchases in response to customer feedback known in real time	Less time and expense surveying customers, collecting responses, and analyzing results

Keep the Legalese Light

Legal and Compliance departments often insist on complex script-
ing and terms-and-conditions statements to avoid very theoretical
risks. Often the customer has to sign or tick to acknowledge having
read the terms and conditions, but let's be honest, very few people
actually read them. We don't! They are written in complex legalese
and almost unintelligible without a law degree. The worst we've seen
ran for over a hundred pages. We've heard customers hang up after a
fifteen-minute sales conversation because the final step in the process
was playing a terms-and-conditions script! What a waste. We have
helped clients time and again to challenge offering these legal statements, instead finding other ways to be compliant yet much more
customer-sensitive.

Rethink the Basics

Some of the most fundamental reasons that it's so hard for companies to deliver "easy" are cultural. For one, it often means sweeping
changes, rethinking the entire way the organization works. Management must have patience and thick skin to break down all the steps to
produce, deliver, and support products and services in order to strip
out redundancy, confusion, and barriers. Most of these problems
stem from issues outside the Customer Service team and therefore
fixing them needs broad organizational involvement and commitment, as we described in *The Best Service Is No Service*.

Walk in the Customer's Shoes

Many organizations suffer from insularity or groupthink, and they
forget to get new perspective by walking in the customer's shoes.
When CEOs do "go back to the floor" they are often figuratively
floored when they see what it's like to be their customer. But apart
from reality TV, how many CEOs actually take the time to do this?
      While meeting with the global head of technical support for a
leading software company, Bill once asked, "What do *you* do when
you need tech help?" The officer smiled and grabbed his handset,

dialed three digits, and got connected immediately to a highly skilled tech agent. Fast and easy!

When Bill pointed out that his customers had to endure long searches to find a number to call, long hold times waiting to speak with someone (often located offshore, harder to understand), and several attempts to get an issue resolved, this savvy global head of technical support winced. He admitted that he had never used his company's website to find the right number, or called it to experience the hold time or go through the offshore agent interaction. He did, however, admit to having a slew of reports that confirmed how hard it was for his customers.

CHAPTER FIVE

YOU VALUE ME

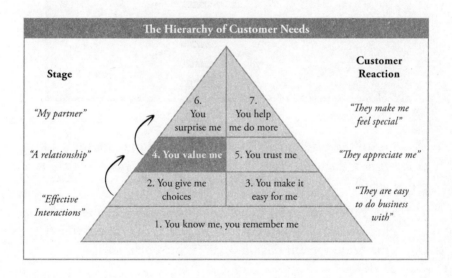

The Hierarchy of Customer Needs

Stage

"My partner"

"A relationship"

"Effective Interactions"

6. You surprise me	7. You help me do more	
4. You value me	5. You trust me	
2. You give me choices	3. You make it easy for me	
1. You know me, you remember me		

Customer Reaction

"They make me feel special"

"They appreciate me"

"They are easy to do business with"

M ost of us have heard this message, sometimes multiple times in a single call, while waiting on hold to speak to a contact center agent:

> "Your call is important to us. All our operators are busy right now so please stay on the line and we'll connect you to the next available customer care representative."

This trite recording is often used in the customer service world—and yet could there be a more hypocritical message about valuing customers than that one? At first it might seem sincere, but when the customer hears it minute after minute, it grows more and more hollow. If the organization truly valued the customer, it would add more agents or find a better way to handle the call volume it receives—or so the customer is left to feel.

Why do some organizations treat their customers like cheap commodities while others treat them like gold dust? Any successful two-way relationship is built on an exchange of value. The challenge is that it's hard to know at the start of any relationship how valuable it will be. Companies in recent years have decided which customers deserve to be rewarded for their value by analyzing which are important and which are not, based on their "recency, frequency, and monetary returns," or RFM.

The companies leading in customer experience today—and performing better because of it—find creative, meaningful ways to make all customers feel valued. They see the RFM model as the equivalent of looking in the rearview mirror to figure out how to move forward. Instead, Me2B Leaders recognize that it's very hard to spot a valuable customer early in a relationship, when data on spending and behavior is unclear. Instead they focus on calculating and managing the potential value that customers can bring to them—in particular, potential profitability based on future spend, including greater share of wallet. They also consider the potential value of positive word of mouth that influences others to do business with the organization.

The old customer segment model completely misses these targets. The new success strategy points toward treating all customers as valuable, or at least having a very clear line of sight on future value and early indicators of potential value. There is also a school of thought, embraced by many Me2B Leaders, that all customers can be valuable if you take the time to build an effective two-way relationship.

Understanding customer value was easier when most business was local and face-to-face. The organizations of yesteryear had personal memory of the length of the relationship with each customer. Local bank managers or garage mechanics therefore knew instinctively how to value those relationships. The storeowner in the good old days might have run a tab for a known and valued customer and only sought payment once a month. Contrast this with large companies today, whose debt collection and credit management processes rarely vary depending on customer history.

Of course, businesses have always had different tiers of service and versions of customer segmentation. Pubs in the United Kingdom used to have a public bar for one class of customers and a lounge or saloon bar for the more affluent clientele. Many rail services had three classes of travel, just as full-price international airline carriers still have today. However, whatever the class, the best of yesterday's businesses showed an underlying respect for all customers, treating them as individuals to be valued, not potential figures in a balance sheet.

That is the essence of "You Value Me," the fourth customer need to be met for Me2B success. Today's customers want more than rewards cards or discounts, whether they're in the company's backyard or halfway around the world. They want to be listened to, they want to have a say in how the company treats them and other customers, and they believe they deserve better treatment the longer they've been loyal to the business.

Sometimes simple gratitude is all that is required for a customer to feel valued and respected. Small gestures go surprisingly far to strengthen relationships with customers, not unlike what you might have experienced in your personal relationships. The Open University research in the United Kingdom, cited earlier, found that expressions of thanks and thoughtful gestures—a very basic way of showing that a partner is valued—were in fact a key factor in successful personal relationships.

Many organizations, however, fail to provide value gestures to the customer. In some organizations, the attitude is worse than negligence—instead, it is clear that customers are a commodity to be exploited. These organizations value neither the customers' time nor their contribution to the business. In this new customer-centric era, that positioning is no longer tenable. Business relationships built on the idea of "the value I can extract from you" will be a thing of the past. This chapter offers a guide to satisfying customers' growing desire to work with companies that take the time and the effort to make them feel valued. We describe five contributors to this overall customer Value Me need in the rest of the chapter, starting with Table 5.1.

You Value My Potential

All customers, not just big spenders, want to be treated well. They want to know that their purchase, however small, is important—and at the very least merits them a quality experience. One way to fulfill

Table 5.1 The Customer's Experience of Success and Failure

You Value Me Success	You Value Me Failure
You value my potential.	You treat customers well only if they have already produced large amounts of revenue.
You value the length and depth of my relationship with you.	You offer me discounts to join and then full rates after a few months. You operate in product silos so that I'm treated differently by different parts of the organization.
You listen to me and act on what I say.	You force me to give feedback in ways and at times that I don't want to. Never follow up on any feedback I give.
You value my time and effort.	You see company and staff time as more important than mine. You make me wait frequently and repeat information and processes.
You make sure your partners value me as you do.	Your partners and related businesses show no understanding of my relationship with you.

this need is to focus on potential value, recognizing that customers who aren't providing much revenue now might become high-value later, if they're treated right. This is widely known by marketers as CLV, or customer lifetime value.

Of course, shifting focus to future profitability is a challenging proposition for most companies. It's far afield from the common strategy today, which emphasizes past customer sales, and requires not only forecasting future value but also weighing it against the future costs of serving each customer. But those who blindly focus on past revenue risk falling into the trap of thinking that past experience will repeat in the future. In fact, every customer is constantly undergoing lifestyle and life cycle changes—getting married, changing jobs, inheriting money. Looking backward causes these companies to significantly underestimate the value of many of their customers—and those customers, quite naturally, feel undervalued or maybe even ignored. At other times, hindsight leads companies to the other extreme, overestimating customers' true current value.

Shifting to an emphasis on potential value (or CLV) is not as mysterious a notion as it may seem. There are many ways to measure potential value, some already being practiced by companies today, even if simplistically. The first is to figure how much a typical customer is worth per year or per purchase, and compare that to acquisition and ongoing support costs. Statistics have circulated for many years in some industries comparing the costs of acquiring a new customer compared to retaining one. That ratio and relative cost is important. In recent mergers, market commentators stated that one company had effectively paid $1,000 per customer. The average margin per customer per year in that industry was $300. Clearly this meant that the organization believed it would keep each customer for at least 3.33 years just to break even. In the same industry, acquiring a customer through knocking on doors or by outbound calling cost in the order of $200 per acquisition. However, acquiring also meant discounting and reduced the margin in the first year to zero. In both of these areas companies had models of the future value of these customers. Simplistic though their models may be, they clearly illustrate that acquisition is an expensive game and that retention activities can be essential to making that cost worthwhile.

In fact, it may be more profitable to invest in a retention campaign than to acquire new customers. Put another way, if you can make the current customers *stickier*—more likely to stay with you—for example, by fixing things that might make them leave, there is a huge payback. David's company recently advised a business that had acquired a smaller business. The plan was to merge the small business into the mother ship—but that started to make less sense when David's team found that the smaller business had a far better customer experience. Keeping the small business separate added costs per year, but analysis showed that losing 250 customers (a tiny percentage)—a likely result of dumping them into the larger company's pool—would cost the company even more. The future value of those customers exceeded the costs of retaining the business as a separate entity.

Bad Stories: Narrow View of the Wallet

One of the tricky issues when determining a company's "share of wallet" (share of the money customers spend on the type of goods and services the company offers) is defining the scope of the wallet. Take booksellers. Is the wallet the entire market's book purchases? Or do you consider that a book is also a form of personal entertainment and education, meaning that the wallet should include alternative forms of entertainment and education, such as magazines or schools? If the former, you might have the 25 percent share of the customer's wallet but if the latter, you might have only 2 percent. It's easy to see how this might expand your idea of each customer's future potential.

Airlines struggle with this concept. Their model rewards frequent flyers, but they don't know enough about anyone's overall travel history to construct a useful "share of wallet" analysis. For example, if a frequent traveler on American Airlines flies 55,000 miles, American might place that customer in a middling level; it's not that many miles. But suppose the airline knew that the same customer was flying another 200,000 miles a year with other carriers, and also that those miles were on routes that American also flies. Better treatment might shift more of those miles in American's direction. Sure, some airlines send surveys to their customers asking about overall numbers of flights or miles per year, but the response rate for such surveys is extremely low. So, instead of valuing the potential for travelers across the industry, the airlines—in general—fall well short and do themselves a revenue disservice by only counting their own miles. If, instead, the airlines collected data from social media, idle conversations with check-in staff, and many other sources, they could begin to construct the potential value of their travelers and then treat them very differently.

Good Stories: Predicting Potential

Calculating the future value of customers becomes a more attractive investment when companies learn to identify the characteristics of higher-potential customers, making it possible to focus on acquiring more of them and investing in their retention. In the 1990s, the National Australia Bank embraced this approach, having recognized that white-collar professionals were very profitable customers. To cater to them, they created a "professionals package" that bundled products and services. They waived fees on certain accounts, believing that these customers—the type likely to take on a large mortgage—would be well worth the investment. The bundled package of products also made these customers stickier since it was harder for them to change banks. As a result of this campaign, the NAB captured more of the most valuable customers in the marketplace than its competitors were able to hold on to.

Lloyds is another bank that has invested in customers with strong potential value. In the United Kingdom, only a subset of students complete the final two years of high school, known as sixth form. These students are more likely to go on to university and well-paid careers. Lloyds ran competitions for sixth formers, with prizes such as a trip to the United States. Anyone who entered received a $10 deposit in a Lloyds bank account. The bank identified a group with good potential value, then bet that £5 a head (along with contest expenses) was a relatively cheap way to sign up members of that group for their first bank account.

Media providers such as DIRECTV use the broad view of "share of wallet" to their advantage. DIRECTV calculates not only its revenue from its subscribers (perhaps $110 per month), but also the amount that its subscribers spend each month going to movies, buying DVDs (admittedly a lower amount year over year), and participating in other forms of entertainment and education. Understanding the larger picture of its customers' entertainment expenses helps the company understand their potential spend. That's important information for helping set prices for sporting events, premium channels, streaming options, and other new products. By deciding that it's in the entertainment business, not the satellite television business, DIRECTV is able to move ahead to calculate and realize customers' true potential value.

You Value the Length and Depth of My Relationship with You

Companies often do not understand the value and importance of the length and depth of each customer's relationship with them. Meanwhile, customers want their loyalty, measured by time and spend, recognized and rewarded. Companies would do well to recognize length and depth of relationships for reasons beyond the customer's experience. A customer who stays with an insurer for five years may be far more valuable than one who stays a year, even if the latter buys more products. Long relationships reduce the high costs of sales and acquisitions, and offer valuable chances for the organization to understand customers better and design products and processes to address their needs. The depth of a relationship matters too. A customer might be very profitable in one product and not another. An affluent bank customer, for example, may not earn the bank much in credit card finance charges or checking account fees, but may have an investment or pension portfolio that generates a large amount of wealth management income for the bank as a whole.

Assessing the entire relationship becomes the only way to determine the real value of the customer. The length of the relationship predates even the first purchase. It includes early inquiries and sales proposals for business relationships or searches and early customer discovery for personal relationships. The depth of the relationship is more than the total amount of sales in any given time. It also needs to include how the customer interacts with the company. For example, some customers are high touch and expensive to serve relative to their spend, while others may have few products but be profitable. This analysis also needs to include the share of wallet and how highly the customer values the company.

Bad Stories: Relationships with Expiration Dates

The advent of airline frequent flyer programs has been one of the biggest developments in customer loyalty in the past twenty-five years. These programs have been hugely successful, and yet they also miss major opportunities to show long-time, high-mileage customers how much they're valued. Beginning with American Airlines and quickly copied by virtually every airline in the world, there are now multiple levels of frequent flyer status that receive increasing rewards, including upgrades, extra baggage allowance, and free flights. But for some crazy reason the airlines decided that their frequent flyers would need to requalify every year on a calendar basis.

This has led to a strange seasonal behavior by some flyers who squeeze in round-trip flights toward the end of the year just so they can keep their status level. To the customer who might have had one off year, it can seem as if the airline is saying, "What have you done for me lately?"—which could be an expensive mistake if the customer's travel picks up the next year with no feeling of loyalty to the old standby. In fact, we have seen some of our LimeBridge business partners move completely away from particular airlines because they just missed a status level. It gets even crazier: We know of no cases where any airline has bothered to contact its frequent fliers who have reduced the number of miles flown year-over-year to inquire why their patronage has changed: Is it because of mistakes made by the airline? Changes in the customer's circumstances that might change in the coming year? Or is it because the silly requalifying rule lost them a status level? Just think how valuable it would be for an airline to obtain and analyze this data.

Many businesses, by no means just airlines, need to adapt existing business processes that fail to take into account the customer's prior history. Customers of insurance companies, utilities, and credit cards are typically charged a late payment fee regardless of their prior track record. When they have paid on time in every prior period for ten, fifteen, or twenty years, the fee is like a slap in the face. We've listened to them complain to contact centers, full of distraught, "*But I've been a customer for fifteen years, I just forgot to pay before I went away on vacation!*" In some instances, the frontline staff might have the freedom or the good sense to waive a fee. But we've never seen a company proactively manage this by measuring customers' good behavior and rewarding it with flexible policy. Generally they count only infractions such as missed payments, not good behaviors, such as "paid on time 146 times out of 146." If they did, perhaps they could send a different letter for a one-off miss or waive the fee for any first-time error.

Customers won't tolerate what they perceive as this mistreatment by banks. In 2014 lawyers in Australia filed a class-action suit against a number of banks for excessive late payment fees. The court ruled that the fees charged by the banks are out of line with the costs involved and ruled in favor of mass refunds. This was the ultimate slap on the wrist to the industry for gouging customers regardless of their behavior. As we went to press a series of other class action cases were lined up for other banks.

Good Stories: Swapping Status

Some airlines are getting it right, recognizing that the overall tenure of a long-term relationship with their flyers is more important than a yearly quota. They have granted these customers permanent status—perhaps not the highest level—in order to recognize and encourage their loyalty. Bill has earned this grandfathered status on United Airlines (where he is a two-million-mile flyer) and Delta Airlines (where he is a one-million-mile flyer), and he and other customers have benefited greatly from this level of recognition—and so have the airlines, with sustained patronage.

Virgin Airlines allows its flyers to waive certain fees and charges based on their tenure with the company—clearly a stab at keeping them as frequent flyers but also smart business in general. Why would any company want to annoy its best customers with nickel-and-dime charges when they can simply fly or shop elsewhere with relatively little friction? Virgin Australia recently went even further than this. In a recent dispute, competitor airline Qantas suffered a series of strikes and disruptions. Many customers had no choice but to travel Virgin Australia. Virgin recognized that transferring meant many customers would miss their frequent flyer status. So throughout the dispute it acknowledged Qantas status in all its lounges; a Qantas Gold customer was treated like a Virgin Gold customer. Qantas customers were delighted by this unexpected treatment, and Virgin got to showcase its lounge experience to new customers.

Anniversary celebrations and appreciation events are an easy way for organizations to recognize and reward the length and depth of customer relationships. Clubs and nonprofit mutual organizations seem to be better at this because they see customers as members rather than sources of profit. (Note: Me2B Leaders such as Costco, REI, and USAA also arrange to have their customers join and become members.)

The Bellevue Club where Bill and his wife are members is a good example. Its retail shop sends a 25 percent coupon for anything purchased on or after a member's birthday, a classic version of an anniversary celebration and, on top of that, the club finds seats at hard-to-get performances like *The Book of Mormon*. The Royal Automobile Club of Victoria in Melbourne, David's club and the leading roadside assistance provider in the state, sends customers birthday vouchers for discounts on meals and other facilities. The cost? Low. The result? Not only "wow!" reactions but also repeat purchases and word of mouth, including all-important mentions on Facebook, Twitter, blogs, and other community forums. As well, RACV customers are color-coded by their years of tenure: five years, Bronze; ten years, Silver, and so on. Each level also comes with a greater discount. This is a true reward for loyalty, offering both recognition and an incentive to stay. The company is acknowledging that when customers have paid twenty years of premiums, they've earned the discount.

You Listen to Me and Act on What I Say

In any relationship, not being listened to is frustrating. It's a major cause of relationship breakdowns. But listening alone is not enough—it needs to be followed by action. The response can take many forms. Let's start with acknowledgment. The customers need to know they've been heard. Then there's tactical action, such as resolving a customer's specific issue. Next there's explaining the context, and why change may or may not be possible. Finally, the company might make a real systemic change to address the customer's feedback.

Customer-centric companies have found many ways to listen and learn from their customers. They value their customers not merely for the financial return that they can bring but also for their ideas and critique as a way to add to or improve products and services. These companies have built sophisticated listening and improvement loops and communicate with customers in a way that demonstrates that they truly value their customers. The best companies don't only look to customers to improve experience, but also to learn how to develop better, more customer-friendly products and services.

By being a good listener, T-Mobile USA has gone from losing subscribers every quarter to entering an innovative corner of the U.S. mobile industry and adding millions of customers to its ranks. The telecom firm crunched sophisticated customer analytical data, but more important listened to its subscribers' constant refrain that one- and two-year contracts were a pain and that they were willing to pay unsubsidized pricing for their mobile devices in exchange for lower monthly charges. T-Mobile responded by changing its entire philosophy to become the "Un-Carrier"—with no fixed plans or terms—and customers are voting in favor of this bold move with their dollars.

Nike takes direction from avid fans to decide on new product development. "When the Nike shoe company asked runners what they wanted from a shoe," said Nike designer Ben Shaffer in *Smithsonian* magazine, the athletes "would describe all the characteristics a sock would offer."[1] So in 2013 Nike knit them a shoe, the Flyknit Racer. With a "seamless mesh upper that expands and contracts with the wearer's foot," the Flyknit Racer is getting rave reviews from customers.

Bad Stories: Hearing Problems

Unfortunately, organizational complexity and dysfunction—all too common—tend to frustrate or even prevent enterprise-wide programs from listening and acting. "Treat every criticism as a gift" is popular among management pundits, yet in all too many cases we encounter situations where customer-facing employees—in retail stores or branches, customer service centers, field support, and so on—say "it's not my job" to listen to what the customer shares with them and forward it upward in the organization.

We have seen this in multiple industries. Staff at airline check-in will tell you to "ring the complaint line." David tried it recently with a train company. He told the ticketing agent that he had a suggestion about how to change the process. The ticketing agent said, "You'll have to pass that to complaints." He responded that it wasn't a complaint, but the answer was the same. Reluctantly David passed his idea on to the Complaints Department. Naturally enough, they treated it as a complaint and asked if the issue was still a problem. He said no, he was just offering a suggestion for evaluation. This just did not compute. The complaint was closed and his suggestion (and time to offer it) wasted. We apply this as a common test of an organization's listening ability: Are the frontline staff able to listen to suggestions, and if so do they have a mechanism to get these suggestions to those that matter?

Surveys seem to offer a tangible way to listen, but they're surprisingly difficult to engineer successfully. Many companies use what we call the "hear no evil" format—fixed-format surveys with no opportunity for open comment. They are not really listening because they have predefined the areas they think are important—an experience that can be very frustrating for the customer who sees it otherwise.

Other companies fall victim to sample bias. For example, one insurance company we observed was delighted with positive survey results. Then we discovered that it only sent surveys to customers with a completed (that is, closed) transaction. Those customers who had unresolved issues or problems that weren't properly recorded on the system were never surveyed. This organization had unintentionally closed its ears to the most unsatisfied customers.

Post-contact surveys are useful only to a point. Oftentimes the customers who've had the worst experiences—for example, the 20 percent we observed at one utility contact center who were on the phone for more than fifteen minutes—don't stick around to spend even more time taking the survey.

Given these limitations, organizations also need to listen in ways that move beyond what customers explicitly tell them about their preferences. They need to read between the lines and look at context and behavior to see what's really happening. Customers who say they are satisfied with the organization's products or services but then never buy again are sending very strong signals to the company—what earlier signals might the company have tracked to understand their true disposition? This is becoming the "sweet spot" for "Big Data analytics," mashing together disparate data sources to divine meaning and predict behavior. We're eager to see the results!

Good Stories: Leaders on the Move

For years management guru Tom Peters taught a management practice called "management by wandering around," or MBWA, that he learned from Hewlett-Packard.[2] He even created calendars for executives with random hours per day grayed out, during which times he instructed them to get out of their office and avoid meetings in order to find out what was really happening in their company and on the front line. It's an important practice, and sadly not as widely adopted as it should be—except maybe on reality TV. U.K.- and U.S.-based TV shows such as *Back to the Floor* and *Undercover Boss* have become cult hits by filming CEOs who have virtually no clue what really happens at the coal face where customers deal directly with their companies. Often the show depicts them returning from the floor to their executive chambers and decreeing that henceforth, the company will be reorganized around the customer's experience. But that's reality TV—let's look at real examples.

Unilever's CEO Paul Polman speaks directly with customers and distributors every time he travels to a country where the company's products are sold to learn firsthand what's really going on. Richard Branson of Virgin does the same. Similarly, former BestBuy CEO Brian Dunn, who started his career in that company on the front line, famously spent time with sales and support staff in retail stores to find out what was selling and what was not selling, and what the staff needed to become more successful.

More typically, executives don't stray far from their office. One of Bill's early consulting clients reviewed his observations of contact center problems with a quizzical look on his face, admitting that he had never encountered any of these issues before. When pressed, he acknowledged that he had not spent any time in the customer service center, even though it was around the corner from his executive office. Bill was flummoxed. Taking his cue from Tom Peters' MBWA calendar, Bill asked the executive's personal assistant to join them. After working through his calendar and canceling nonessential meetings, voilà! He now had four hours a week available for customer-facing education. Two weeks later, the executive effusively shared how much he had learned from recent visits to the service center—problems, new issues, great suggestions—as well as a healthy respect for how hard it is to be a customer service representative. Suffice it to say that it was much easier after this education for him to approve targeted investments to improve customer experience and customer service agent experience, and everyone benefited.

You Value My Time and Effort

Many in the customer experience management industry believe that surveys are the key to customer improvements and showing the customers that their opinions are valued. However, by constructing long and complex surveys or surveying customers too frequently or inappropriately, they instead demonstrate that the customer's time and effort aren't valued at all.

Meanwhile, customers voluntarily give organizations plenty of feedback, but outside the mechanisms that the companies have put in place. Customers are now providing customer reviews, star ratings, and opinions or reactions in other forums. Organizations that listen to their customers speaking to other customers in these forums (an essential characteristic of Me2B Leaders) are demonstrating that they value their customers enough to seek out and listen to their opinions in the forum in which they've chosen to express it.

We've already described the need to make sales, service, and support interactions low effort for customers. "Value my time and effort" extends that idea to the methods that companies use to solicit input and feedback. Sending out a survey request, especially one with no explicit reward for completing it, is essentially begging a favor, asking the customer to invest time to help the company. Me2B Leaders are very careful to recognize this fact and find ways to get customer feedback while asking for the minimum of time and attention.

Every single question in a customer survey should be scrutinized for the amount of effort it will require of the customer. (As should the value of the survey itself.)

The Hyatt Hotel Corporation launched a new brand called Andaz in 2007, rapidly adding properties in Asia, North America, and Europe. The minds behind the new hotel chain have built its process design around a two-part goal: remove all the barriers that prevent guests from having a great experience at the hotel, as well as the barriers that prevent hotel employees from providing great experiences. The result? Customers feel valued at every step of their stay. This has led to reducing complexity around checking in, billing, and services, and increasing staff flexibility to meet customer needs.

The Andaz team understands that while smart process design can help meet those goals, hotel employees truly have to understand what it's like to be the customer, to be on the receiving end of the experience. Months before the opening of a new Andaz property, the management team practices "imagining the customer" and invites the hotel employees' family and friends to stay at the hotel before the official opening to experience it themselves.

The Andaz team has also paid careful attention to customer preferences, and has reengineered standard processes accordingly. For example, the team discovered that many guests objected to the nickel-and-diming with mini-bars. At Andaz all nonalcoholic beverages, candy, and treats are free. Similarly, noticing that many guests needed a clothing item pressed when they arrived, the team made it a complimentary service.

Bad Stories: Brain-Stumping Surveys

One of the worst instances of not valuing customer effort that we have seen is also in the hotel industry. A hotel we observed asked customers to provide information not only about frequency of staying in its own hotels but also about the number of times they have stayed in each of its competitors. OK, we get it: The survey designers are trying to determine potential value. But they asked customers to remember and list how many room nights they had spent in each chain in the past year—not an easy task for a frequent traveler—and not a task that values their effort. (Last year's travel night totals are something most of us would rather forget!) Perhaps a single question such as *"How many nights do you typically spend away from home a year on business?"* would have been sufficient to get a read on potential value. On top of all that, this hotel asked each customer for the number of nights spent as a guest of that hotel chain—clearly information that it already has on record. By making the survey overly complicated, the hotel surely received fewer responses—and probably alienated more than one customer with its careless approach in the process. When companies deploy clumsy surveys that force customers to work hard, customers don't feel empowered. They feel disrespected.

Good Stories: Clever Customer Empowerment

When websites first launched support knowledge databases, using them was a daunting process. The articles rarely matched the search terms used by the customer. Customers were forced to go through page after page of articles, often without finding one that solved their problem. Meanwhile, users had no fast mechanism to report results and improve the system. Fortunately, companies such as Pitney-Bowes and Apple found a way to improve the process. They reduced the number of articles displayed in response to a search request, and added a new feature: They asked customers "how valuable was his article for you?" Today Amazon asks the same sort of question for each review of a book on its website, helping prospective buyers decide which reviews are worth reading. Providing easy feedback mechanisms to let customers weigh in quickly empowers them. Instead of feeling squeezed for their opinion, they see the value and are happy to make the small effort.

Earlier we slammed overly long customer surveys with no apparent return for the survey takers. But even with lengthy surveys, clever companies have found ways to ease the demands on their customers' time. Implementing a "percent completion" bar on each page lets customers know how far they have progressed, which offers a practical benefit and also a sense of accomplishment. Other companies have added pause features so that the customer can leave and come back without having to reenter any data. The percent completion bar is now common, the pause and return feature still rare. While both appear to be straightforward and obvious, most companies have not figured out how to implement them. The Hyatt Hotel chain, where customer surveys do offer these features, gets a higher than average response rate.

Travel booking sites Booking.com, Wotif.com, and TripAdvisor have made it really easy for customers to give feedback through surveys. Their feedback systems comprise only two or three questions and allow customers to provide comments if they see fit. As a result the volume of feedback they obtain is far greater and probably the demographics less skewed toward those who have time for long surveys. Survey data—for example, about experience of a specific hotel—is a major value driver of the sites, so it's important that they get it right. To build confidence in that data, they share how many customers have contributed to the rating. They also reward participating customers with discounts on future bookings.

You Make Sure Your Partners Value Me as You Do

Even among Me2B Leaders, very few companies have figured out how to make sure that their business partners view and value customers the same way they do. It is the most challenging and least used way to make customers feel valued.

And yet it's important. Business is becoming more intertwined than ever before. Companies around the world use third-party outsourcers to handle their customer service calls. Cable TV companies use independent organizations for in-home installation and repair; major airlines subcontract short-haul routes to companies with the same logo but different management and ownership; chains license their brand to franchisees. Whenever these partner companies operate on behalf of another organization, it's imperative that they equally understand and employ the value proposition that customers bring to the party. They need to have the same access to customer history, issues, and opportunities, as well as the ability to participate jointly in collecting and applying customer information.

Bad Stories: False Alliances

Unfortunately, all too often a company's partner cannot access the same customer data and treat customers in the same manner. Take airline alliances. Oftentimes the larger airlines' lower-cost service partners don't recognize the status of their partner carriers' customers. For example, one airline asked a hundred top-level frequent flyer passengers to travel on their low-cost sister carrier after a five-hour delay. When passengers complied (and what choice did they have?), they found that none of the perks they were promised when they bought their tickets was honored; for example, they were hit with baggage restrictions and charged for meals and entertainment. That doesn't feel like an alliance that serves them; instead, it looks like a business relationship that serves the airlines at customers' personal expense.

Franchise operations fall into the same trap, often sharing the same corporate logo but operating under different scenarios and even different mottos and slogans. In one of the major U.S. airports, Bill spotted an outpost of his favorite coffee franchise only to discover it didn't take the company's prepaid card and had menu variations, such as more limited sizes for drinks. (Bill likes a "Jumbo" iced tea.) Same logo, different experience is always a recipe for customer frustration—and a disaster for brand reputation.

Good Stories: Consistent Customer Experience Across Franchises

The McDonald's Corporation is essentially a franchise business: 80 percent of McDonald's restaurants around the world are owned by local managers and not by the company itself. McDonald's might not be on your short list of favorite restaurants, but it's one of the world's most successful companies. It has done a fantastic job creating consistent customer experience on a global basis while allowing for local differences in cuisine, sizes, and ingredients. One of Ray Kroc's early mantras, taught at the company's "Hamburger University" to generations of newly minted store managers, was "QSC&V": Q for quality, S for service, C for cleanliness, and V for value. The company monitors many touch points and data points to ensure that it is delivering all these elements. Through a very clear operating program, training, and monitoring, McDonald's has kept in place all of the fundamentally successful aspects that made its outlets a hit in the 1950s and 1960s while now partnering with small business owners all around the world.

Similarly, but on the higher end of the scale, Hyatt Hotel properties are operated almost exclusively by local owners. Hyatt requires very strict adherence to quality standards, logo-based products, central reservation systems, and the like, making sure that its partners value the customer by offering a consistent experience. Few guests ever realize that each property is independently owned and managed—which proves the partnerships' success.

Why "You Value Me" Is So Important

In any relationship, being valued *matters*. Whether it is personal or professional, being valued meets an underlying psychological need for belonging. The relationships we have with businesses are no different. Of course, we don't necessarily need to feel valued with each and every transaction. However, the more we deal with an organization, the longer the relationship lasts and the higher the value, the more we expect our value to be recognized and rewarded.

"You Value Me" can have impacts on many financial drivers, as shown in Table 5.2.

Meet the Challenge: You Value Me

This challenge is hard for many organizations because the four steps involved are complex and costly, though simple to state.

Invest in Long-Term Thinking

Investing in future value doesn't produce an instant return, and it is hard for organizations that have grown up seeing customers as

Table 5.2 The Benefits of Clearly Valuing the Customer

Customer Need Met	Potential to Increase Revenue	Potential to Reduce Cost
You value the length and depth of my relationship with you.	Increased loyalty among value customer segments More targeted marketing spend	Less expense to attract new customers or retain upset ones
You value my potential.	Targeted marketing to customers with greater potential Increased customer lifetime value	Avoid wasted spend of marketing dollars on customers who have already delivered value
You listen to me and act on what I say.	Increased customer retention Growth by reputation and word of mouth	Reduced investment in market research Reduced costs of waste and effort
You value my time and effort.	Faster feedback and quicker action on customer turn-offs	Reduced survey and analytical processing costs
You make sure your partners value me as you do.	Customer retention	Lower support costs Less expense to hold on to current customers

commodities to be managed for the lowest cost to suddenly change their attitude and see customers as something to be nurtured. As we discuss later in the book, it often takes a disruption like a new leader or a business crisis leading to a rebound to bring about such a major rethinking, but companies can take important steps to valuing customers by taking a long-term focus.

Invest in Big Data

The data and analysis to deliver on this customer need can be complex, requiring the scope of the new phenomenon of Big Data predictive analytics. Understanding your customers well enough to know the depth of their relationship and their potential isn't easy. It requires analysis of buying habits, demographics, and other behaviors to create profiles of who is valuable and who is not. As such, every organization must design strategies, processes, and products that are effective with those groups—never an easy task, but easier with Big Data.

Seek Multidimensional Feedback

Valuing customers requires organizations to do what we can only describe as multidimensional listening. It's no longer sufficient to rely on just one feedback mechanism. Organizations need to bring together a whole host of feedback sources if they are truly to be seen as good listeners. Customers may say something to a staff member, they may send a complaint, they may blog, they may comment on social media on numerous platforms or just write a letter. Companies must find ways to capture and process all that feedback, and this new field of EFM (Enterprise Feedback Management) will help ensure that customers feel valued.

Align Measures to Long Term–Customer Value

Parts of an organization or its partners may have goals that conflict with the way the business wants to manage certain customers. For example, managing an outsource provider to meet cost goals may mean looking for efficiency over service goals for all customers. To overcome this challenge, organizations need to look for and refine contradictory goals. Some have done this by finding measures that are better aligned with broader customer objectives. For example, measuring an outsourcer or service area on resolution rates is likely to drive behavior different from the results of rewarding them for shorter contacts. Measurement can get even more complex if a business wants different customer types to be treated differently, which clearly requires measures tailored to the treatment of each group of customers.

CHAPTER SIX

YOU TRUST ME

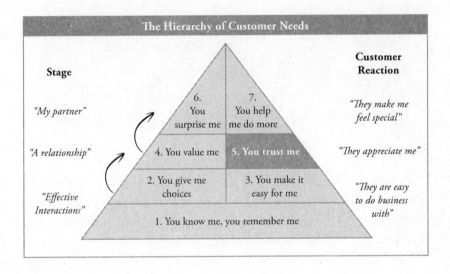

The Hierarchy of Customer Needs

Stage

"My partner"

"A relationship"

"Effective Interactions"

6. You surprise me

7. You help me do more

4. You value me

5. You trust me

2. You give me choices

3. You make it easy for me

1. You know me, you remember me

Customer Reaction

"They make me feel special"

"They appreciate me"

"They are easy to do business with"

It's frustrating enough to face what feels like arbitrary inflexibility when dealing with a company. But it can quickly escalate to infuriating when the apparent reason for the inconvenience is that the company doesn't trust you to act with integrity.

This is an all too common experience. Most organizations over the past twenty years have been following command-and-control edicts that emphasize efficiency and routines designed to root out variation—for example, the Six Sigma model and other forms of process standardization. The trouble is, applying command and control to frontline customer interactions means narrowing the options available to customers in an effort to minimize the chances of errors or undesirable consequences. For example, a formal wear company may accept returns only within fourteen days of a sale (for most people, an uncomfortably short window) to decrease the likelihood that a customer will wear an outfit for a big event and then return it. These limiting, inflexible rules are often meant to protect the company from unscrupulous customers. Unfortunately, they create poor experiences for everyone, and force frontline staff to be insensitive in situations when they might be accommodating.

Me2B Leaders, intent on creating exceptional customer experiences, recognize that trust, always important in quality relationships, is a two-way street. While they might apply command-and-control thinking to manufacturing, product and system design, or shipping, they expressly ignore it when it comes to the customer experience. The value of trusting customers is weighed against the potential costs—to use our earlier example, the lost sale and the damage caused by someone who used the company for a free rental. They also recognize the need to trust—and in doing so empower—their frontline employees to make decisions that favor the exception over the rule.

Of course, unscrupulous customers are out there, and we know that you cannot (and should not) take trust to extremes. Before organizations grew in scale and complexity, it was far easier for businesses to trust customers and for customers to trust businesses. The relationships were closer and communities were smaller. Reputations were therefore more available and vulnerable for both consumers and businesses. Neither could afford to be distrusted in the community, nor did they want to challenge trust.

However, we've seen that many organizations today are at the other extreme: They seem to distrust by default and put controls in place for all customers and situations even when risk is negligible or absent. Companies that take customer relationships seriously have recognized that these controls and impositions are costing more and doing greater damage than the actions they were trying to control. They have found ways to operate differently. We explore five of them in this chapter. To join the Me2B era, it's time to rethink the balance between trust and control following the five successes and failures in Table 6.1.

You Don't Tar Me with the Same Brush

We have found that many organizations treat all customers like fraud suspects. One scam or theft creates a prevention process for all subsequent customers, and soon this becomes the "way we have

Table 6.1 The Customer's Experience of Success and Failure

You Trust Me Success	You Trust Me Failure
You don't tar me with the same brush.	You treat all customers as not worthy of trust because of the actions of a few.
You don't impose an arbitrary policy on me, and you allow exceptions.	You have no room to maneuver even in a situation that is exceptional.
You trust my version of events without my jumping through hoops.	You force the customer to prove things with documents and physical evidence.
You enable me to trust you.	You provide misleading or dubious data and fail to keep some (or most) of your promises.
You trust me to advise others.	You stamp out customer commentary in social and other media.

to do business." Me2B organizations have worked out ways to manage the exception rather than the rule. Constantly focusing on the customer's experience has led them to build more intelligence into their processes and place greater trust in the front line.

Even companies in industries in which fraud is a real threat have found solutions to manage the trust-risk balancing act. Take the insurance industry. The value from an insurance product to the customer occurs at the time of a claim. However, the financial health of insurance businesses depends on their having appropriate control of claims. Unfortunately for the customers, that can mean that the protection they were promised and have paid for over many years can be hard to obtain, thanks to the inspections, approval process, paperwork, and generalized distrust that make claims so hard. A worst-case example can be seen in Christchurch, New Zealand, where four years after the 2010 earthquake, many policyholders whose homes were demolished were still unable to rebuild their homes due to claims disputes even though the earthquake was clearly the cause. In the United States, Hurricane Katrina conjured up similar horror stories years afterward.

Fortunately, other insurance companies are finding better ways to do business. Australian insurance business Suncorp faced a series of destructive weather events, including Cyclone Yasi and extensive flooding in Brisbane and the surrounding areas. After Yasi, claims calls rose 50 percent in a week. Experience of prior cyclones in 2006 had shown Suncorp that normal processes couldn't cope, so it was prepared to try something new. It changed the process to triage claim calls and put many claims through a fast-track process with limited paperwork or proof. Effectively, it trusted the customer throughout the process and offered faster response and more immediate funds to those in crisis situations. It has since used this same process in other more recent storm events, to great customer acclaim.

Some insurance companies now allow small-value claims of certain types without detailed proof. The companies worked out that the value of trust (or easing the customer's experience) can be great enough to make it worthwhile to both customer and company to price products to compensate for the very small percentage (perhaps 1 percent) of fraudulent claims. They have also added systems to warn or detect any customers who try to game this system, for example by claiming for the same or like items multiple times.

Bad Stories: One-Size-Fits-All Policies

Generic processes apply fraud protection across transactions where fraud is extremely unlikely. Here is one of the most obvious examples: When paying bills such as credit cards for some companies, customers must go through the same identity process as they do for any other transaction—but how often does someone fraudulently pay someone else's bill? We'd invite that kind of criminal over for dinner! You'll also find it's often easier to pay online or over an IVR or even in person at the branch than it is over the phone. Billing details and money to pay are often all that is required in some channels, but in many contact centers that's not enough. We've often heard of customers trying to pay bills on behalf of relatives or friends and being turned away.

Banks, which tend to be hypercautious about fraud, frequently make the mistake of generic protection policies. One customer we know wanted a debit card in her partner's name. The customer was known to the branch staff and had many joint accounts with her partner—and yet the rules said that the partner would have to set up his own debit card. So the customer had to take away a form, get it signed by the partner, and then return to the branch: no trust and no net gain. The generic fraud protection rule had no override feature for staff, no matter what the situation. We would have suggested an override with simple controls or checks to prevent cases of customer-employee joint fraud.

Good Stories: Wear the Risk

In another case of highly inconvenient policy to manage low risk, utilities often require customers who share rental properties and thus share payment responsibilities to present documented proof—paperwork from the rental company—to show that they're all on the lease. But utilities such as AGL and Origin Energy in Australia, and Puget Sound Energy in Seattle, have realized the exception cases where customers try and dodge responsibility by passing it between residents are quite rare. They decided it was better to get someone signed up quickly than to force all customers through a complex documentary proof process involving multiple calls and interactions with landlords. After the policy change, debts didn't increase—and customers got their lights on faster.

Zappos, Amazon, and Marks & Spencer are three companies famous for their return policies. Amazon allows customers to download return labels and send goods back without any proof. It trusts that few customers would go to the effort of ordering and paying for goods and then return them. If some customers changed their minds, then the cost would be minimal—and more than compensated by loyal, happy customers who place orders more freely knowing that a return, if needed, won't be a headache. Zappos has the same philosophy: It is famous for letting customers return goods up to one year out. The high-end online fashion company Net-a-Porter does the same, as does Shoes of Prey. These businesses have turned the risk of shopping online—that customers cannot touch and try their goods—into an advantage. Customers become quickly loyal when they understand that the company is willing to shoulder all the risk on their behalf.

Famed British retailer Marks & Spencer established its returns policy many years before the Internet was born. The initial Marks & Spencer stores had few fitting rooms where customers could try on clothes. The store therefore allowed people to take things home, try them, and if necessary return them. This became part of the value proposition even after the bigger stores added fitting rooms. Customers loved the freedom to try items on at home. The policy not only established trust, it also encouraged buying without fear, buying gifts for others, and impulse purchases.

The Goring Hotel, a well-known five-star establishment in London, trusts its customers—who represent "the top end of town," to use the British expression. While many hotels insist on large deposits for conference bookings and events, the Goring does not. The customer's word is sufficient to book the facilities, and payments are made after the event. This is unusual even among luxury hotels and resorts.

The Australian Taxation Office at times shows great flexibility to taxpayers who may hit short-term cash flow issues. Small and medium-size businesses receive very flexible terms for large payments. The agency understands that tax payments can significantly impact the cash flow of a small business. If a customer offers to pay within several weeks of a deadline, this is accepted. Background processes check that customers can live up to their promises, but the trust shown is valued by businesses and helps oil the wheels of the economy.

Vashon Island, close to Seattle (where Bill and his wife, Lori, have a weekend cottage), still features "honor stands" where local farmers display their eggs, fruit, and vegetables without anyone tending the stand, and often without any prices—just what you think is right. Twice in one year, money was stolen from the open tackle box that served to collect payments at Karen Biondo's stand, but even then it still made financial sense for her to leave the stand unmanned. Most of the time, customers are honest and the box is left alone. More recently, a neighbor made her an industrial strength cash box, solving the problem of theft entirely.[1] Of course, people could still steal the produce, but again, the value of trusting the majority is greater than that risk.

You Don't Impose an Arbitrary Policy on Me; You Allow Exceptions

We have worked with a lot of companies where the regulation or compliance team—trained and rewarded first and foremost to be risk averse—has been allowed to control and standardize all the key processes. This leads to one-size-fits-all processes that staff must follow in all instances, even when they can see they make no sense. This is admittedly similar to the last section, "don't tar me with the same brush," which is about everybody being forced to do something that should apply in only a few situations, but here the focus is on situations where companies would improve customer experience without undue risks by empowering frontline employees to occasionally waive rules. This is the flip side of the earlier problem. The rule is right for maybe 90 percent of situations, but the remaining 10 percent desperately need frontline staff who can make exceptions for special cases. A common cause is that these exceptions reach some people that the organization knows it can't trust because they're not adequately trained. As a result, the company trusts no one.

In some cases, companies that deal well with exceptions have set up operating models where certain problems and situations are given to more experienced staff who are trusted to take these exception decisions. These employees, often called "Tier 2" specialists, have higher-level limits and the ability to override system or standard recommendations. Sometimes this is linked to the value and history of a customer. For example, many airlines have fees that in theory are not changeable. However, Virgin Australia allows frequent flyer lounge staff to change flights for the highest-value frequent flyers regardless of the fare they have booked. In effect, it has a separate policy for some customers, recognizing their exceptional value to the airline.

Table 6.2 Mistrust Versus Arbitrary Action

Customer Need	The Norm	The Exception	What the Company Does
You don't tar me with the same brush.	90 percent need no check.	10 percent need a check.	Checks 100 percent though only 10 percent need it.
You don't impose an arbitrary policy.	90 percent need a process X.	10 percent need an exception to process X.	The 10 percent can't escape process X.

Table 6.2 summarizes how "tarred with the same brush" and imposition of an arbitrary policy differ. The first applies an unnecessary process to 90 percent of customers. The second won't let 10 percent of customer who need to bypass the process get away from it even though they should.

Bad Stories: Stranded

Many airlines around the world have a standard policy for flight leg cancellations. If a customer has booked a multisector fare and then misses one leg of the flight, the remainder of the trip gets canceled.

David had a trip planned with several international connections. He took the first long international leg, but then changed plans and didn't take the shorter international flight with that airline as it arrived at his destination too late. He alerted the check-in staff to the change during his first stop. Unbeknownst to him, the airline promptly canceled both return legs, stranding him in another county. He called the airline, but the policy had kicked in and the staff could not override it. It took David two days and many phone calls and threats to get his return trip rebooked. How happy will he be to fly with that airline again?

On further investigation David found that this is a standard policy with many airlines. If you miss one leg of an outbound trip, the whole return is canceled regardless of where that leaves you stranded. It seems extraordinary if a customer has already taken part of a trip to cancel all subsequent legs, but that is how it works. We're still trying to figure out why that is the standard process in the industry.

Good Stories: Trust the Front Line

Empowering frontline employees to make smart decisions can often result in win-win exceptions that serve both the customer and the company. A popular restaurant had a policy that large bookings (eight or more) required a deposit that was only refundable with two weeks' advance notice. They adopted the policy after being hurt by too many last-minute cancellations leaving empty large tables. A customer called a week out to see if a booking for ten could be canceled. The staff member on the phone knew that it was highly likely that the restaurant would get enough bookings during the week so that it wouldn't take a loss. At a restaurant where the rule was "enforce the policy with no exceptions," the staff member might have refused the customer's request, making any further visits highly unlikely. Instead, this restaurant trusted employees to waive the policy when merited, so the staff member made the refund, more or less guaranteeing the customer's loyalty long into the future.

Customer-centric companies are also flexible when good customers face unexpected hardship. Southern California Edison (SCE), a U.S. utility company in a state bordering Mexico, occasionally gets plaintive calls from frantic customers saying that their wife, husband, parent, or partner has been deported to Mexico, and even though they are American citizens they will soon join them across the border. They tell SCE that they will need several weeks to get their affairs in order and won't be able to pay the current invoice. While some companies might push even harder to get the money quickly in such a scenario, fearing that this customer might skip town permanently, SCE chooses to trust that a customer who would make such a call will eventually pay. It therefore allows its front line to waive the rules—sure, it's humanitarian, but it's also good business.

Similarly, in Australia, all three major utilities have hardship teams and policies for customers in difficult circumstances— regulation requires some protection for consumers so they never lose essential services. Sometimes these utilities even match the payments customers make with their own payments so as to help them reduce major debts. They also help customers obtain all the associated government grants and provide energy audits and advice to help reduce consumption. These hardship policies are great examples of appropriate exception treatments.

You Trust My Version of Events

It's amazing to us how often organizational policies and processes force customers to repeat steps that they have already completed, or fail to trust their feedback about how a product or service has performed. This often amounts to treating customers like children and puts frontline staff in an embarrassing position. By insisting on the policy, for example to provide documentation for certain claims, they are essentially telling the customer, "I don't trust your version of events." Often this leads to wasted time and massive frustration for customers, as was the experience of one customer who called because he couldn't get his digital TV set top box working. After several reboots he called the company and was immediately told to reboot the machine. He explained he had done so already, more than once, without success. "I'm sorry," said the agent, "you'll have to do that again with me on the phone." After pushing back, the customer finally gave up and spent five minutes doing another reboot, with the same outcome. The events annoyed the customer to such an extent that he terminated the contract.

Me2B Leaders such as Costco, REI, and Vente-Privee have taken trusting their customers' stories to great levels and have demonstrated the business case for operating this way—unparalleled customer loyalty, strong revenue, and incredible word-of-mouth marketing. It's amazing how much a little trust, particularly in a stressful time, endears a company to a customer.

Bad Stories: Better Off Dead

Ham-fisted policies that don't trust the customer are even worse during times of emotional hardship—for example, bereavement. A major utility had a policy that customers had to send a copy of a death certificate to transfer accounts from one customer to another—adding unneeded hassle at a most difficult time. Working with the utility, we were able to introduce a process where the word of relatives or executors was accepted in such a situation.

PEOPLE AT THE BRANCH TENDED TO THINK THE COMPANY'S REQUIREMENTS FOR PROOF OF DEATH WERE A BIT OVER THE TOP.

Good Stories: Benefit of the Doubt

The health fund AHM was the first in Australia to allow Internet-based claims, in the ultimate example of trusting the customers' version of events. Claims were paid, for the majority, without detailed checking of paperwork. The company did spot audits and defined business rules to determine exceptions that needed checking. However, when customers said they'd had a treatment, the insurance provider trusted their word.

Customers are especially appreciative when companies give them the benefit of the doubt when something goes wrong. A Subaru car dealership had a policy of not releasing new vehicles until payments had cleared. With such a high-value transaction, this policy was understandable. But when one customer went to collect a new car, he found out on arrival that his bank hadn't cleared the payment in the time expected. This was distressing for the customer, but not really the dealer's fault. Nevertheless, rather than making the customer go through the hoops of returning again to collect the vehicle, the dealership delivered the car to the customer as soon as the payment cleared. The customer was thrilled and became even more loyal to the brand. Subaru fans call themselves "Subaru'ers," and their blog postings are very popular thanks to stories like this one.

You Enable Me to Trust You

The list of outlandish claims that companies foist onto consumers is long: Food items claim to be healthy when they are clearly not; get-rich-quick schemes draw in the naive; cosmetic companies claim benefits based on dubious science. We could probably write a whole book about how bad marketing makes it nearly impossible for customers to trust companies.

Some companies have learned that transparency and honesty make for the best marketing, and they have learned to support what they claim with genuine testimonials. Others rely on the power of customer communities to promote their products. But social media is open to abuse, with services available for hire. Even well-intentioned restaurants and hotels inflate their ratings by getting friends and family members to publish reviews on influential websites. (What can we say? Like all authors, we made sure the first few reviews of our first book were by people we knew.)

There's a second kind of false claim made by companies, instances where something is promised in good faith, but the company fails to follow through. If a customer is told that the company will "reply in three days" or "someone will call you back" or "a refund is in the mail and will reach you shortly," then that needs to happen. As soon as a commitment is broken, all trust is lost. Avoiding this breakdown of trust requires integrated, consistent processes where the frontline staff understand how things work and what commitments they can make and keep. It also requires consistency of delivery and expectation management. In the event of failure, being proactive and quickly rectifying the situation can help restore trust.

Some of the biggest and best companies now know that trust is easily lost. Take, for example, Toyota and Volkswagen. For decades both companies served as the gold standard for reliability. But after major product recalls around the world, that trust rapidly diminished, despite the reputation that preceded it. No company can rest on the laurels of past trust—like everything having to do with relationships, trust is dynamic and waxes or wanes with each and every interaction.

Bad Stories: Backlogs

Earlier we mentioned a utility company that migrated to a new, deeply flawed system, resulting in its contact center being flooded with questions and complaints. At the peak of the chaos, it had nearly 500,000 customers with severely delayed bills. Thousands of others had bills that were wrong, and some of the discount processes weren't working. The frontline staff was besieged. But what made things much worse was that management didn't give the frontline staff any information on how bad the problems were. People were operating in the dark and had no mechanism for getting things fixed. They fumbled their way through the calls, saying things like, "I've escalated your issue to another department." Those requests sat untouched in a long backlogged queue, but the staff didn't know that. Customers got increasingly frustrated, saying things like, "But you said you would fix things last month and I've already taken you through this twice. Why should I invest more time to tell you about your problems?"

Companies also lose trust when they refuse to take responsibility for and manage their own mistakes. Our featured utility company was guilty of this fault, too. At no time did it admit the size of the backlogs or their implications. It also tried to minimize the financial damage. In some states in which it operated, it had a legal obligation to provide customers extended payment terms for the delayed bills. But it only admitted this to customers when pressed. A more transparent business would have sent a letter with every late bill apologizing and explaining the extension in payment terms to the customer. That kind of admission and transparency might have maintained some trust. Instead, hiding the issues and its legal obligations lost this company many customers. It may have helped with short-term cash flow but it caused many customers to leave.

A well-known automobile company made the same mistake when, over a two-year period, stories started to emerge about one of its models. Customers reported that the engine on certain models would cut out completely. This was extremely dangerous since the cars would lose speed quickly and unexpectedly on freeways and other major roads. The media and public raised the issue but the company line was that no problem existed. Eventually the company recalled over 5 million vehicles globally, obviously a very costly exercise. If the recall had been swift and precautionary, the cost might have been offset by reducing the damage to trust in the brand and product, or even maybe increasing it by being so swift to protect customer safety at any expense. Finally, trust was eroded once more when it emerged that the company knew there was an issue and had changed the part involved without changing its serial number (knowing that would highlight that the issue was known in any future inquiry). By that point, many customers had decamped to other brands rather than try to sort through all the falsehoods.

Good Stories: Enduring Reliability

Trust from customers is very valuable to any brand, allowing these companies to gain and retain customers and sometimes even charge premiums, as in the case of Hilti, a Liechtenstein-based company that makes power tools. The company operates in a very crowded and competitive product landscape, and yet in some countries it has nevertheless created a position in which it can charge a premium for its tools. Hilti earned a reputation for reliability worth paying for by offering lifetime guarantees of service and replacement for business customers that competitors don't seem to be able to match. Business customers need the assurance that a working product will be available when they need it. Today the Hilti brand represents an investment in peace of mind. It's not the cheapest product, but it has become the most trusted. Profits have doubled in four years as a result.

Providing exceptional products that show truly innovative solutions for persistent problems is a strong route to customer trust. Dyson, a U.K.-based company, is a great example. Of course, the reliability of its products has been a major asset in gaining trust. (It even shut down one of its customer support contact centers because the company was getting fewer calls, as we detailed in our first book!) But the incredible trust customers have in Dyson products seems to be equally rooted in its reputation as a great innovator.

The Dyson brand has expanded into many products beyond the initial vacuum cleaners, such as heating units and bladeless fans, exploiting its engineering excellence in related products. Its air blade hand-drying technology has been a hit all over the world and seems to dominate public restrooms. Why? Traditional hand dryers were noisy and ineffective. They also seemed to break down frequently. Dyson air blades are almost as fast as using a towel and rarely break down. Dyson has become a trusted brand whatever it chooses to make. Each of its products has an engineering "wow" factor that excites customers. Its vacuum cleaners showed the spinning working parts while its hand dryers have a rush of air that is impressive. We'd argue that its growing reputation for innovative inventions is its other secret: Customers assume that if a company is smart enough to innovate, its products must be reliable, too.

Other companies build trust the old-fashioned way: By delivering on consistency, uniformity, and quality of product over many years. Heinz is an excellent example—it has often appeared at or near the top of customer satisfaction ratings in the United States. Heinz baby foods are among the most popular in the world. Many Heinz products, such as baked beans and ketchup, have icon status. The high levels of trust it has with customers have allowed it to extend its product range annually. It now has market-leading products in more than fifty-nine countries and it sells 650 million bottles of tomato sauce per year.[2]

You Trust Me to Advise Others

Over the last six years the Internet social sphere, blog postings, and communities have exploded many times over, enabling organizations to take advantage of the incredible experience and perspectives possessed by their customers. When companies value their customers enough to expose their ideas and suggestions to other customers, everybody wins. It has been shown that customers often trust and value the opinions of other customers more than they do the company itself.[3] Enabling customers to advise other customers pays off with knowledge sharing instead of staid knowledge bases, more positive loyalty to the organization from those customers—both the advisers and the advisees—and often increased revenues or reduced rates of customer contacts. This level of trust that customers have for each other (what we earlier defined as C2C) means that customers can assist each other and reduce contacts to the organizations. Some companies fear customer initiative, but we believe that it is a great self-service opportunity, as well as a way to deflect issues so that the company itself doesn't have to handle them.

Bad Stories: Skeletons in the Closet

One of the luminaries and early proponents of a social media connection with its customers has taken what we believe to be a dangerous turn. Whenever one of its customers complains online, for example on Facebook, Twitter, or public blogs, the company initially engages directly with the customer for all to see, but then invites them offline and proceeds to delete the original conversation. This is almost as if a lost ballgame is no longer in the standings.

Taking commentary offline will only make customers wonder what needed to be hidden, and it also risks the possibility that the offended customer who was taken offline will come roaring back with additional negative comments.

eBay was one of the Internet pioneers of public rating systems; all sellers were rated by customers. This made service issues very public. We held workshops with some eBay sellers and found that they had an interesting variety of approaches to these customer ratings. When some sellers received a poor rating, they got annoyed and tried to dismiss the buyer's comments as unfair. In many ways, they were in denial of the customer's right to comment. Other sellers had a smarter approach. They contacted those who had made a negative comment and tried to work with them to fix the problem. If customers were happy, they asked them to change their ratings. This seemed like a far more enlightened approach.

Good Stories: C2C Support

Earlier we mentioned how companies such as Apple and Amazon are wisely limiting the search results in support features instead of providing a tidal wave of possible answers to customer queries. Apple has taken this one step further by featuring customers' opinions juxtaposed with its own knowledge base information so that the Apple customer can decide whether to follow customer commentary in a blog, on Facebook, or via Twitter, or delve into the substantial and usually very informative Apple information. Sometimes customers post their own YouTube video showing how to use a new Apple product or feature, load an item back into a box (Bill resorted to this when he packed his large Apple monitor when he and his wife moved back to Seattle from Iowa), use a new app, and more. While perhaps not as high in quality as an Apple-produced video, these customer-developed recommendations are often more highly prized and valued.

As we mentioned earlier, C2C communication has been one of the most exciting new developments in the customer experience and support world in the last five years. Online customers are now able to provide advice that's in some cases backed by experience superior to what the company can offer via support teams. We have seen large corporations such as Dell convert their internal knowledge system to one populated actively by their in-house and outsourced technical support representatives and, to some extent, by customers themselves. This collaboration is accomplished by using a wiki, which enables immediate rewrites or overwrites by individuals who believe that they have a better, more current, or more relevant answer to share. That level of control and agility makes the support staff feel more engaged and willing—if not eager—to use the knowledge tool.

We're also impressed with new co-browsing software from companies such as BevyUp; one of its innovations allows its consumers to view each other's screens and shop together online and even comment on the items that they see on each other's screens. This has led to significant improvements in sales conversion rates, average order size, and reductions in return rates because of better fits at point of purchase. The C2C movement can cut the cost and effort that the companies themselves have been putting into building information systems and support systems. It represents the new wave of self-service.

DIRECTV, the North American Latin American leader in satellite TV and other media, was an early pioneer inviting its customers to comment on products and features and provide support to fellow customers. Along the way, one of DIRECTV's customers began to get a huge number of positive comments from other customers because of his extensive knowledge of the system's remote control device, one of the more challenging elements dealing with any TV system. In the site's online community space, this customer began to style himself as the world's foremost expert on remote controls and offered his knowledge for free to any DIRECTV customer: how to program your remote, how to use the quick keys, and how to find your favorite shows.

When DIRECTV discovered that this customer was playing such a key role with other customers, the company could have intervened to shut him down. Instead, it took a smarter route: It encouraged him by sending him new remote control devices before they were generally available so that he could break them down, (re)program them, and be prepared to provide advice when the rest of the DIRECTV customers got the new remote. Minimal cost and maximum return for the company, in the form of a learning experience for the company and its more than 30 million subscribers.

Why "You Trust Me" Is So Important

A customer's trust is valuable and precious. Besieged by marketing messaging from all angles, customers start new relationships with their guard up. Companies must earn their trust, and it is easy to lose. If a customer has one poor experience, it may take months or years to rebuild that trust, and it may never get back to the same level.

As with the other Me2B customer needs, the importance of trust becomes obvious when we think about companies as being in relationships with customers. Look at personal relationships: Loss of trust in marriages due to affairs or erratic behavior often spells the end. Even when relationships do survive after trust is lost, they are forever changed, typically for the worse.

Few of us like not being trusted. We believe our honor and values are being questioned if another party in a relationship shows no trust for us. This is why organizations need to be so careful. If a customer says, "I did X," for example, made a payment, and the company responds by saying "prove it," the relationship is immediately on a different footing. The sense of fair and open exchange disappears. The relationship can quickly become adversarial and may well end badly.

When an organization extends trust not just to customers but to employees, it gains yet another advantage. It can eliminate unnecessary scripts and confining rules, freeing the front line to listen more closely to customer requests or complaints and do the right thing in response. Me2B Leaders might track the concessions or rebates given, but they don't limit them. In the end, surprisingly, interactions are shorter without the mandated scripts and both employees and customers feel better about the experience.

Airlines like Southwest and Virgin extend this same trust factor for their frontline staff at airport check-in or the gates, upgrading harried travelers or passing out free drinks or airport meals vouchers without limits or controls. When we fold trust into the equation, as a core part of the organization's process and thinking, profits are even higher than under the command-and-control model. In addition, customers are happier and employees more engaged and even more committed to doing the right thing.

The net result of this increased trust is not only improvements in brand reputation but also improved loyalty. Customers value organizations that show trust in them. As we've shown, the trade-off in time and effort is usually positive if the organization can reduce checking and identifications. Of course, there may well be an occasional fraud or an unnecessary return or product upgrade. However, above all, organizations need to evaluate the balance of this equation:

The cost of fraud compared to (The extra effort to control the fraud

+ the good will and loyalty from

customers available from

trusting them)

As we highlighted in stories like Amazon, Marks & Spencer, Nordstrom, REI, and Zappos, it's often cheaper to trust customers to return things than have checks and validations along the way. We often see instances where frontline staff must get approvals, escalate issues, raise work requests, or go on hold because the company doesn't trust them to make a reasonable decision. All these steps have a cost. There may be added layers of cost from the areas that then check adherence to these processes or build the validation and checks into software, and the hidden costs in this type of command-and-control process can be identified and removed when trust enters the environment.

Understanding the balance between fraud or issue prevention and the positive benefits of customer trust through reputation and loyalty is harder. The loyalty effects may take time to measure.

Table 6.3   The Benefits of Clearly Trusting the Customer

Customer Need Met	Potential to Increase Revenue	Potential to Reduce Cost
You don't tar me with the same brush.	More focus on the exceptions that can hurt revenue Increased loyalty Reduced customer frustration	Reduced time for non-exception customers
You don't impose an arbitrary policy on me.	More focus on the exceptions that can hurt revenue Increased loyalty Reduced customer frustration	Reduced complaints and escalations Reduced handle times and transaction times
You trust my version of events.	Increased loyalty Reduced customer frustration	Less activity on each contact Reduced repeat contacts
You enable me to trust you.	Brand loyalty Word-of-mouth marketing	Less time wasted checking what customers claim or say to you
You trust me to advise others.	Increased revenue by customer word of mouth	Reduced staffed service costs

Equally, taking away a check or control may not produce an immediate flood of fraud issues or costs. We therefore recommend pilot testing changes to see what happens. In our experience, the flood of frauds or issues rarely occurs but the goodwill and loyalty is apparent quickly. Table 6.3 summarizes the benefits.

Meet the Challenge: You Trust Me

We see three common reasons why it's hard to demonstrate trust with customers. Likewise it's important to take specific measures to meet the challenge for each one.

Reduce Controls

It is hard for companies to implement trust because systems and processes are rarely designed to work that way. Processes of checking and hierarchical approval have been in place for many years. Audit and control mindsets have dominated some organizations as they grew through the last century. It's much easier to add a check or review than take one away. Furthermore, moving away from checks and controls puts more faith in frontline staff. Companies are also reluctant to reduce controls because they are scared of bad news and bad publicity. However, with the power of publicity also swinging toward the customer, there is now more risk around bad experiences damaging brand and reputation. Companies that break through their conventional thinking and decide that it's cheaper and better to forget about most controls, such as Costco, find that they create lasting bonds with their customers.

Don't Fear Precedent

Many companies also fear setting precedent. The concern is that a rule relaxed for one customer may open the floodgates for others. We think that because of the damage that can be done by customers' sharing stories of narrow rules and policy-driven processes, this concern for precedent issues should be ignored. We've seen very few examples of customers looking for loopholes and telling others to exploit them. A customer who is in exceptional circumstances will appreciate that the difficulty is acknowledged and dealt with appropriately. For example, customers who are beneficiaries of a company hardship policy and have payments extended or waived because they are in financial difficulties rarely tell other customers that this is how you can get bills and fees waived. They appreciate that their circumstances are treated sensitively and appropriately.

Break Down Calcification

Finally, the systems and processes for this kind of control have been baked in over many years. It's hard to make the systems flexible enough to allow exceptions and have sufficient overrides close to the customer front line. It's easier to design prevention mechanisms that degrade the experience for all customers, rather than create more sophisticated business rules that spot exceptions or handle customers differently in different situations. Creating such flexibility requires more complex software, better use of data, and more sophisticated process design. Other powerful tools include removing some rules altogether and trusting frontline staff. It's better to identify and discipline staff who are abusing this trust than to mistrust everyone.

CHAPTER SEVEN

YOU SURPRISE ME WITH STUFF I CAN'T IMAGINE

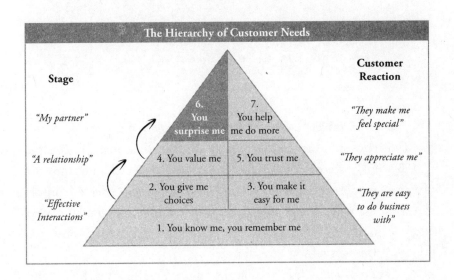

The Hierarchy of Customer Needs

Stage

Customer Reaction

"My partner"

6. You surprise me

7. You help me do more

"They make me feel special"

"A relationship"

4. You value me

5. You trust me

"They appreciate me"

"Effective Interactions"

2. You give me choices

3. You make it easy for me

"They are easy to do business with"

1. You know me, you remember me

No news travels faster or lasts longer than the story of a creative, well-executed surprise. Consider this one: During the 2013 holiday season, the Canada-based airline WestJet got into the Christmas spirit by offering a Santa video kiosk at a selected airport location. As with all Santas, this one asked children and adults what they wanted for Christmas. What the passengers didn't know was that WestJet was taking careful notes.

When passengers arrived at the baggage claim after their flight, they were shocked at what they saw: large, spectacularly wrapped presents coming around the carousel with their names on them. Imagine their further delight to find that these presents fulfilled the wishes they had expressed to Santa only three hours earlier! A logistics team at WestJet had worked feverishly to source and obtain the wide array of gifts—from socks and undies to flights home for Christmas to wide-screen TVs. The laughter, tears, and joy were recorded for all to see. It may have directly impacted only two hundred passengers, but the event has had over 36 million viewers on the Internet.[1]

While that story might well represent the ultimate in "surprise and delight," satisfying most customers' needs doesn't really require anything so elaborate. In the good old days, a local butcher might have surprised a regular customer by saying, "*I slipped a couple of our new sausages in with your roast, for your breakfast.*" There's no reason that today's companies can't do the same—and in fact, some do. The New York City–based online grocer FreshDirect, for example, occasionally throws in a free full-sized sample or a few extra bananas.

What makes surprises so alluring isn't necessarily their content or grandiosity. Even a small kindness, when it's unexpected and freely offered, can change the course of a customer's day. Somehow the unexpected aspect, the surprise, is much more important than the thing itself. Being taken unaware changes the emotional response. The customer is suddenly aware that there are real people on the other side of the transaction, thinking about how to make the day just a little bit better. This awareness and appreciation deepens the relationship.

"You Surprise Me" sits at the top of the Me2B customer hierarchy along with "You Help Me Do More," which we explore in the next chapter. It builds on the experiences delivered by the other five customer needs. Organizations need to demonstrate the other needs consistently before they attempt to surprise the customer. As they move up the hierarchy, their relationship with customers matures to the point where they can get a surprise just right. On the other side of it, any customer who's dealt with a company with ease, who's been given choices, and who's felt trusted and valued is open and ready to be impressed and surprised by something the organization does. In familiar terms, it seals the deal. It can also sometimes work to offset bad experiences in which a company has slipped on its delivery of the other needs. However, that should be the exception, not the norm.

Despite literature on delighting and *wowing* customers, the vast majority of organizations have yet to embrace this practice—and we partially agree. Getting the simple things right consistently is a better place to start than going for wow from the outset. The Hilti Australia power tool company found that being consistent was the wow that its customers wanted. Customers were delighted that tool repair and delivery timetables were always met.

Cost-cutting and efficiency drivers around methods such as Lean and Six Sigma seem to be the antithesis of surprise and positive investments in customer relationships—and yet even they have something to contribute. Lean projects should get rid of wasted contacts and effort, to help free up the time and resources for surprise planning. Six Sigma projects seek to reduce variation—a noble effort when applied to variations that aren't good for the business or customer. Standardization of processes doesn't need to exclude positive surprises.

The goal here isn't to surprise or delight every customer on every interaction; no one expects that. In effect, any company that delivers an easy, trusted, and value-filled interaction is on some level surprising and delighting customers, who all too often have had an entirely different experience in their commercial dealings. Imagine if a rail commuter purchasing a weekly ticket was told at the counter or on the website that there was a cheaper ticket available. They would be surprised by the interaction despite its routine nature.

"Surprise me" is about going a step further: identifying those moments—not just anytime, but the *right* time—and those offerings that provide the greatest opportunity to deepen customer relationships. Me2B Leaders are always on the lookout for creative ways to generate "wow!" reactions from customers and employees, and to weave surprise and delight into the long-term relationship experience.

As we discuss in Chapter Ten, it takes conscious design to create a culture in which the frontline staff feel empowered to take charge in providing a unique experience. The organization needs to hire people with the right attitude first and also set up an environment that enables these events to happen. The Virgin organizations all over the world are famous for hiring on attitude and training the technical. Staff with the right attitude do these kinds of things because they find them intrinsically rewarding. However, it's important that organizations also don't create obstacles that prevent these kinds of acts, such as restrictive measures or oversight that discourages such behavior. Managers need to share positive stories as an important way to encourage these behaviors overtly. Nordstrom lives by this. Instead

Table 7.1   The Customer's Experience of Success and Failure

You Surprise Me Success	You Surprise Me Failure
You do more than I expect at key moments and delight me with random acts of kindness.	You do the bare minimum to satisfy me and say it's not your problem.
You make the complex world simple for me.	You make everything more complicated.
You treat me like a new customer all the time.	You treat me as a commodity once I'm on board, and only give the best deals to attract new customers.
You only surprise me when it is appropriate.	You surprise me when it is inconvenient.
You do things I didn't think or know were possible.	You just meet my expectations.
When you fail me, you do more than just fix it.	You barely fix problems you make.

of a long and boring employee manual, the company simply says, "Do the right thing," and then Nordstrom regales its associates with stories of actual events that build on this behavior.

In this chapter we explore six parts of this need as set out in Table 7.1.

You Do More Than I Expect at Key Moments

Not all surprises are created equal—or rather, timed equally. It turns out that you need to catch what SAS's former chairman, Jan Carlzon, has called "moments of truth," the critical customer moments and interactions during which a surprise has real and lasting relationship impact. Bill likes to call the phenomenon "2 + 2 = 6," because the return on the investment is greater than would be expected.

The companies that do this well use the ingredients and then produce a new direction that produce "wow!" or "gee, I didn't know that!" reactions. Some industries naturally produce more of these situations.

Insurance, by its very nature, encounters customers in situations where things have gone wrong (a car accident or house damage) or in an unwanted situation (health or medical insurance). These are all great opportunities to deliver surprises since they are so unexpected. But a first interaction or early stage of a relationship is also a chance to surprise. It's interesting how companies fail to take these opportunities. Banks, for example, know when customers are about to move into a new home. What a great opportunity to exploit this unique and critical time in the lives of their customers. But few, if any, send a bottle of champagne or a welcoming bunch of flowers, or indeed make any gesture to the life event they have enabled. With mortgages providing great profit margins, this is an unexploited opportunity to surprise customers.

Random acts of kindness are not only welcomed, they are relished. Coffee shop patrons might tell the barista to keep the change or to apply it to the next customer's order; the barista might toss in chocolate mints to the order so that the customer can sample the new item. On a larger scale, companies that send credit notices or rebates for loyal patronage, or waive fees, produce "wow" reactions that customers wind up telling their friends and family about every chance they get.

Bad Stories: Missed Opportunity

The irony of insurance claims is that it is often the wronged individual who has to do all the work in third-party claim situations. The driver does nothing, while the person who was hit has to obtain quotations to prove the legitimacy of the claim. What a great opportunity for a company to surprise the third party by waiving some of these requirements! The last thing they want after the stress of an accident is to take their damaged vehicle to two approved assessors and then wait for approval. Medical insurers also miss prime opportunities to make a surprise with emotional impact. When new parents file claims for maternity costs, why not send congratulations, and perhaps a toy or an appropriate book? Or even better yet, they could send a book on child health or some other form of practical help for new parents.

Good Stories: Going the Distance

The provider of mobile travel SIM cards TravelSIM received a call from a customer asking if the SIM was working since he had experienced issues while traveling. The agent did the basic checks, establishing that the card was active and working. But then he went the extra mile. He looked back through the attempted call logs and identified what the customer was doing wrong both on SMS and international dialing. He walked the customer through the correct process, and then referred him to appropriate instructional material on the company's website for the future. Finally, he talked him through the techniques he could use to have cheaper calls while traveling. The customer was totally surprised by the comprehensiveness of the research and the support. None of these extras was expected, but all surprised and delighted him (and now David can share his story!).

A frequent flyer on one of the Virgin-branded airlines got a call a few hours prior to her planned flight. The flight had been canceled due to weather delays, but the call wasn't to deliver bad news. The agent asked if there was any chance that the customer could get to the airport fifteen minutes earlier, as she could then be reticketed on an earlier flight. The customer said "Absolutely!" and made the earlier flight, so instead of being inconvenienced she actually got home sooner than expected. The airline turned a potential negative experience into a positive one by surprising the customer with proactive contact and an unexpected, unrequired solution.

When sales clerks go above and beyond for customers, especially for new customers or those they don't even know, the results are extraordinary. This is from a letter written to CEO Blake Nordstrom:

> I am writing to you regarding two amazing associates in your Austin
> Barton Creek store. This past week I travelled to Austin Monday
> night for important meetings early Tuesday morning. When I first
> went through security in Toronto, I opened my suitcase and, much
> to my chagrin, realized that I had forgotten shoes. Because it was
> evening and many hours of travel ahead of me, I was wearing flip
> flops of all things. When I arrived in Chicago, I went to the lounge

and called ahead to your Austin store. Gabe in your men's shoe department answered the phone and I told him my problem. I was hoping that he could send some shoes over in a taxi to my hotel. Gabe would hear nothing of it. He asked me instead to visit your website and took me through the shoes he had in stock in my size. He then told me (he wouldn't take no for an answer) that he would meet me at my hotel, whatever time I arrived, with 4 or 5 pair of shoes and we'd conclude the transaction then. I told Gabe that I wouldn't be at the hotel until midnight but his response was simple and very "Nordstrom." "I am 24/7 for my customers. Just call me on my cell phone when you arrive." The end of the story is no surprise. Gabe and Clancie were waiting for me in the lobby of my hotel at midnight. We tried on 4 pair of shoes and I purchased one pair. The next morning I told the story to an audience of 40 people and continued the cycle of storytelling that befits only your customer service.[2]

Remember Nordstrom's one-line operating manual? "Do the right thing!"

You Make the Complex World Simple for Me

Many customers now have multiple electronic devices such as computers, mobile phones, and tablets. Add wireless and multiple family members to the mix, and the average home is a pretty complex technical environment. The financial world is equally complex: We have accounts, pensions, insurance policies, credit cards, loans, Internet banking, and so forth. Customers juggle dozens of accounts and logins. David has more than 250 IDs and passwords. This has indeed become a complex world.

In this environment, customers typically expect complexity—providing an excellent opportunity for organizations to surprise them with simplicity at key moments. The methods here aren't so different than those employed in "You Know Me, You Remember Me" and "You Make It Easy," but these instances hinge on giving the customer the impression of the company having gone unexpectedly further. Some companies are even building value propositions around simplifying complexity; for example, e-tailers like Amazon are opening "drop boxes" to provide for same-day delivery, and companies offering interchangeable parts such as universal phone chargers or battery packs with fittings for any computer.

Bad Stories: Universally Frustrating

In an attempt to simplify complexity, some technology companies now make what they call "universal remotes" to control the plethora of entertainment devices such as televisions, DVD players, amplifiers, digital recorders, and the like. However, these devices only function correctly if they are configured correctly, and the whole setup is placed squarely (and uncomfortably) on the customer's shoulders.

At the start of the process for one particular remote, users first have to download two programs, a process that rarely succeeds on the first attempt and introduces inevitable confusion. If successful, they then need to obtain precise model details from all existing devices—far from simple, since the model numbers are generally located behind or underneath the devices. (Customers with a wall-mounted TV are really in for it!) Finally, customers need to custom-configure the inputs, yet another challenging process with potential for error. Even for the successful few that make it through the gauntlet, it's a time-consuming, confusing, frustrating process that the company evidently didn't spend any time thinking about how to make easier. The process is as complicated as one could imagine—no simple step-by-step guide, no friendly online how-to video, no pictures to provide a visual walk-through. So the net result of a device meant to simplify a complex world is many hours of frightful complexity. We would wager that a high percentage of universal remotes are never used.

A well-known online music store has built-in controls that prevent more than five machines logging on to a given account. But over time, this presents families or individuals with multiple issues. Many PCs and laptops have about a three-year shelf life, not to mention unexpected failures, so a family of four could easily get through more than five machines within a few years and hit the limit. Unfortunately, when that happens, it's very difficult to figure out how to disable the retired machines. The information is buried in the site, as is evident in the store's customer support forums, which are littered with customers confused and looking for this assistance. The problem could be easily resolved with an automated message such as, "*You have exceeded the number of machines for this account, which of the following machines would you like to disable?*" The user could then log in and uncheck devices from a list.

Good Stories: Smooth Moving

Bill recently downloaded an album he'd purchased on Amazon to a new computer. He was amazed when Amazon asked him, "Would you like us to rip all the albums you have bought from us onto this new device?" Why yes, he would! In one stroke, Amazon had removed the complexity of getting music files up and running on a new device, without making customers do any work or even have to search for the new functionality. Of course this "surprise me" process could not have happened without Amazon's renowned "You Know Me, You Remember Me" capabilities and the company's penchant to "Make It Easy" for its customers.

The logistics and mail company Australia Post has been forced to recognize the speed with which its business is changing. Because mail volumes have been declining, the business has regrouped around package delivery. It has introduced a surprising innovation: On any package, a customer can now add a "video stamp." This exploits QR-code technology to link to a video greeting made by the customer—an especially friendly feature for sending gifts. What a great way to surprise customers with a clever feature by exploiting a technology that they may not have even have known existed.

Approximately 14 percent of U.S. households move every year, creating the major administrative hassle of shifting service providers and updating account information. The U.S. cable industry has simplified that process for its customers by having providers share data so that account details are readily transferred. Then they go one step further, connecting with the U.S. Postal Service, utilities, and other organizations to make the rest of the move work smoothly with a service called CableMover.

You Treat Me Like a New Customer All the Time

Customers certainly aren't dumb, so why do so many companies treat them that way? Many companies launch marketing campaigns offering discounts to new customers—meanwhile loyal customers are well aware of these campaigns and disappointed or even insulted by them. Loyal customers should be rewarded, not penalized as the company chases new customers, trying to entice them to switch over.

Customer-centric organizations know they have to do better; "bait and switch" is unacceptable. These companies proactively inform customers when there's a better plan or a more cost-effective promotion available. Sometimes they automatically place the customer on the new plan, perhaps even refunding the difference over the past several months. Who doesn't like the "surprise!" of a refund? Instead of giving new customers all the best deals, these companies put existing customers first. Customers feel valued and their loyalty and likelihood to recommend increase dramatically.

Bad Stories: Encouraging Churn

The Australian Victorian state utility industry is one of the most competitive in the world: 30 percent of customers switch providers each year. This is hardly surprising, given that many of the companies offer new customers discount products that give them 10 to 20 percent lower rates in their first year. Many customers eagerly exploit these rates, switching once again as soon as the deal ends to a new provider offering a slightly better deal for them. None of the companies offers a discount based on loyalty, and only a few offer discounts for longer than one year. The only way a long-time customer ever gets a break is by threatening to leave, at which point a "save team" has the power to offer incentives. Without a process in place to reward loyal or valuable customers with a better deal, the churn cycle continues.

Mobile and data plans offered by telecommunications companies are well known for disappointing, rather than pleasantly surprising, loyal customers. These plans often offer calls, SMS, or data up to a cap for a fixed monthly charge. If you exceed the cap, penalty rates kick in and can cause large bills. But if you use *less* time or data than allotted, those unused minutes don't roll over to your next bill. That's the case in Australia, anyway; some U.S. providers do allow "rollover minutes" at least for talk time. It's like a one-way penalty: Use too much and we charge you at penalty rate, use too little and we get to absorb the unused credit. Some Australian companies are at least starting to offer better warning systems that tell a customer when a cap is approaching, while others now have "all you can eat" plans with no caps.

Good Stories: Treat Customer Loyalty Like Customer Acquisition

Despite the ineffective approaches that we have described in some telecommunications companies, others do seem to get it. In Australia, Telstra uses analytics to identify valuable customers who are on the wrong plan. It calls customers to advise them of this and help them switch to plans that are a better fit. It recognizes that far from being profit cannibalization, this is the best way to keep loyal and profitable customers. In the United States, the former market challenger carrier MCI also found intelligent ways to surprise the customer. It had processes in place to recognize product features that customers weren't using and turn them off (for example, if a customer wasn't using overseas dialing, MCI canceled the feature and then sent an automatic refund). When MCI called these customers to inform them, there was often a shocked silence, followed quickly by "wow!" and a thank you. Occasionally, the customer requested that the service be restored despite the lapse in use, but in all cases, customers were pleased to know the company was looking out for them.

As we have mentioned, cable and satellite TV providers all have attractive introductory offers to land new customers—for example, a season of free NFL channels worth $30 a month. One of these providers decided it didn't want to treat new customers better than old customers, so it provided every existing subscriber with the introductory NFL offer, without them even having to ask for it. It has now elevated this practice to being the second of four "Founding Service Principles": "We will make all new services and features available first to existing customers, if possible without them having to bother themselves to request them."

David is a member and season ticket holder of the Melbourne-based soccer team known as Melbourne Victory. They are contracted to play some games at a very large stadium, which often has extra seats. For a recent game, the team decided to fill some of those extra seats by rewarding fans: David got an SMS that offered him a free additional seat for the upcoming game merely by texting "yes" in response to the SMS. The club then e-mailed him an additional ticket at no charge, allowing him to bring another family member. The club pleasantly surprised him again later that season by e-mailing him an offer to buy back his seats for a particular game if he wasn't planning on coming. The game was likely to be a sell-out, so having extra seats to sell was good for the club—but it was also good for any members who couldn't go and would have lost the value of their reserved seats. These two examples show methods by which loyal customers can be rewarded for loyalty in ways that surprise them.

You Only Surprise Me When It Is Appropriate

Poorly timed surprises can damage a relationship rather than enhance it. In some industries, it is obvious that certain interactions need to be handled delicately. Notification of a life insurance claim, for example, is unlikely to be a good time for sales-related conversations on other financial products to which the claimant has now become entitled. To give a lighter example, "Would you like free fries with that?" is probably not the right surprise at the right moment for a customer who has selected a low-fat food product.

It's hard to define black-and-white rules to protect against poorly timed surprises. Certain interactions may be a great opportunity for a value-added offer or some unexpected customer education—except that the specific customer contributes unknown variables that make it inappropriate, such as being in a rush or having recently had a poor experience. *A surprise only improves the relationship if the customer values it.*

The organizations that succeed in delivering surprises train their staff to be aware of the context for the customer. They provide options so that both the content—the offer, the freebie, the value-add—and the timing of the surprise can be tailored by the customer as needed.

Bad Stories: Unpleasant Upgrades

A large software company we know automatically runs updates to its software as customers power down their computers. The focus is on making sure customers always have the latest and best code available. The trouble is, the timing can be a real problem when a customer wants to power down quickly and go get somewhere, board a plane, or head into a meeting. Why not let the customer decide when to install updates? A later version of this company's software became even more controlling, warning customers that it would power down in ten minutes to install updates. At least there's a warning, but shutting down on its own schedule is tantamount to being rude to the customer, who may not be in a position to take a break.

On a recent flight, a frequent flyer was offered a free upgrade. He was thrilled—and then completely disappointed when it turned out the airline wasn't going to offer the upgrade to his traveling partner, who wasn't a frequent flyer. The situation might have been avoided since the same IT system that recommended the upgrade was also capable of checking the booking to see if the passenger was traveling by himself. It's tantalizing to have the promise of First Class, only to see it pulled away unless you're willing to leave your partner back in Coach.

Good Stories: Welcomed Assistance

Several years ago e*Stara introduced an exciting new tool to online retailers and their customers. After a customer spent a certain amount of time on a high-value page (called *dwelling* on the page), the tool popped up a box offering the customer the opportunity to have someone from customer service or sales call and provide assistance. Customers responded avidly when they realized they could select the timing for the call back ("now," "in 5 minutes," or at a time selected by the customer). They also loved a feature that allowed the agent who called to know which web pages they had already visited, greatly simplifying the conversation and increasing conversion rates! Since the success of that tool, other companies have developed even more helpful (and surprising) solutions, including new versions of co-browsing that allow two or more consumers to see what is on one another's screens and comment together on possible purchases, a practice called *co-buying*. Co-buying simplifies collaborative shopping, ideal for customers such as a prospective bride and her bridesmaids who may need to confer on dress colors and designs.

You Do Things I Didn't Think or Know Were Possible

The ultimate surprise comes when a company seems to do the impossible. Often this involves rethinking part of a business so that it behaves in ways a customer doesn't expect. It is behavior you see most often among innovators and challengers that aren't so invested in the old way of doing something.

We all now accept airlines' frequent flyer programs as the industry standard, but they didn't exist until American Airlines came up with the revolutionary idea that loyal customers should be rewarded with extra benefits including free flights and upgrades. Sometimes new inventions are the ultimate customer surprise. Frontline agents who know their products backward and forward can often pull off "wow" feats by revealing new capabilities or features to customers. All of this harks back to Amazon's often-cited mantra that it intends to "Be Earth's Most Customer-Centric Company." When pressed for his definition of this, Amazon founder and CEO Jeff Bezos would tell Bill and other executives, "It's a delicate balance between listening to the customer and inventing for the customer."

Bad Stories: Making the Possible Impossible

It's extremely frustrating when a customer is told something is impossible when they know for a fact that it can be done. David had that experience while traveling with his family on a partner airline to the one in which he has frequent flyer status. On the outward leg, he and his family were allowed into the frequent flyer lounge of the partner airline, as had always been the case. But on the way home, three weeks later, they arrived at the same lounge and were told that only one guest could accompany him, unless he paid a large fee; that was the rule and they couldn't break it. Although it turned out that this *was* the rule, it had never before been enforced. David and his family therefore knew what was possible and were denied it, leading to a very tired, cranky group.

Good Stories: A Better Test Drive

As we've mentioned already, Subaru has developed an avid following of "Subaru'ers." (Full disclosure: Bill's wife, Lori, and David's wife, Sue, both love their Subarus.) Subaru is known as one of the leaders in four-wheel-drive technology. All its cars, from sedans to off-road vehicles, are fitted with it. Some of its dealerships realized that many potential customers weren't seeing the full value of the vehicles because they didn't really understand the cars' capabilities, so they sent customers out for test drives with a well-trained mechanic as a demonstration driver. He demonstrated the anti-lock braking as well as features designed to autocorrect the car if it was unbalanced or risking roll-over. Customers had known these features existed, but never understood their impact. Showing them firsthand became a persuasive feature of the sales process.

When You Fail Me, You Do More Than Just Fix It

When a company fails at something it promised to provide or perform, or something goes wrong, fixing it isn't enough anymore. Just as in any relationship, a partner who fails to meet expectations needs to make it up to the other person. A nice surprise on the upside makes an excellent and high-impact peace offering.

Addressing the issue first means assessing the scale of the damage, then considering the appropriate reparation. Some companies just throw money at these problems, offering financial rebates as goodwill gestures. The trouble is, this can feel like a quid pro quo, reimbursing customers for their effort, not an instance of a company truly going the distance to restore the relationship. Careful thought and analysis of customers' needs—either as a group or individually—could produce unique surprises that offer greater impact.

For example, consider the impact on a customer after getting a series of incorrect bills. It takes time to correct the problem, plus there's financial hardship. Extended payment terms help manage the inconvenience to the customer, and an apology or even a rebate takes reparation one step further. However, to restore the relationship entirely, the organization might need follow-up action timed with the next bill. It could call the customer to make sure that everything on the new bill is correct, and perhaps point out a small discount. Only at that point does the customer feel surprised by the level of attention and care given to the error. Everything prior to that point was just fixing the problem.

Some organizations have created recovery units whose sole goal is to fix broken relationships via special treatment and offers. Unfortunately, these units tend to be examples of too little too late. Companies that lead in Me2B customer experience don't need this type of unit, both because failures are rare and because they have created a culture that produces recovery surprises *before* relationships are nearing the point of failure.

Bad Stories: No Sheets, No Clothes

A customer rented a touring camper van for his family holiday from a well-known rental company. He and his family reached their first-night destination only to find that the company had not provided linen or bedding, even though they had been booked. The company had made a mistake and the customer needed help, yet the response to his call was tepid at best: The customer was told to buy bedding himself, for which he would later be reimbursed. Who wants to go shopping for sheets in an unfamiliar area on the first day of vacation? No further gestures were made to make up for this major inconvenience. Meanwhile, the customer had called from a location only two hours from where the camper had been picked up; delivery of the promised bedding shouldn't have been out of the question.

Anyone who has been through lost luggage with an airline knows that it's traumatic. Airlines generally offer only cursory support, such as a small wash bag or pair of pajamas, plus (one hopes) convenient delivery of the missing bags. The staff that handle these types of queries at airports appear to be trained to deal with the loss as routine, rather than address and ameliorate the inconvenience and emotional stress the problem causes customers. They certainly aren't empowered to offer customers recovery surprises. We even ran across one U.S. airline that decided to handle lost baggage inquiries with an offshore contact center, exacerbating an already traumatic situation.

Good Stories: Make It Right

As we all know, the airline industry can be hit with weather and other uncontrollable events that drastically impact customers. Qantas Airlines decided to try offering some form of institutional-ized recovery for international customers who had suffered a bad experience, regardless of whether the cause was within the airline's control. Customers who had experienced a bad delay or cancellation received recovery calls and letters offering extra frequent flyer points and other bonuses. The airline tracked the impact of this activity and found that the average spend per customer by recovered customers was higher over the next six months than those in a control group where no recovery occurred. Overall, the recovery efforts saw a positive return.

Losing something in a cab is a moment of truth for cab companies because customers are in a difficult situation, but only some recognize how important that is. In Melbourne, Australia, David left his wallet, including credit cards, in a cab and had no receipt. Not knowing which company he'd been dealing with, he called each of the cab networks in the area to talk to their lost property area. Two told him that they had no lost property function; drivers were told to drop any lost property into a police station. David was distressed. How would he know which police station to call and how often? If the wallet was not visible in the cab it could be days before it was found. David's surprise here was that these companies had no process for what must be a frequent event that is distressing.

Silver Top, the third company, was different: Not only did it have a lost property department and process, but its agent said he would get a message to all drivers immediately asking them to look for the item. "Call us back in an hour and we'll help you from there if we have it," he said. David hoped he was with this cab company, and he was lucky. When he called back they had found it. They connected him to the driver, who returned it in exchange for the extra fare. The company may well have received a small booking fee for that extra fare, but the much bigger win comes from the huge amounts of loyalty and goodwill produced by helping customers at such a vulnerable moment. David now actively recommends Silver Top to everyone he knows—and all the readers of this book, too.

Why "You Surprise Me with Stuff That I Can't Imagine" Is So Important

Some might say that *businesslike* means boring, plain, and basic. But if businesses are serious about wanting positive, long-lasting relationships with customers, they have to go beyond bland and transactional interactions. Surprises that require some initiative and are proactively offered stop customers in their tracks and create an emotional impact that deepens relationships. Being successful at this will produce lasting change for companies, perhaps even more than filling the other customer needs for Me2B success. It can reverse negative attitudes immediately, and turn regular customers into loyal and positive brand advocates. These extra acts live a long time in the customer memory and are retold many times, especially in this new era of social media. Few of us tell friends and colleagues about things working well, as expected. The stories we share are the outliers, and it's better for a business to have those outliers be positive surprises, things that were unexpected and welcome. Having customers market your business is also cheaper and much more powerful than any planned marketing campaign, as word-of-mouth marketers have espoused for many years.

As the story about WestJet playing Santa demonstrated, surprises can also broadcast powerful marketing messages and give employees the chance to experience something more meaningful than the routine day-to-day business. Empowered employees stick around longer, and costs such as recruitment and training fall. Table 7.2 summarizes the benefits of doing surprise right.

Meet the Challenge: You Surprise Me

Creating the machinery for customer surprise experiences isn't easy. Several reasons explain why it's hard to produce these invaluable surprises, but meeting the challenge with the steps outlined here is well worth any efforts.

Empower Staff

In most cases organizations lack an environment in which individuals are encouraged and allowed to perform customer support actions independently. Employees need sufficient training and skills to assess what will be effective and when, and more important, they need to know that when they exercise their power their management will back them up. This staff empowerment also requires flexibility in the measurement system to allow staff to do things that might take

Table 7.2   The Benefits of Offering Welcome Surprises

Customer Need Met	Potential to Increase Revenue	Potential to Reduce Cost
You do more than I expect at key moments and delight me with random acts of kindness.	Increased word-of-mouth marketing Improved customer retention and lifetime value	Reduced contacts requesting special treatment
You make the complex world simple for me.	Increased word-of-mouth marketing	Reduced unneeded contacts Reduced product returns and waste
You treat me like a new customer all the time.	Increased lifetime value from customers	Reduced marketing and discounts to new customers
You only surprise me when it is appropriate.	Controls impulse to "give away the store"	Reduced complaints Reduced wasted investment in the relationship
You do things I didn't think or know were possible.	Increased word-of-mouth marketing	Less need for marketing or promotional expense
You when you fail me, you do more than just fix it.	Increased word-of-mouth marketing Extended lifetime value Improved customer retention	Reduced follow-up contacts

longer or cost more without penalizing them. It's a delicate balancing act for companies to encourage individual behaviors and surprising acts but also get people to follow routine or standardized processes that deliver speed and simplicity for customers. That can mean helping staff by making it clear which processes require speed and simplicity and which have room for more surprising acts.

Develop Creative, Forward-Thinking Teams

A second reason it's hard to implement surprises is the lack of creative, forward-thinking teams. Just as with individuals, organizations need to assess what will make a difference to customers and when it will be appropriate to deliver these differences, and then adapt process and sometimes technology to make it possible. It needs people in the organization who are focused on *what could be* rather than *what is*, asking questions like, "Wouldn't it be great if we could also do X for the customers?" Companies need to encourage such questions and thoughts from product and service creation through support over the long haul, often by blending departmental representatives in development, testing, rollout, and service functions as done at Amazon and other Me2B Leaders.

Think Long Term

Shifting to a culture of surprises requires two approaches that most organizations sorely lack: long-term thinking and leaps of faith. As we see in the financial press, most organizations are fixated on next quarter's earnings. Executives find it really difficult to justify investments that don't pay off right away. The effect of a great surprise might not show up until down the line, when the customer contemplates the next purchase. Surprises also require a leap of faith. It's hard to predict their effect, and then sometimes it's hard to tie that effect directly to revenue increases.

Some organizations are better placed to practice the art of surprise—for example, those that are privately owned or mutually owned like Bupa or USAA and don't have to worry about public markets or shareholders. It's easier for these companies to take on longer-term bets. But it's also easier as we've pointed out for member-based organizations like Costco to behave this way because they too are thinking about the long term, while also striving to satisfy quarterly returns.

CHAPTER EIGHT

YOU HELP ME BE BETTER AND DO MORE

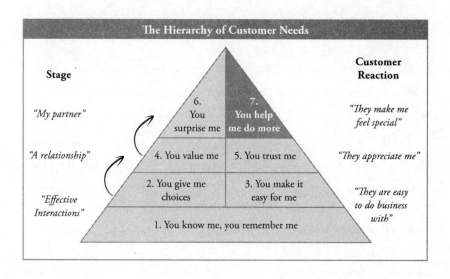

The Hierarchy of Customer Needs

Stage

"My partner"

"A relationship"

"Effective Interactions"

6. You surprise me

7. You help me do more

4. You value me

5. You trust me

2. You give me choices

3. You make it easy for me

1. You know me, you remember me

Customer Reaction

"They make me feel special"

"They appreciate me"

"They are easy to do business with"

Richard Branson was once asked to describe his general attitude toward business. "I have always said there is no point in starting your own business unless you do it to try and make people's lives better," he answered. "I have often started my ventures out of a sense of frustration at what is on offer and with a view of creating something that will shake things up."[1]

Branson's attitude captures the essence of the final Me2B customer need: "You Help Me Be Better and Do More." It is the most aspirational of them all, akin to the highest two levels in Maslow's hierarchy of needs, esteem and self-actualization. Organizations focused on this level of customer need look beyond the immediate consumption of the product or use of the service to consider the *context* for that consumption. They search to discover the intrinsic reasons *why* customers shop, search, buy, use, travel, and stay, especially when the items are not essentials but rather discretionary purchases or services. They ask how the products are serving the customers' broader goals or deeper needs of identity, community, or philanthropy.

If the company gets it right and finds ways to represent and serve that broader context, it is selling much more than a product. Customers begin to associate the use of the products and services, and the company itself, with their own goals and values. Companies that meet these broader aspirational needs become indispensable, and customers start to recognize the relationship as something special, stronger: a true *partnership*, one that creates a virtuous circle of benefits for all involved. Sometimes, improving the customer's life even means sacrificing revenue in the short term for a long-term relationship, for example, when an energy company finds so many ways to help customers reduce their electricity consumption to make the world a greener, cleaner place that it reduces its own revenue. However, when customers experience that contribution, it reinforces the notion of being in partnership.

Identifying and serving these greater needs requires a deep understanding of the customer, which is why this need sits at the top of the Me2B customer needs pyramid. As with the customer needs discussed earlier, fulfilling the need for self-improvement came more naturally in the past when local providers had more intimate knowledge of the customer. A local storeowner or bank manager knew about the customer's life and naturally looked for ways to help, and then could readily see the results.

As organizations grew, adding more channels of delivery and becoming more remote from the customer, focused assistance became much more difficult. As we've already noted, many companies focus on quarterly profit maximization and increased shareholder value, using formulas that have worked reasonably well in the past but now may not be sustainable. These old models encourage vast amounts of product trial, capture a small percentage of actual purchase, accept some annual loss or attrition, and fill the bucket by developing more products or finding ever more prospects and customers. Meanwhile, relationships with customers are more or less transactional; customers focus on price and organizations struggle to deliver the margins they require as a result.

That model is breaking down since customers are changing providers more often and becoming even more price aware. Customers are in control and can use the Internet to find the best deal, whether it's around the corner or halfway around the world, making it ever harder for companies to sustain profits. Meanwhile, as we've said, technology creates a new opportunity to understand customers' individual context with the help of the data they share.

No customer wants to feel exploited. Companies need to think of themselves as in long-term relationships with customers, in which they help the customer achieve far more than the immediate use of the product. (Note again that we are not saying "customer relationship management"; CRM assumes that the organization is in charge and we've shown how that is no longer the case.)

Most companies would benefit from adopting this broader view of the good they're providing to customers. In financial services, investment and wealth management companies need to help customers grow their wealth and use their money wisely. Professional services companies such as IT consultancies need to ensure that their clients are using their services to achieve their objectives rather than just helping the companies pursue their internal revenue targets. In retail, serving broader needs can be as simple as helping customers use the product to improve their lives. For example, many successful hardware chains run free workshops helping customers perform projects, and they provide a whole series of self-help guides on common projects such as installing shelving or building a shed. These gestures show customers that their business is valued and that the company has taken an interest beyond the product sale.

Table 8.1 presents five ways all companies can help their customers be better and do more.

You Support Me Beyond the Product Sale

Quite often products or services help customers pursue a life goal or experience. In some industries, this association is more plainly evident—and thus recognized and supported—than others.

Table 8.1 The Customer's Experience of Success and Failure

You Help Me Do More Success	You Help Me Do More Failure
You support me beyond the product.	You do the bare minimum to sell this product or service.
You coach me to use things better.	You leave me on my own and hope I work it out.
You help me use less of your stuff.	You sell me things I don't need.
You help me look forward.	Once you have sold to me, you move on to the next sale.
You help me get things that I didn't think I could.	You only care about the purchase of these products.

Online florists, for example, know that their products are generally purchased for special occasions such as anniversaries, birthdays, and holidays. They therefore include gift cards (often themed) with every purchase, and also offer other gifts and services supporting the broader event, such as chocolates and balloons, or guaranteed delivery on a particular date. Some of them also recall that date the following year, sending notes or e-mail reminders, reinforcing the first of our customer needs.

Hotel concierge desks are a highly recognizable instance of a business recognizing the need to serve the customer's broader experience. In theory, hotels are selling a simple, concrete good: an attractive, comfortable place to sleep. A concierge service isn't part of that, and often hotels have no direct financial upside from providing such a service. However, a traveling customer has broader goals to serve—enjoying a vacation, seeing the sights, or perhaps (for a business trip) wining and dining business associates. Enter the well-trained and savvy concierge, who sizes up guests' needs and can offer completely customized options accordingly, for example suggesting nearby restaurants for families with kids in tow. Some companies start this process even earlier by looking to identify and support the customer's broader needs at the time of the booking. A simple open question such as "Can we help you with any other aspect of your trip?" can create new opportunities to serve.

Bad Stories: Difficult Times

Health insurance companies are in a very privileged position: Their customers are experiencing life's most significant moments. We mentioned pregnancy and birth earlier, but these businesses are also dealing with other stressful changes, such as major operations and accidents. They are in a unique position to help the customer adjust and move through these situations. In the pregnancy and birth scenario, insurance companies are not only facing a new potential customer on the way, but also the health recovery for the mother, and in the case of a first child, radically changed life circumstances for both parents. Instead of offering services and support for this critical situation, many health insurance companies only touch the customer in one way: Sending out the bills. If anything, their claims processes are designed to minimize any risk of excess claims, taking the most narrow view of what serving the customer requires.

Few situations could be more distressing than a fatal car accident, and yet judging by their actions, general insurance companies fail to recognize the severity and the need for sensitive care. We've seen cases of companies badgering the grieving family with taxing administrative requests or, worse still, sending renewal requests to the deceased six months later. Too many organizations have failed to build a process that respects difficult situations. A claim for a scratched bumper is totally different from one involving a fatal wreck, and that difference should be reflected and supported by the claims process.

Good Stories: Whole Event Support

Virgin Atlantic was the first airline to recognize that the customer's journey started at home and ended in a destination other than the airport. To attract business customers, it added the option of pick-up from home and drop-off after the flight. Recognizing the time pressure and travel fatigue of business class passengers, Virgin also made it easier to check in and clear airport security. In Australia, the Sydney Virgin lounge is adjacent to the taxi line and has its own check-in desk and security gate, saving customers from the longer lines that await other passengers. The net result for frequent travelers is a better overall experience, less painful travel, and fewer stress-inducing delays and unknowns. Emirates Airlines has taken this one step forward with an entire terminal in Dubai dedicated to business class and first class guests.

Both the United Kingdom's Nationwide Building Society and Australia's National Australia Bank created customer kiosks to sell financial products. Home loans are key products for both institutions, so both built add-on services in the kiosks that didn't just promote mortgages but instead supported the customer's entire home-buying process. Self-service videos took the customer through every stage of the home-buying process, including searching for a property, handling the auction and buying process, and working through technical processes such as mortgage settlement. The multimedia kiosk service also offered tools such as home loan calculators, so customers could work out what value property they can afford given their income and expenditure, and what size loan the companies will finance. These whole-event support ideas then migrated to the Internet sites of both companies.

You Coach Me to Use Things Better

Many companies are obsessed with reducing handle times on calls, e-mail, or at the counter, since they believe that moving faster saves them money. They are very happy to send customers e-mail and correspondence about new products or services since they believe that offers like these increase revenue. But Me2B Leaders provide quality coaching and information to their customers regardless of the time investment with one goal as their highest priority: Helping customers use the product so that they get the most value and have the best possible experience. Unfortunately, companies driven by short-term profit motives or other organizations obsessed with cost-cutting often ignore this opportunity since it can reduce revenue or increase costs in the short term. This is a false economy, because customer education pays off in multiple ways. It reduces the need for and length of expensive customer support calls. It leads to repeat purchase and recommendations, since customers value the product more highly. Finally, if customers aren't well-educated or don't understand how to use a product, they may well cause brand damage by complaining online.

Many companies offer coaching and education only after a customer has a problem. More forward-thinking Me2B organizations coach proactively, for example at Intuit, building tutorials, demonstrations, and various levels of help and support directly into software. This requires understanding both customers and products well enough to anticipate coaching needs and layer support and education into the sales process.

The health insurance industry has frequently populated the "Bad Stories" in this book. However, in this area of customer support some of these companies have started to invest well. First off, they coach customers toward physical activity and a healthy lifestyle by subsidizing exercise or sports equipment. Some policies include free checkups every year to help with prevention and early intervention for medical or dental needs. Many services offer customer health phone lines that customers can call, staffed by nurses or even doctors who provide information and advice. These services literally help customers "be better and do more" and also offer peace of mind. Meanwhile, the companies benefit when claims drop because customers are taking better care of themselves. We're also now seeing a return of home visits by doctors, a sure-fire throwback to the good old days. But it makes a lot of sense today—preventive medicine, analyzing home environments, and checking family ailments all play a big part in providing a better outcome for customers.

Bad Stories: Out of "Touch"

When a major software company launched its latest operating system, it tried to be forward-thinking by designing the software to handle touch screens and touch-based devices as well as traditional keyboard and mouse-driven PCs and laptops. However, the touch screen interface launched as the default—an unfortunate choice, given that the overwhelming majority of installed desktop machines, laptops, and other devices don't have a touch screen. The customer backlash was quite dramatic. Customers didn't like having to take the extra step of navigating to the conventional interface, which felt clumsy and also lacked the options and ease of the new touch-screen version. Eventually the company had to redesign the configuration and support for traditional keyboard-controlled computers. It failed to anticipate the needs of different user groups or build in a variety of options for help and support. Its reputation suffered as a result.

Many people now store music on multiple devices. It's a predictable requirement that they will want to transfer music from device to device as they retire devices or buy new equipment. Despite the sensitive copyright issues involved, most customers aren't pirates, they simply want flexible access to their music. One of the popular music download sites doesn't offer any help or support for this clearly recognizable need. Disgruntled customers therefore are forced to figure it out on their own, or with help from independent C2C websites where customers help each other.

Good Stories: Quality Education

The TiVo digital video recorder has been a very successful product, particularly in the U.S. market. The product had several features that helped customers use the device better, essentially building customer training and education into the product setup process. TiVo included simple graphics to walk new customers through installation and first usage. Once they booted up, customers could play a series of how-to videos that explained product features and usage. Finally, once it's up and running, the TiVo software helps customers find and watch new shows by monitoring past recordings and then automatically recording similar programs going forward. For example, if the customer often records a cooking show, then the device will automatically record other cooking shows. A customer who doesn't like any of the TiVo suggestions can simply ignore them; soon they will erase automatically.

During Bill's time at Amazon, posters on the walls of customer service centers reminded the agents, "Have you educated a customer today?" That meant that they were to conclude calls or e-mail responses with advice about what to expect next, suggest follow-ups, or share information about how callers could resolve a problem themselves the next time it came up. This conscious fifteen-to-thirty-second investment more than paid for itself by reducing repeat calls. It also helped customers run with the solution, often producing unintended benefits such as the discovery of partner-provided tools.

Despite the benefits, Bill was at one point pressured to cut back on this small form of customer education. A successful holiday free-shipping promotion had led to dramatic increases in call volume, leading some of the Amazon executive team to think that saving those thirty seconds was the solution, but Bill argued that keeping it was important. Amazon's marketing senior vice president David Risher agreed on the grounds that skimping on customer education when things were busy would lead to even higher call volumes as time progressed. This short-termism would have meant that the seasonal peak would be even *bigger* the following year. Bill and David won the argument, and in the following year Amazon's support contacts per order shipped dropped significantly, and the company for the first time won the coveted #1 services score in the American Customer Satisfaction Index.

Online gaming company Blizzard Entertainment provides in-situ support tools in games such as World of Warcraft, offering help without forcing gamers to leave their quest or lose momentum. On other websites, pop-up advice panels provide very convenient education, allowing customers to view the tips and move on without having to switch windows, place a call, or launch an online chat. These responsive guides require comprehensive understanding of customer paths, so that companies correctly anticipate where people might get stuck.

Apple revolutionized the high-tech shopping experience with its Apple Stores, and then added the Genius Bar to help coach customers to use its products and software ... for free! Many companies are copying Apple's model with varying degrees of success. Verizon Wireless has transformed its 1,700 U.S. retail locations into technology-lifestyle centers it calls "Smart Stores." Experienced specialists host *free* (there's that word again) in-store classes, and Verizon's customers are gushing: "It's awesome. I love personal instruction. It's 10 times faster than to learn any other way."[2]

You Help Me Use Less of Your Stuff

In an era where up-selling and cross-selling are apt to be poorly used or overused, customers often complain: "No, I would *not* like to buy that other stuff." This presents a real opportunity for companies to show their respect for the customer's dollar and time by helping people use *less* of a product or service, rather than pushing them to buy more. This behavior helps the customer see the company as an unselfish partner but is anathema to many businesses. As discussed earlier, many organizations resist this type of thinking because they're focused on short-term revenue statements rather than long-term relationships and sustainable profit. But with customer cynicism toward large organizations on the rise (for example, in 2013 Ford found that customer brand trust had fallen by 50 percent since 2001), it's increasingly important for companies to find ways to demonstrate that customers, not shareholders, come first.[3]

Customers love it when companies help them, seemingly at their own expense. For example, when a retail salesperson tells a customer that a cheaper model will satisfy their needs, the customer immediately feels that the salesperson is operating with their best interests in mind. This creates trust, and also suggests to the customer that the salesperson has confidence even in the less-expensive products—nothing on offer is *cheap* in the negative sense.

Bad Stories: No Motive for Less

Many business process outsourcing companies (BPOs) claim that they partner with their clients. However, few of their contracts are designed to help their clients use less of their services. In the case of service calls, most contracts are set up to pay the outsourcer based on cost per handled call minute: The more calls that occur and the longer they take, the more the outsourcer profits, which encourages the worst behavior—the opposite of helping the customer use less of a service. The same is true in a back-office environment. Here the outsourcer needs to partner with the client to make the processes more effective and reduce their cost, but many are paid per transaction or per customer. If the outsourcer does make the process cheaper or more efficient, the benefits aren't shared with its clients. That's no partnership. Some BPOs like Sitel are breaking out of this mold with "gain share" and other progressive pricing schemes that guide them to pursue "Help Me Use Less of Your Stuff," for example, reducing the need for customer contacts or finding process improvement solutions.

In sunny spots around the globe, many people are installing solar water heating and solar panels to generate electricity. In Australia, government regulation, subsidies, and buy-back credits have encouraged this growth and more than a million panels have been installed in a country of nine million homes. However, while the electricity retailers do sell the panels and offer solar-based products, customers who do the right thing for sustainable energy are often charged higher rates for the electricity they use—a penalty for using less of the product. In fact, customers who have only a few panels end up paying more for their electricity than those with no panels at all.

Good Stories: The Highest-Value Service

As we noted earlier, TravelSIM offers SIM cards to use when customers travel globally. The company actively advises customers how to avoid paying too much for their calls when traveling abroad, explaining how those calling the phone can pay local rates when calling the user of the SIM card. Using a toll-free number, the customer's friends or family members wind up with the much lower local rates instead of international rates for their calls—a classic case of a company recognizing that it can benefit its customers by encouraging them to use less of their stuff, or in this case pay less for what they use. They help the customer and friends and family of the customer.

As we've also noted, T-Mobile's innovative "Un-Carrier" strategy has shaken up the U.S. industry, for example with its new

"Simple Choice Plan"—which Bill recently added when he traveled to Tokyo, Seoul, and Singapore. Bill wanted to limit his roaming charges but was delighted to discover that for a small one-time change fee, under Simple Choice Plan he would no longer pay any international roaming charges and enjoy a lower monthly fixed rate for all his favorite features. As with TravelSIM, this is almost the antithesis of many of the telecommunication companies that charge high global roaming and call forwarding rates.

In Chapter Six we describe how David's company helps utilities make moving in easier for customers sharing leases. The program also ensured that customers were getting set up with the highest-value service. As part of the process, the customer service agent asks whether anyone in the household is entitled to a government concession or discount—if so, the agent sets up that individual as the primary account holder to qualify for the discount. The agents also explain all the methods customers can use to obtain discounts, such as setting up direct debits to ensure they receive rebates and discounts for making payments on time.

Last year in classically rainy Seattle, Bill went to one of several local REI retail stores looking for a waterproof jacket. Since he's always been satisfied with REI-branded products, he started there. Watching him rifle through the racks, one of REI's experienced "Green Coat" retail sales specialists approached him to offer assistance. After hearing Bill's planned usage—a sixty-minute group run every Sunday as well as hikes during midwinter squalls—he steered Bill away from the REI racks to a national brand that had recently released a new waterproof jacket that he recommended for Bill's punishing outdoor activities. Bill ultimately bought a second jacket for himself from this manufacturer (at REI, of course), and then a third one for his wife, Lori. Clearly, REI sometimes wins by steering customers to the best available product in the store, whether it carries the house mark or not.

You Help Me Look Forward

Companies today have complex and powerful information databases, R&D labs, product development gurus, and data scientists. With all this firepower you would think they would be able to predict what customers need and to educate them on their future requirements. However, it doesn't happen as often as it should for several reasons. First, it's often in the vested interest of the company to do so only when it creates the need for further products and services. In addition, several challenges face companies seeking to provide this kind of guidance:

- Building credibility with the customer to make such recommendations acceptable when they are seen to be in the interests of the company.
- Identifying when and how to have these conversations or promote these products.
- Locating regulations and compliance issues that might restrict how and when these conversations occur.
- Packaging the information or discussion so that customers understand why it's in their interest.

The wealth management industry is well placed to have such discussions and build better relationships as a result. Since they hold their customers' savings and pensions they can predict what level of retirement income each customer can expect, and therefore what else these customers need to do to meet their future needs. Some countries have been moving to a "fee for advice" model in which advisers are paid solely for recommendations and all commissions are removed. However, retirement funds and savings companies should be able to help customers by predicting the position of the customer upon retirement and demonstrating what that means.

There are many other situations when organizations should be able to predict likely future needs of customers. We've included some in Table 8.2.

Bad Stories: Start the Relationship Again

A few years ago when a well-known online movie rental company created its next-generation product, it really blew it. Under its old model, customers rented DVDs via the Internet and got them delivered by postal service. Its new model allowed customers to stream a subset of movies online with no physical DVD required. While this

Table 8.2 Occasions for Prediction

Life Event	Future Need
Getting married	Saving for a home
Having a child	Saving for school expenses and university
Child reaching age sixteen, eighteen, twenty-one	Changed insurance position, independent banking
Major asset purchase	Extended insurance position

was a logical next step, making it possible to watch the DVD in two modes, the company forced its customers to register all over again for the new streaming service on a completely different website and provide information that the company already had for the original postal delivery. Talk about making it hard! We couldn't imagine a worse way of introducing customers to your latest and greatest service. The company threw out its source of competitive advantage, the fact that the customer already had an account. By forcing people to sign up again, the launch made it just as easy for customers to try someone else's service. In the process, this company lost 60 percent of its market value in short order, and while its stock price has largely recovered, customers are still wary.

What action should a company take when engaged in a customer relationship that seems poised to self-destruct? We've watched customer support agents in the credit card area of a major bank handle phone calls from customers who have maxed out their cards, and it's an alarming experience. Rather than help customers create structured plans to get out of debt, they sit by as customers revolve debt month by month, struggling to pay the highest rates of interest that credit card suppliers charge—bankruptcy seeming an inevitability if something doesn't change.

Instead, banks might suggest moving the card balance into a personal loan that forces the debt to be paid off over time, and packaging this with a credit card with a far lower credit limit to remove the temptation to rack up yet more debt. That would serve the customer's future and build a longer and more sustainable relationship.

We have heard stories of one or two banks that encourage customers to merge their credit card debt into a secured home loan, another example of a more responsible approach to working with struggling customers.

Good Stories: Forward-Looking Engineering

Intuit provides several brands of accounting software for businesses small and large, and the company keeps abreast of regulatory changes affecting accounting practices. As a result, Intuit can proactively advise businesses of needs for upgrades and changes, leading to tremendous customer loyalty. Intuit has focused obsessively on both hot metrics for tracking customer satisfaction: "Would you recommend us to a friend?" (known as Net Promoter Score, or NPS) and "How hard was it for you to do this process?" (known as Customer Effort Score, or CES). Is it a coincidence that Intuit's founder Scott Cook once served on Amazon's board of directors?

Basecamp provides project management software in the cloud. Its product is well written and intuitive, but on top of that, the company demonstrates impressive support for "What will I need next?" After you create your first project in the application, Basecamp helps you make best use of what you have just created with coaching on the next steps in the process, for example free advice on how to write a kick-off message. The company is working with its customers to help them do better by anticipating their future use of the product.

You Help Me Get Things That I Didn't Think I Could

Earlier we discussed supporting customers beyond the product itself. Helping customers get things they didn't think they could obtain is another example of finding ways to serve customer needs more broadly. Top companies are recognizing and meeting exceptional or unusual needs that their customers may not have articulated because they didn't know the option existed.

Perhaps it's no surprise that many of the companies that are doing this best are membership organizations. These companies tend to be relationship-focused; their members are their shareholders, and therefore they never have to manage any apparent conflict of interest. They are also well acquainted with their members and their needs, and therefore can often anticipate what their customers might want or aspire to achieve or become.

Bad Stories: Make the Customer Pay

Online ticketing sites are now common all over the world. In theory they offer convenience, allowing customers to book tickets in their own time and avoid lining up to collect them. Often these sites offer three choices for acquiring the tickets. The cheapest, easiest choice is printing at home. Having the tickets sent by post or collecting them at the venue are typically the more expensive options, and are definitely more time-consuming. But we don't like two things about these services: First, even the print-at-home option often has a hidden transaction fee of $5–$10, meaning that customers are being charged for doing the work and providing the equipment themselves. Second, for many events at sports grounds all that the customer really needs is a simple ticket with a bar code to scan at the admission gate. However, the companies send ticket formats that contain rich graphics with lots of colors and branding and advertising for the event. Customers have to waste printer ink on complex images that serve no purpose.

In Australia, the United States, and most other places airline lounges will not let even their gold-level frequent flyers use the frequent flyer lounge if they aren't flying with that airline on that day. Some might say that is a reasonable policy if the customer has chosen to fly with a competitor airline, but the airline with the lounge may not have had a flight that suited the customer's needs. Doesn't it make sense for the lounge to allow access when the customer wants to use it, especially since the customers prepays a hefty sum every year to join the lounge network, and not when the airline feels like making it available? This would suggest a trusted, ongoing partnership rather than a quid-pro-quo arrangement.

Good Stories: Places to Go

The Royal Automobile Club in Victoria offers a city facility with dining rooms, gym and swimming pool, library, pool and snooker lounge, and much more for its members. It also owns golf courses and resorts. The club is part of the broader RACV group, a mutual association that also provides roadside assistance and insurance. The executives who run the club recognize that the membership base wants access to services and events that they might not be able to obtain for themselves, and they are constantly searching for ideas and services that will serve their customers and their families. Club members receive a fantastic monthly brochure full of events and ticketing opportunities—for example, members can get tickets for hot events in Melbourne such as the Open Tennis and the Melbourne Cup racing carnival, as well as invitations to dinners or lunches with relevant speakers such as leading Australian sportsmen and other personalities. The club recognizes the demographic of its membership base and also offers travel such as cruises or guided trips around Europe, as well as unique offerings such as a guided tour of some of the leading private gardens in the state. Not surprisingly, membership has been growing by nearly 20 percent a year as word of mouth spreads about the extensive benefits of membership. Nearly all new members come from referrals from existing members, fantastic testimony to RACV's ability to help customers get things done that they didn't think they could. American Express treats its customers as valued members, and not just in name. For example, the company makes exclusive tickets available to different membership levels, including the best seats in town for sold-out concerts and sports events. For its highest-level members, American Express also offers travel benefits supported by experts who can help plan a reception in Marrakesh or an intimate party in Manhattan.

Jim Bush, who leads AmEx's impressive global customer service operations, was recently asked whether the company's agents work from scripts when helping customers. His response:

> No scripts. Information is presented to the care professional—we call them 'customer care professionals' because that's what they are. They're not service professionals; they take care of customers. We present the profile of who that customer is and other information relevant to that particular interaction. That allows the care professional to be conversant and pull out their personality and match it to the personal needs of the customer.[4]

Why "You Help Me Be Better and Do More" Is So Important

Creating a true partnership by serving a customer's broader needs is the ultimate differentiator for any organization. As with "You Surprise Me," it often is completely unexpected by customers, and therefore even more appreciated. Customers who see a company taking steps to keep money in their pockets, save them time, and make their lives better are much more likely to stick with the company and tell others about their positive experiences. Opportunities to expand business with the customer must be carefully chosen, always with the customer's best interest and perceptions in mind. Companies need to build a strong enough relationship that they have permission to suggest new services—another reason why this driver sits at the top of the Me2B pyramid. Many transaction-based industries risk the perception that education can come across as aggressive up-selling, but that risk can be managed.

Serving customers holistically will become even more important as intermediation between customers and providers increases. As the Internet creates more brokering-type services that enable comparison shopping, organizations are going to need to find more ways to create loyalty. They will need to look for ways to partner with the customer and may have to think more creatively to do so, as shown in Table 8.3.

Table 8.3   The Benefits of "You Help Me Be Better"

Customer Need Met	Potential to Increase Revenue	Potential to Reduce Cost
You support me beyond the product.	Increased lifetime value of customers Increased repurchase and share of wallet	Limited acquisition and exit costs
You coach me to use things better.	Increased brand and product loyalty and re-purchase	Reduced inbound support needs Fewer complaints
You help me use less of your stuff.	Increased re-purchase and share of wallet	Lower advertising and marketing costs
You help me look forward.	Increased re-purchase and share of wallet Improved word-of-mouth marketing	Reduced direct marketing
You help me get things that I didn't think I could.	Increased lifetime value of customers Improved word-of-mouth marketing	Fewer returns and lower levels of refunds and complaints about purchases

Meet the Challenge: You Help Me Be Better and Do More

This pinnacle Me2B customer need is hard to satisfy, which enhances its payoff when done well. Four steps will help you meet the challenge of helping customers be better and do more.

Understand Fundamental Customer Needs

To serve customers well beyond the initial sale, organizations need to understand customer needs in depth, putting themselves firmly in the customers' shoes and understanding what customers will value during various life events. Getting there often requires a redesign of internal sales and service processes, and most organizations have huge inertia that inhibits change. Meanwhile, customers may resent intrusions into certain areas so each add-on has to be carefully considered.

Remember That Timing Is Everything

Getting the timing right for a valued-added service, offer, or educational opportunity is critical. In face-to-face sales channels, the organization's staff need to listen carefully for timing signals and clues to the customer's situation and frame of mind. Blanket rules such as "always offer X" fail to serve the wide variety of customer experiences and needs.

We recently observed a situation where every customer service agent was forced to ask for a new sale at the end of the call. Even though they met with minuscule success (8 percent), some executives attempted to argue that it was still worth $500,000 in profits—when in fact it represented a 92 percent failure rate, with all the attendant customer pushback and upset.

Rethink from the Outside In

Organizations that do not rethink their products with a longer-term perspective—and with that, weigh some complex financial trade-offs—are planning with limited information. Using the credit card example, a relationship with a high-debt customer may be very profitable; a solution that serves the customer more responsibly may be less profitable in the short term but deliver more in two to three years hence when the customer has paid off a debt rather than spiraling into bankruptcy.

The financial return from long-term thinking that serves the customer relationship more broadly comes from a variety of sources:

- Reduced support costs and fewer complaints
- Enhanced customer loyalty driving repurchase decisions
- Recommendations and positive word of mouth
- Lower customer churn, with less marketing and other acquisition costs

These financial benefits are often not easy to quantify, and few organizations will support extended customer service on the basis of its being the right thing to do. Companies must have an accurate model of customer lifetime value (CLV) since they may be trading off short-term margins for a slightly lower margin stream over a

longer period. To help quantify the benefits of some of these investments, organizations need to understand and be able to quantify the
following:

- The cost of churn and lost customers, especially among the best customers
- The amount of additional potential self-service use
- The cost of complaints or contacts associated with being on the wrong product
- The length of relationships last today, and how long they could last

Seek More Perfect Knowledge

Even though "You Help Me Be Better and Do More" sits at the top of
the pyramid, it relies heavily on the foundation customer driver, "You
Know Me, You Remember Me." In many instances, companies lack
the business intelligence to understand the customer's broader needs.
For example, if a telco wants to shift customers to a lower-usage
plan when they've shown a pattern of not using their minutes or
data allotment (as we've portrayed earlier and heartily endorse), it
would need billing systems that could monitor usage over a rolling
twelve-month period, compare recent usage levels and trends, and
also account for other seasonal variations. This requires very sophisticated software—certainly available, but not yet in place in many
companies today, and not likely to be in place until the Big Data
analytics are implemented effectively. To meet this last need, organizations need to know how the customer behaves and be able to
process that information against current and potential products and
services. That is possible, but it does require complex systems and
analytics and should therefore emerge as a more common behavior.

CHAPTER NINE

WHAT DRIVES ME2B LEADERS

In the preceding chapters, we lay out the blueprint for building extraordinary customer experiences that power performance in the Me2B marketplace. Now we'd like to explore why some companies know that their customer rules, and others haven't figured it out yet. By examining the characteristics and underlying impetus of organizations that truly serve the customer, we hope to prepare boards and senior management teams to make the often sweeping strategic changes required to serve customers and compete in today's frenetic marketplace. For start-ups and those contemplating new businesses, these observations may also help clarify strategy.

Organizations that meet the seven needs we describe provide an exceptional experience for their customers and exceptional returns for shareholders over a long period, as well as dynamic and exciting places for staff to work. For example, if we plot the stock performance for four of the Me2B Leaders we profile, it's clear that they have beaten the S&P 500 by large margins (see Figure 9.1). You might say, "Sure, but Apple and Amazon have awesome products, that's why!" We'd agree with you, but think about it: These companies, and others we've mentioned, are also doing well because people enjoy and appreciate the experience of doing business with them. Many companies offer great products; Me2B Leaders offer great products *and* great relationships along with them.

When looking at organizations that are successfully serving most or all of these customer needs, we see four distinct though not mutually exclusive groups:

- *The Naturals*. Customer focus is in these companies' gene pool. They were created with customer-centricity as a core principle, and it infuses everything they do. It comes naturally to them.
- *The Challengers*. For these companies, customer focus has become a key differentiating strategy to beat the competition.
- *The Rebounders*. These companies neared the point of failure, were shocked into action, and survived. That action included a dramatic, customer-focused change in strategy.
- *The Defending Dominators*. These companies already dominate their markets without the benefit of a strong customer-experience focus. They are now shifting strategy to defend their patch—and why and how are important insights.

The Naturals

Me2B Leaders in this first group were born that way. Their founders put the customer's experience at the heart of all key decisions from the very beginning; it is both the culture and the operating manual for the entire organization. These companies' leaders and their employees believe deeply and passionately that investing in the customer will have bankable returns, and they are happy to sacrifice both short- and medium-term revenue for a long-term goal. Funnily enough, they wind up with both superior current returns and sustainable revenues over the long haul.

The Naturals don't ebb and flow in terms of their commitment to the customer. That isn't to say they are perfect. Apple is a Natural, serving customers its unique products and culture straight back to its

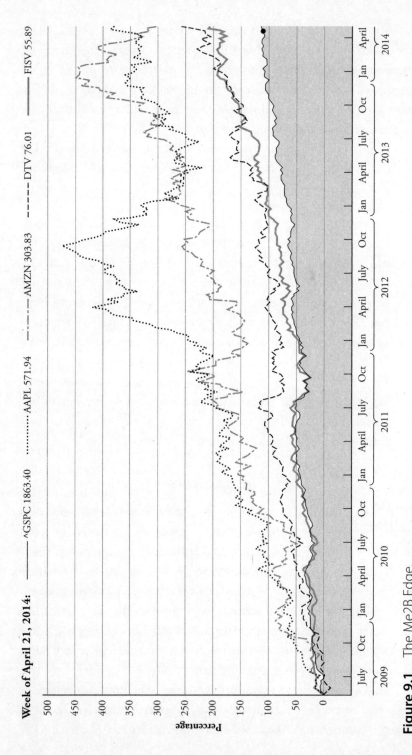

Week of April 21, 2014:

——— ^GSPC 1863.40 ⋯⋯⋯ AAPL 571.94 ——— AMZN 303.83 – – – DTV 76.01 ——— FISV 55.89

Figure 9.1 The Me2B Edge.

Source: Yahoo! Finance Compare feature, May 18, 2014.

modest start in Steve Jobs' garage in Palo Alto. However, Apple lost its way in the '90s—until Jobs returned. Even today the company sometimes disappoints customers by exploiting its monopoly or near-monopoly position, for example using its proprietary music format on its devices, a choice that is commonly seen as pro-company, not pro-customer. Overall, however, the Naturals are distinguished by their belief that customer focus and company growth are indelibly linked.

Amazon's Jeff Bezos' first letter to shareholders in early 1997 clearly reflects the customer-focused ethos of the Naturals (and note his use of "will continue to" as a two-year-old start-up):[1]

> Because of our emphasis on the long term, we may make decisions and weigh tradeoffs differently than some companies. Accordingly, we want to share with you our fundamental management and decision-making approach so that you, our shareholders, may confirm that it is consistent with your investment philosophy:
> - We will continue to focus relentlessly on our customers.
> - We will continue to make investment decisions in light of long-term market leadership considerations rather than short-term profitability considerations or short-term Wall Street reactions.

At an executive staff meeting, Bezos once made a point to have a prominently empty chair, a reminder to his team to "make sure that we keep the customer uppermost in all of our decisions, since our customer can't attend our decision-making meetings."[2] The approach had its naysayers among outside pundits and analysts. At the peak of the dot-com boom in 1998 and early 1999, many experts claimed that Internet-based companies were different and could challenge standard financial analysis that focused merely on profitability.[3] However, seventeen years later, it's clear that Amazon's customer investments have paid off and the organization delivers against conventional measures of profitability and return on assets.

Because they were built on customer-centric principles from the ground up, the Naturals have found every opportunity to bring the customer point of view into their business. Companies like

Costco, Kohler, Nordstrom, Vente-Privee, and Yamato Transport have a whole series of reports and feedback mechanisms to connect their executives with customer issues, compliments, criticism, suggestions, and insights; they also hold regular meetings at every level of the business to discuss customer issues. For example, at Costco, the department vice presidents (such as for food service) respond daily by phone to customers who give negative feedback in the stores, often asking questions that might reveal better ways to serve Costco members. The Naturals also have embedded processes that serve the seven Me2B customer needs and empower staff to deliver them.

Led by Visionaries

It's no accident that many of the Naturals have CEOs who are now household names, some in their home country and some internationally: Jeff Bezos of Amazon; Steve Jobs of Apple; Richard Branson of Virgin; Tony Hsieh of Zappos; Jacques-Antoine Granjon of Vente-Privee; Yasuomi Ogura of Yamato Transport. The companies in this category that aren't led by their visionary founder generally have leaders who are still directly connected to the original founder's principles.

USAA is one Me2B Natural without such a single prominent figure. But it's unique in that it was effectively a mutual organization, focused originally on the welfare of fellow military officers. That focus is what created its customer culture. Even today USAA's tag line, "We know what it's like to serve" (in the military), resonates with current and former U.S. military officers and senior enlisted staff and their families.

The Naturals worry less about competition and more about extending their share of each customer's business with great products and service. In Amazon's case, the company has expanded its business with customers by moving into new product categories, or even creating new markets such as the Kindle, cloud services, and Fire TV. Apple is famous for inventing new devices that we never knew we needed—such as the iPod and the iPad, which are now must-have items. None of these inventions came from a reaction to the competition; they emerged from a combination of ingenuity with deep customer knowledge.

Culture Communicated in Value Statements

These companies don't just have energetic, forward-thinking leadership. They also have enshrined their values into clear statements that resonate across the entire organization. They even extend across the larger ecosystem of suppliers, distributors, and other business partners—a key learning for companies that aspire to customer experience excellence. These value statements permeate everything—hiring, training, executive-level decision making, and so on—enabling staff to do the right things by the customer.

Ceramics products producer Kohler developed four "Competencies" more than fifty years ago, and they are still a core part of how it operates: Build Trust; Set High Standards of Performance; Drive Continuous Improvement; and Focus on the End Customer. When we visited Vente-Privee's head office and main customer support center outside of Paris, we were struck by a poster we saw soon after entering, which displayed the company's eight values in bold red font:

> *Responsabilité* (Responsibility)
> *Diversité* (Diversity)
> *Mixité* (Multiculturalism)
> *Confiance* (Trust)
> *Transparence* (Transparency)
> *Creativité* (Creativity)
> *Innovation* (Innovation)
> *Respect* (Respect)

When we asked CEO Jacques-Antoine Granjon what these values mean to him and how they were developed, he didn't stop until forty minutes later! Clearly these values are part of Vente-Privee's secret sauce.

Blizzard Entertainment, one of the huge success stories in multiplayer online games, convened its senior management to chronicle why the company had grown so successfully and so fast, and to convey to its employees what they could do to sustain that growth and success. Today the company proudly displays its Mission Statement and its Eight Core Values everywhere—surrounding the statue of one of its famous characters outside its headquarters building, on the walls of its training center, and on its website—something that precious few companies elect to do.

"*Blizzard Entertainment's eight core values represent the principles and beliefs that have guided our company throughout the years. These values are reflected in employees' decisions and actions every day.*"

Blizzard's core values: "gameplay first; commit to quality; play nice, play fair; embrace your inner geek; every voice matters; think globally; lead responsibly; and learn & grow."

Blizzard uses these values in its hiring process and induction and training, as well as in everyday decision making to break ties and ensure that the customer comes first. By sharing these values publicly, Blizzard explicitly lets its avid gamer population know how their "epic entertainment experience" is to be delivered and experienced.

Yamato Transport wears its value statement on its sleeve—that is, on all its trucks and across its warehouses: a yellow oval with a black mother cat carrying her kitten in her mouth. In Yamato's words:

> The black cat logo, in 1976 developed by the founder Mr. Yasuomi Ogura himself, has become the national symbol for transport in Japan and will be all over the world. In the eighties Yamato Transport established networks in South-East Asia, the U.S.A. and Europe, which were further greatly expanded.
>
> Today you will find the black cat at your service right on the spot where you need it. After 90 years it still stands for care and reliability.[4]

The Challengers

The second group of Me2B Leaders features companies that are challenging the incumbent players in their markets, consciously deciding that they want to focus on improving their customers' experience in order to dislodge the incumbents. The telecommunication firm iiNet, a challenger to the large established players in Australia, is a classic example. (Note it fits into the "Naturals" category as well.) The Challengers are similar to what are frequently called *disruptors*, but their innovations are specifically focused on improving customer experience and satisfaction.

The Challengers see that offering the customer a differentiated level of service is a competitive advantage, enabling them to attract customers from incumbents and then hold on to them. Richard Branson adopted this as a business development strategy, launching not one but a series of new companies in markets (music, airlines, train travel, and more) where he believed customers were being poorly served.

Any industry dominated by companies where the norm is average or even poor customer experiences offers ample opportunity for customer-focused Challengers to emerge and thrive. Even in industries with high barriers to entry, such as airlines, savvy Challengers such as JetBlue and, in an earlier era, People Express (1981–1987) have broken through. The Internet has enabled other businesses to enter some markets with a lower-cost entry point, leading to a wealth of Challengers. For example, AppliancesOnline in the United Kingdom and Australia is competing with conventional big-box white goods stores by offering superior customer service (and price) without the expense or hassle of expensive brick-and-mortar stores. It fills customer-need gaps in areas such as guaranteed delivery ("You Give Me Choices"), and quality installation ("You Help Me Do More"). Other notable examples include Amazon (also a Natural), Make-MyTrip (an India-based travel company), Zillow (a real-estate listing service), and Egencia (a business travel service, part of Expedia, itself a Challenger).

That said, the true Challengers from our Me2B point of view aren't *primarily* trying to compete on price—they're distinguishing themselves with a higher-level customer offering. U.K.-based financial services leader first direct, for example, did not offer the cheapest option for its products when it entered the market. However, it did provide a wider range of contact channels and differentiated service.

On its website, first direct introduces a digest of its many awards with, "We love making our customers happy, but every now and then it's nice to get an industry pat on the back too."[5] These awards include Moneywise Winner: Best Current Account for Call Centre Services 2013; Winner: Best Current Account for Online Service 2013; Most Trusted Credit Card Provider 2013; Most Trusted Mortgage Provider 2013; and the MoneySupermarket "Supers" Award. The "Supers" award goes to financial services companies that have provided the very best in product and service. Winners are chosen by customers of the site as well as independent judges.

Finally, an important note: What makes these companies successful as Challengers is that they actually *deliver* a differentiated experience rather than simply using it as a marketing pitch to grab attention in industries in which customer treatment is poor. For example, in Australia after telecommunications deregulation, a major player promoted itself as having better service than the old monopoly. It really was rated slightly better, but the improvement was insignificant; for customers, not much changed. In contrast, the Challenger iiNet doesn't look to traditional telecom firms or ISPs for competitive analysis where customer service is concerned. Instead it tries to match the higher service ratings and NPS of the best performers across *all* industries, therefore trying to exceed the performers in its own industry by a substantial margin. That is true Challenger behavior.

Here are some special characteristics of the Challengers, focusing on their agility and how they build the case for change.

Agile Early Adopters

Challengers are usually known to be young upstarts. They have entered the market because they see an opportunity and have found some new or differentiated way to serve customers in a given niche or industry. Because they start smaller, these companies can be more agile and adaptive, and they tend to be early adopters of new channels and innovations.

Like the Naturals, these companies are usually entrepreneur or founder led. In fact, Naturals are really just Challengers who have succeeded to the point that they are now large market leaders. Amazon began life challenging brick-and-mortar booksellers and is now *the* dominant player in that business as well as many other categories of online retailer.

A few interesting exceptions can be found in large companies that have either bought or incubated a Challenger brand without absorbing it into their own operations. In Australia, for example, the market leader Commonwealth Bank acquired the challenger brand Bankwest but largely left it alone to continue running itself and delivering the unique customer experience that had been so well received in the marketplace. The logic is clear: If a brand can create a competitive challenge, it's better to own it than be run over by it, even if it ultimately cannibalizes the parent brand. It's still a net gain if it is just as successful at taking market share away from competitors. In the United States, the science and technology company Danaher has done this with great success, acquiring more than a hundred specialty manufacturers and often retaining their original brands, such as Fluke.

Making a Clear Business Case for Change

Challengers are useful in convincing skeptics of the value in a customer-centric strategy. These companies are succeeding in winning market share and growing at the expense of incumbents. While Challengers might absorb losses in their early days, companies like Amazon and T-Mobile demonstrate that this strategy can lead to solid profitability. Challengers can cherry-pick profitable customers and therefore leave incumbent companies with underperforming (less profitable) customers. Any stakeholder of incumbent players who doubts the danger of underserving customers should take note.

The Rebounders

The Rebounders have come close to closing down or had a severe slide in market share or customer satisfaction, or have otherwise been shocked into action—what we like to call a near-death experience.

They've reversed the slide into oblivion by increasing or resuming their focus on customer experience.

Tom King's turnaround of British Airways (BA) in the 1990s is one of the most famous examples. BA had lost market share and brand value. Customers started returning when King reoriented the company around quality delivery and restored pride in the brand. In the United States, Home Depot, JetBlue (also a Challenger), and Starbucks are among the best-known examples. Other former leaders worldwide, such as Hewlett-Packard and Vodafone/Hutchison, are still struggling to regain their former customer-focused glory.

There are many reasons why companies reach the brink. Sometimes a critical systems failure is to blame, as was the case with Vodafone/Hutchison in Australia. The merged group underestimated the scale of network required across both customer bases with the rapid growth of data traffic. The poor network coverage and reputation damage that Vodafone suffered led to the loss of nearly 2 million customers in two years. From this near death the group is trying to rebuild itself with renewed customer focus and passion, but at the time of writing its restoration remains a work in progress.

Often long-term neglect or a change in the market creates the threat. For almost ten years in Australia the Coles supermarket group was outperformed by its main competitor. It lost market share, neglected stores, and watched as margins fell. But under new management, the company was completely refreshed. New store formats, new logistics and systems, and a three-year campaign offering customers great bargains on house brand staple products such as milk and bread changed performance. For ten quarters, the stores have achieved above sector growth and have gone from market follower to market leader.

Earlier we mentioned that Australia Post had created the option to connect online video greetings to mailed packages—this is just one smart innovation launched in reaction to the death of its core business, mail and letters. The mail service has had to rethink its customer proposition around parcel delivery, billing services, and other logistics capabilities. Branches, which have to operate under Australian law, have been totally revamped with customer-friendly features such as twenty-four-hour box drops for parcel pickup and other clever and customer-satisfying services. Left alone, these expensive assets would have become liabilities.

New Leadership, Failed Mission

New leadership that fails to respect the core values that made a company successful has threatened the future of many businesses, requiring them to restore old policies, rebuild culture, and re-earn their customers' trust in order to survive.

This was exactly the story of the home improvement store Home Depot. Over the years, led by visionary founders Bernard Marcus and Arthur Blank, Home Depot earned a very loyal customer base by flooding stores with its orange-coated staff to help shoppers select the best DIY tools, products, appliances, or electrical fixtures. These reps really knew their stuff, and customers trusted them. When Marcus and Blank retired in 2000, they turned to an external executive to take the reins. Over the next several years the company's vaunted reputation for outstanding customer experience took a nosedive as the new CEO shifted focus from customer experience to efficiency, cost-cutting, and workforce reduction. Employee and customer morale withered. In 2007 Frank Blake was brought in to engineer a turnaround, and he has since focused on reinvigorating the brand's customer service culture and improving the in-store experience. The satisfaction scores shown in Figure 9.2 are dramatic, illustrating Home Depot's drop and later resurgence as a Rebounder.[6]

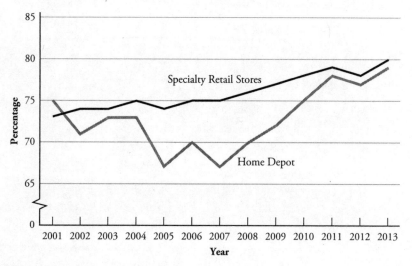

Figure 9.2   Home Depot's Rebound Success.

Starbucks is another high-profile rebounder. After dominating the coffee shop market for years, rapid growth (including many third-party franchise operations) led to inconsistent service, alienating many of its loyal customers. When CEO Howard Schultz took back the reins he focused on reclaiming what had made the company so successful. In his 2011 book *Onward: How Starbucks Fought for Its Life Without Losing Its Soul*, Schultz relates how the company forged "The Transformation Agenda" to re-instill earlier core values, such as "inspiring and nurturing the human spirit," that had propelled the company to its amazing growth and iconic status.[7] He focused the company on "Seven Big Moves," among which were engaging and inspiring employees (which Starbucks calls "partners" to recognize their key value) and igniting "emotional attachment" with customers.

Shortly thereafter, Starbucks created a new customer service mission statement and stitched it inside each barista's ubiquitous green apron. "We create inspired moments in each customer's day," the aprons read, with four simple yet clear and powerful action verbs: *Anticipate, Connect, Personalize, Own.* These "crew minders" have helped restore Starbucks' reputation by reengaging what Schultz has always recognized as its most critical value driver: the baristas, not the coffee.

A Testimony to Transformative Leadership

The positive lesson exemplified by Rebounders is that a negative position can become a powerful motivator for change, particularly with the right leadership to transform indifference into meaningful action for customers. A rebound often requires a leadership transition. It's very hard for leaders who have taken a company to the brink to recognize the error of their ways. More commonly, they are unseated by an unhappy board of directors and replaced by someone with clearer customer direction.

This group also demonstrate the importance of re-invigorating the values, often customer-focused, that made a given company successful in the first place. Often these organizations have the institutional knowledge to create great customer experiences, but it needs to be rekindled and supported. Meg Whitman, the CEO of Hewlett-Packard (HP), has been leading her organization to "rediscover the HP Way" as it was articulated in the largely forgotten one-page, five-point paper that co-founders Bill Hewlett and David Packard wrote in the 1970s to help shape the company's values as it was growing overseas. At the time Packard was famously quoted as saying, "Somehow, we got into a discussion of the responsibility of management. [Then board member Bob] Holden made the point that management's responsibility is to the shareholders—that's the end of it. And I objected. I said, 'I think you're absolutely wrong. Management has a responsibility to its employees, it has a responsibility to its customers, it has a responsibility to the community at large.' And they almost laughed me out of the room."[8]

For organizations that can't look into their history for a guide to improving customer experience, we encourage thinking back to the "good old days," an excellent source of ideas and models for dealing with today's business challenges, as we've seen throughout this book. Bill calls this searching for "wooly mammoths and [the edible heart of] the artichoke," or looking deeply into a company's own history for solutions to today's business challenges.

The Defending Dominators

In many industries, dominant brands are facing competition from new upstarts—the very kinds of companies detailed in our Challengers group. Their best defensive tactic is to reorient strategy toward the customer. This means that they have to get over this new bar that the Challengers have set for customer experiences. Besides meeting a very specific competitive challenge, it provides a second boost by combating complacency with a strategic point of focus. Hence we have the fourth and final group, the Defending Dominators.

Beyond Defense

Upgrading the customer experience isn't just a defensive tactic. Some successful, unchallenged companies have improved customer experiences as a growth measure to increase the share of wallet from customers and reduce waste in the business. From the point of view of a new CEO, it seems to be a sensible strategy to align the troops and continue down the "domination" path. What are employees more likely to rally around, a mandate to build better customer relationships or one to improve efficiency in the workplace? We put our money on customer relationships! Trying to persuade an already dominant and very profitable company to cut costs is hard. Employees see the profit and revenue levels and may question these goals. However, a Lean or effort-reduction program that emphasizes the goals for customers is an easier sell and a more effective rallying cry.

Driven by both causes—the pressure of Challengers and a canny leadership strategy—nearly all Defending Dominators have benefited from having a new CEO at the helm. Just as with the Rebounders, we have rarely noted an incumbent CEO more than a year into the job suddenly see the light and switch course. It is nearly always a point of strategic difference of a new CEO and a new team, often in stark contrast to the old way.

At Telstra, the CEO prior to David Thodey had spent big on technology, yet customer numbers kept declining and the reputation for service was poor throughout Australia. The complaints team numbered almost five hundred people. Thodey and his team made improved customer outcomes a central focus. Goals included slashing the number of complaints in half and reducing call volumes. Three years later these initiatives began to show real results: Telstra gained market share in key sectors like mobile and data, customer interaction volumes declined, and the share price rallied consistently as a result and hit historic highs.

Rallying around the customer even has been seen to motivate change in government institutions, where there's no risk of losing anybody to competition. The U.K. Revenue Office has focused on reducing waste and customer effort, and on "treating customers fairly," to great effect. The benefits include much lower costs to support U.K. "customers" (note that they are no longer called "citizens" or "residents"), less pressure from Members of Parliament in response to customer complaints, and higher levels of tax receipts.

In government there has also been a trend to create improved service offerings. In many North American cities, including Toronto and New York, the "3-1-1 Initiative" (started where Bill grew up, in Baltimore, Maryland) created a single access point for a range of government services. This has been mimicked by initiatives like Smart Service Queensland and Services New South Wales, which in turn have created unified government access points. Customers benefit, and so does the government, thanks to reduced complexity and maximized economies of scale. In some instances complex and expensive telephone number maintenance and IVR systems have been shut down, a solid proof point that better service models save money.

Customer Service and Efficiency Gains, Not Either/Or

What many of the Defending Dominators demonstrate is that improving customer experience and efficiency gains can be achieved in parallel with each other; one doesn't need to happen at the expense of the other. Earlier we've mentioned the Australian market leader Commonwealth Bank, led by New Zealander Ralph Norris. Norris and his team completely refreshed the branch network with a modern layout fronted by concierges who help resolve queries and direct traffic. The bank also ran a major education campaign to teach front office staff how to assess customer needs and sell more to them. In parallel, Norris launched a range of initiatives aimed at reducing complexity with simplified loan applications processes and reduced administration. Other customer investments included an almost-instant loan approval process and best-in-class self-service on web and mobile phones. These positive investments reduced the bank's cost-to-income ratio to its lowest level ever and raised the products-per-customer ratio more than 30 percent. The bank now has the highest profit level of any Australian bank and pays substantial dividends that have led to increased capitalization, demonstrating the potential for customers, staff, and shareholders to win with a customer-focused strategy.

At British Telecom a Lean focus has also produced remarkable outcomes. BT slashed customer interactions by making processes easier and more reliable, reducing costs and increasing loyalty. In an era in which new devices and services tempt customers to switch, BT's strategy has been to remove the problems that might test customers' loyalty.

Can Other Companies Change?

It is possible for companies to become more customer-centric if they don't share one of these four characteristics? Sure, it's possible, but it's rare. In government and government-owned businesses, maintaining or improving reputation can be a major driver of customer focus. However, often it takes poor publicity or a crisis to motivate a government body to rebound in response to the reputational risk. You might consider them "reputational rebounders."

We have seen a number of companies outside these four groups launch the rhetoric of increased customer focus, only to fail to translate it into real benefits for customers. Before too long they stumble and fail.

The companies in each of these groups have clear strategic purpose. The Naturals don't have to think about it, they just do it; it is their central organizing principle. For the Challengers, they've decided it's their best, maybe only, course for growth and acquisition. For Rebounders, renewed customer focus represents the strategic response to past issues or competition, a strategic correction. And the Defending Dominators recognize it as the best strategy to maintain their hold on their patch.

What this suggests is that the strategic rationale for an organization's customer experience strategy needs to be quite clear. Companies that declare themselves customer-focused without making a strong strategic case rarely stick to the path. These companies find another, perhaps more quantifiable or immediate strategy that overtakes customer focus, such as cost cutting or growth through acquisition.

In Chapter Ten, we describe the four foundations companies should endeavor to put in place to execute successful Me2B strategies and meet the seven customer needs.

CHAPTER TEN

THE FOUNDATIONS OF ME2B SUCCESS

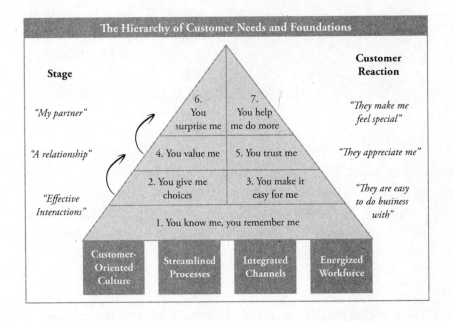

The Hierarchy of Customer Needs and Foundations

Stage

"My partner"

"A relationship"

"Effective Interactions"

Customer Reaction

6. You surprise me
7. You help me do more

"They make me feel special"

4. You value me
5. You trust me

"They appreciate me"

2. You give me choices
3. You make it easy for me

"They are easy to do business with"

1. You know me, you remember me

Customer-Oriented Culture

Streamlined Processes

Integrated Channels

Energized Workforce

If you aspire to meet the seven critical customer needs that companies must fulfill to thrive in the Me2B era, it is fairly straightforward to select which of the four kinds of successful companies yours most resembles. What do you need to do next? This chapter explores what a company needs to build to make the Me2B experience work.

Foundation One: A Customer-Oriented Culture

Companies can't become Me2B Leaders without a strong employee culture that embraces the belief that customer relationships are central to success. It's particularly critical for the more sophisticated Me2B needs ("You Trust Me," "You Value Me," "You Surprise Me," and "You Help Me Be Better and Do More"). Delivering these experiences relies on having a culture that enables frontline staff to

The Four Foundations of Me2B Customer Experience Excellence

1. Customer-oriented culture ...
   rather than measures and strategies that work against the customer.
2. Streamlined processes ...
   rather than exception-oriented thinking and inward-looking design.
3. Integrated channels ...
   rather than discrete profit centers.
4. Energized workforce ...
   rather than teams hired for capabilities and not attitude.

go off script and to recognize when they need to deliver extra without being told. For example, they need to know it is OK to waive a charge or offer something unusual to thrill a customer, all without seeking permission. That kind of culture only emerges when leadership consciously nurtures it through role modeling, messaging, policy, measurement, and constant reward and recognition. Good examples include these three Me2B Leaders that have become famous for being customer-centric:

- Amazon, with the "The Just Do It Award," its sixteen-year-old tradition of celebrating employees who take initiative.
- Zappos, which celebrates "Customer Heroes," where "executives pick a 'hero' each month and award them with a parade, covered parking spot for a month, a $150 Zappos gift card, and a cape."[1]
- Yamato Transport, which in its "Strategic Board of Management" meeting held every Friday, asks "*Is it convenient for the customer?*" and "*Is there only one solution?*" These questions lead to the study of new products and services, and emphasize that not only executives but every employee of each business is responsible for achieving that goal.[2]

Organizations often make building a customer-oriented culture a strategic goal, but then many of them fall far short.

Effective Me2B Leaders do much more than make bold declarations that their company will become "Earth's Most Customer Centric Company" (Amazon) or "Dedicated to creating the most epic entertainment experiences, ever" (Blizzard) or commit to "Service First, Profit After" (Yamato Transport). They don't just make these bold declarations, they follow up with specific actions that help change take root and grow.

For starters, the Me2B Leaders create measures to align the entire organization consistently around new customer-oriented objectives. This consistency is critical. It only takes one contradictory measure, or one major project that appears to lack a customer focus, to undermine a culture. One of the measures that Commonwealth Bank CEO Ralph Norris used to achieve total consistency was a simple common metric for his entire leadership team: A large portion of their bonuses hinged on the bank moving from #4 to #1 in the Morgan Banking customer satisfaction rankings. The goal was common to everyone in the leadership team, whether or not they controlled customer facing-products or processes. Financial incentives shouldn't be the only way leaders motivate change, but they do tend to move people to action.

Successful Me2B Leaders avoid success metrics that present customer experience averages. It sends a negative message if, for example, a company achieves certain service goals by averaging the poor and the good service periods; for example, contact centers might rejoice about hitting 80/20 (80 percent of calls answered in the first 20 seconds), but what if 5 percent of the callers have to wait ten minutes or longer before they can speak to an agent? This sends the message that some customers and some experiences don't matter. A true customer culture only develops when a company starts to show that each and every experience counts.

Walking the Talk

Executive leaders influence culture by the way they themselves behave. Constantly talking about customer issues and showing an active interest in customers has a ripple-down effect. Jeff Bezos demonstrated this trait in the early days of Amazon when he insisted on spending a day a month in the contact centers helping with e-mail. Richard Branson is notable for working with frontline staff in his Virgin airline businesses, and he's also always open to hearing customer issues directly from staff members and customers. The Ritz-Carlton hotel chain, renowned for its customer focus, is also known for founding CEO Horst Schulze attending all new property openings and greeting employees by name.

Walking the talk doesn't work as a stunt. To have a lasting impact, it needs to be practiced with clear meaning and intention over time. One large telco we know made a video about the day the leadership team visited the contact center. They even showed the video at a public conference to prove that the leadership team was serious. The company's leaders were interviewed and testified to how much they had learned. But this event, so rare as to be recorded for posterity, didn't achieve the cultural change that the leaders had hoped to produce because it was a one-off exercise.

Still other companies fall prey to what we call the "Under Nines Syndrome." In soccer the younger players (under age nine) tend to swarm the ball and chase it helter-skelter around the field. Leaders mirror this when they home in on one isolated issue and pursue it doggedly for a while, only to abandon it for the next agenda item. For example, we watched one company pursue revenue for one quarter, then focus full-force for the next six months on invoice timeliness and related correspondence, only to drop that abruptly in favor of credit and collection. This ball chasing was very distracting for the whole business and made managers reactive and confused. No one knew where to focus, and follow-through was understandably poor. The projects and initiatives achieved temporary results and then performance slipped back as the goalposts moved.

Praising Positive Customer Outcomes

Senior executives can make a big difference when they showcase examples of the behaviors that they would like to see throughout the organization. Sharing stories in which employees have given customers great experiences in monthly e-mail messages or other broadcasts to staff sends clear cultural signals. Having frequent awards and prizes for these behaviors is another important way to support the culture shift. The utility AGL congratulated staff for having achieved the lowest complaint rate in the industry; this gave the group the chance to acknowledge and enjoy a common achievement, but also showed that the leadership cared about it.

Yamato Transport has created a program called the "Compliments Bank" that collects customer compliments and presents them to the employees on badges that they proudly wear on the outside of their shirts or blouses, with stars designating higher recognition levels.

Anecdotes and stories resonate much more deeply with employees than hard-to-grasp gross-level metrics such as "net gains" or "revenues per employee." Such figures are useful for dissecting financial statements but offer poor material for storytelling, a far more effective way to gain currency for an idea.

Vente-Privee loves to collect and share stories about serving its customers above and beyond their expectations, reinforcing to its advisers their critical role in providing incredible customer experience. Vente-Privee's Director of Service Relations Laurent Tupin related one of his favorite such stories to Bill in an e-mail note:

> A member once contacted us as she had accidently returned the wrong item in a parcel. Indeed, she sent back her favorite Victoria Beckham jeans instead of the Replay ones she had ordered on VP. She insisted on it because it was a gift she received for her birthday. She seemed so sad and really wanted us to find a solution. Due to the numerous parcels we had in our warehouse, it was like looking for a needle in a haystack. We explained that we would do our best but we could not promise that we would be able to find it.
>
> Over the following days, we asked people in the warehouse to look for the item in the entire Replay stock: that is to say more than 3000 blue jeans of the exact same color! The logistics team searched piece by piece to try and find the member's jeans according to the

description we were given. After many long hours of searching, we managed to locate them. We sent them back to the member; she was so happy and could not stop praising us!

Elsewhere Tupin has stressed that employee empowerment is a requirement to deliver the level of customer service expected by Vente-Privee. "The relation [with the customer] is personalized and the adviser is autonomous in his drafting and his choice to [grant a] refund," he wrote in the French online magazine Strategies.fr. "Autonomy is the only means of motivating the advisers so that they are devoted to the customers."[3]

Prioritize Investments for the Customer

Where companies invest their time and money sends a clear cultural signal to staff. For example, the frontline staff know whether or not they have the infrastructure and tools to get the job done for the customer. When systems and process are antiquated and not up to the task, employees conclude that management's last concern is customers and any messaging to the contrary falls flat. Staff- and cost-cutting measures that seem to make it more difficult to deliver great experiences have the same effect if management can't connect them to an improved customer outcome. Even with apparently positive measures, such as a software-led transformation, it's important that customer benefits are clearly articulated.

Contrast these approaches with one taken by companies that save costs by investing in process improvements that clearly benefit the customer through speedier resolution and other performance improvement. This sends a very different message. The health insurance company Medibank Private made a point of directly connecting every new process and structural change to intended customer benefit and, as a result, the staff became enthusiastic advocates of new programs instead of resisting the changes. T-Mobile USA decided that key investments in its contact center agent desktop, social media program, web support, and related areas merited a multiyear capital plan program status, signaling their critical importance to the company's success.

ON THEIR FIFTEENTH WHITEBOARD, THEY STARTED TO SUSPECT THEIR CUSTOMER JOURNEY MAY HAVE BEEN EXCESSIVELY COMPLICATED.

Foundation Two: Streamlined Processes

Process design is critical for all seven customer needs but it is most important to the first five. Process design has been emphasized at many businesses since Hammer and Champy's 1993 landmark book *Reengineering the Corporation*. The Quality Circle, Lean, and Six Sigma movements also placed an emphasis on process design. However, sometimes these movements have been kidnaped to focus on efficiency and repeatability rather than customer-friendly process. Risk aversion has also led to process design that creates poor customer experiences.

Table 10.1 summarizes examples of the critical role that process design plays.

Table 10.1 Effective and Ineffective Process Design

Need	Good Process Design	Poor Process Design
You know me, you remember me.	Use of known or historic data streamlines processes and makes them less effort for customers and staff. This also makes them cheaper.	Customers have to repeat information on every transaction or interaction. Other data is asked for and not used.
You give me choices.	Call center staff explain and educate on other options. Automated channels also explain other options. Customers can start a process in one channel and complete it in another without repetition.	Each channel restricts the customer to its own process. Staffed channels are not integrated with new and automated mechanisms.
You make it easy for me.	The key knockout questions are always up front in every process. Customer time and staff time are both tracked and not wasted. Proactive contact is used to keep customers informed.	Application forms are designed around the organization's desire to capture data and not to build the most effective process for the customer. The processes put customers to work and customers have to chase completion of processes.
You value me.	Business rules and associated processes flex depending on the depth or length of relationship a customer has with the company.	Frontline staff constantly follow and quote nonsensical rules even to the most valued customers.
You trust me.	Customers are not asked for proof except in rare cases and even then the history of relationship may overcome the lack of specific proof.	Customers are constantly put to work to provide proof of their version of events, for example, by providing copies of bank statements and other documents.
You surprise me with stuff that I can't imagine.	Processes are designed so that staff can step outside the process for the right reason. There is always an override.	Quality-checking processes penalize staff for doing something different even if customers love it.
You help me be better and do more.	The processes are designed to recognize the customers' broader purpose and context and can support them in this situation.	Processes are designed and streamlined only around the company's perspective.

Design in the Customers' Shoes

When well executed, Six Sigma emphasizes process steps and how their repeatability is critical for customers—but it doesn't necessarily ensure a low-effort, high-quality experience. The best way to do this is to design in the customer's shoes, rethinking processes entirely from the point of view of the customer's experience. Direct feedback can play a role, but simply thinking in terms of meeting the seven Me2B customer needs is often all that's needed.

The Fluke division of Danaher, which produces test and measurement equipment for a wide range of industries, has had good success applying customer feedback. Fluke asked some of its business customers to tell them how to lay out the company's web support pages. That interaction excited these customers so much that they now participate in an ongoing program to provide feedback to make the company's web support easier to use.

Exception Handling and One-Legged Parrots

It's amazing how often process design can be driven by exception conditions. We see situations where 99 percent of customers are asked to go through extra hoops to protect an organization against a 1 percent downside scenario, instead of identifying the exception conditions quickly and either tailoring process to address those instances, or accepting and planning for related costs.

The best companies design for the norm, not the exception.

Amazon illustrated this when it introduced downloadable return labels. While some customers might return goods even if they were exactly as promised, Amazon accepted that risk in order to create incredible convenience for customers whose purchases really did fall short. The company found unexpected benefits from this program, too. When customers reported a defective product Amazon pulled it from being available to order online, sending an alert to the supplier, all the while trusting that the customer was right. It has worked well both for Amazon and for other customers (sparing them from getting a defective product)—easier and cheaper for all concerned.

The Three-Year-Old Child Tactic

Processes seem to grow over time; new details get added and it all becomes more and more cumbersome. In our experience, the best answer to this complexity is to adopt the mantra of a three-year-old child and ask "why?" ad nauseam. *Why is this step needed? Why do we have to it that way?* Often the reasons are lost in the mists of time. Some companies routinely cleanse information data repositories (when *FAQ* stopped meaning "frequently asked questions" and turned into "fumbling all questions"), while the Me2B Leaders dismantle databases and replace them with dynamic wikis and social media-based information sources.

We once observed a health insurer insisting that customers who wanted to suspend their policies while traveling had to send in proof of travel. We questioned why people needed to send in such documents. Customers who suspend their policies create no risk of fraud or confusion; they are waiving the right to claim in that period. Additionally, the itineraries that were faxed and e-mailed in were simply ignored anyway. Faced with the question of why, the insurer eliminated the requirement. It was easier for customers and cheaper for the fund.

Why? turns out to be a very powerful question. When companies get stuck in their own way of thinking and lapse into risk-control mode, questioning the cause of every step in every customer interaction is a possible cure.

Foundation Three: Integrated Channels

Integrating channels is absolutely essential for the first three customer needs. As noted, not being remembered in the move across channels is a key cause of customer frustration. Imagine the irritation, for example, of completing a complicated form online only to be told you have to start again in a retail outlet. Technology needs to create organizational memory across channels, or else it fails the "You Know Me, You Remember Me" test.

Channel integration is equally essential to "You Make It Easy for Me." It should be easy to move between channels, and companies should guide but ultimately let customers decide what channel works best for a given process. This is where "You Give Me Choices" comes in. It may well be easier to sign a form in a branch, but not if the customer has to take two buses or drive forty minutes in traffic to get there. Two minutes spent registering online will be far less effort. Customers need choices, and those who work in the channel, and the channels themselves, have to be aware of all the other channels to make that presentation possible.

Newer companies often have an advantage over older ones because they don't have the legacy of channel growth and development. Also, it's easier to present a unified and standardized way of dealing with customers if you just have a website and handle chat instead of six or seven channels that older institutions have added and developed separately as each wave of technology emerged. First was face-to-face, followed by call centers, e-mail, web forms, chat, social media, and so forth. Frequently these channels all have separate owners in the organization, and they are on their own separate technology platforms too. In many instances, organizations don't even know how difficult they would be to integrate—because no one has tried!

It may not be easy, but we've seen organizations embrace mechanisms that make it possible, including conscious integrated design processes, technology that links and integrates, strategic channel design and deployment, unified agent desktops, and the removal of organizational and measurement barriers to integration.

Across, Not Down, Channel Design

Business processes are generally designed within channels, that is, down the length of a silo rather than across the breadth of the organization and all channels. As each new channel emerges, new processes are designed for that channel. Often measurement and organizational systems have driven this. Process design has tended to tackle the problem of "*How do I get this work completed in this channel?*" or at best, "*How do we get this work done for the organization?*" However, a few organizations do stand back and ask, *"How do we design this process across all possible channels to expand customer ease and choice?"*

In our first book we highlighted the New York Department of Motor Vehicles (DMV) as a success story, and it still stands out from the pack today. As web services started to take off at the turn of the century, the registration and licensing authority in the state of New York wanted to take advantage of the new channel but realized that certain transactions could only be handled in the office, such as photos, signatures, and license plate collection. This meant that the DMV was stuck handling these kinds of transactions on site—but by integrating the two channels, it *could* shorten the length of customer visits. The DMV then launched "E-Z Visit," allowing New York state drivers to complete forms online and then finish the required transactions in the offices. Like other organizations, the DMV also encouraged customers to handle other transactions online—paying a registration renewal, updating details, and getting answers to simple inquiries—promoting those concepts heavily through a "Skip the Trip" campaign. But "E-Z Visit" was the true standout, a great example of thinking through processes across channels. This kind of interaction is being mirrored today by omni-channel retailers that allow customers to order online but collect or return in-store.

On the flip side, other organizations blindly or mindlessly apply the legacy thinking of the older channels to new channels. One of the worst cases we have seen was an e-ticketing system rolled out by an Australian state rail service. With some fanfare it told customers they could book tickets online (in about 2008, nearly ten years later than the airlines). However, customers discovered that to use the system, they had to book five days in advance of travel because the company still insisted on printing the tickets and putting them in the mail! This was astonishing in an age where airlines were moving to ticketless travel. The real irony was that each ticket carried a unique booking reference, which could have eliminated the need for a ticket entirely by allowing a guard on the train to merely validate that reference against a booking sheet. Now, six years later, customers still have to collect a paper ticket to travel. (And incredibly, they don't even have the option to print it at home!)

Technology Bridges Not Barriers

Technology has too often been the barrier to effective design for customers. Operating across multiple products often means staff (and by extension, customers) have to navigate a plethora of systems—if each product set has its own software, it's not surprising if they can't talk to each other. Technology can also create barriers between channels. If a branch, contact center, and back office can't see each other's transactions because they're each on separate systems, there is no way they can collaborate effectively.

In a recent positive trend, some organizations have developed web applications for customers and then started using them internally after realizing they were superior to the ones customer-facing staff had to deal with. A major credit card company, for example, developed a fast, easy-to-use self-service application for its customers and then used it to replace the interface in the call center as well. This uniformity between the call center and the customer app made the call center staff's job much easier. Later this same interface was also given to branch staff, adding a third common and unified channel.

We also see obstacles consciously built into system design. One utility let its Risk Department drive a new system configuration. The risk group was concerned that the support staff could both set up an account and maintain it in a way that could be financially beneficial to their friends or family, for example issuing a credit of some kind. As a result they separated system access so that customer-facing staff had no access to the parts of the system that manipulated financial data. That made it secure, but it also meant that simple requests like issuing a refund on a credit balance were tightly controlled, to the great inconvenience of customers. The IT security folks rigorously defended the closed systems, arguing that changes would "violate security standards," as though these were some sacred documents that could never be broken.

In recent years, integrated multi-channel or omni-channel systems have burst on the scene, finally making it possible for the technology to be the bridge across the customers' journey in the phone, e-mail, and other channels. Early adopters such as Virgin America Airlines and BestBuy discovered that not only did their customers like being recognized no matter which channel they chose but their agents had a much easier time handling issues. The logical conclusion of implementing software that brings products and channels together is to revisit the entire organization's sales and service structures. If the system works across channels and products, shouldn't the organization work that way too? Technology can play a key role in creating better structures and processes for customers, but it's not a total fix.

Strategic Channel Design

Some organizations think through the uses and benefits of each channel and make smart decisions about when to link them, applying truly strategic channel design. In insurance claims, for example, some organizations, such as USAA, can text or send e-mail messages to members with their claim number and other details for motor vehicle accidents. This recognizes that customers will probably have easier access to text messages than to e-mail when they take their car to a mechanic for repairs. Having the claim reference on the spot is convenient for the customer and repairer.

In the support arena, Apple has integrated channels by blending community exchanges with customer-made YouTube instructional videos and its own support information, providing a much richer and more relevant set of possible solutions.

As consultants, we look at five areas that add up to excellent design within a channel and across multiple channels: usability, knowledge sharing and search, portal depth, customer experience, and strategic emphasis. Getting all five elements of strategic channel design right isn't easy. After all, different channels require different processes. For example, identifying a customer in a face-to-face environment can involve anything from viewing an ID to a signature or, more recently, fingerprint and retina scans. Contact centers, on the other hand, have to rely on customers' identifying themselves through security questions or nascent technologies like biometrics (voice prints). Some of these differences are accidents of history or possibly constraints of yesteryear rather than today's reality. With new technologies in use today, some constraints of particular channels may have passed and the possibilities need to be revisited.

What we also find interesting is that mechanisms are not always picked up and redeployed between or among channels. In Internet banking, for example, extra security has been added to prevent identity theft in situations like resetting a password or entering a high-value transaction. This is often referred to as two-factor authentication. Some of these mechanisms include sending a customer an e-mail message that requires a response. But few contact centers have picked up on this kind of technology even though it may be just as applicable; they could ask customers for their password reset questions, just as in the online process. This again seems to have been caused by the way channels have developed separately.

Removal of Organizational and Measurement Barriers

It is typical that new and interesting channels evolve independently from the channels that already exist. In the 1990s as websites and e-commerce started to emerge, many companies set up new divisions and appointed e-channel executives to run them separately. There was a sense that the new world should not be polluted with the old. While almost all companies have recognized the error of keeping the web and phone channels separate, some are still posing the silly question, *Who owns social media, Marketing or Customer Service?* We think that the answer has to be "Customer Service, of course!" The CEO at T-Mobile USA got tired of the conflict and decided at one point that Customer Care would own the entire web development and the social media–community support area in order to focus squarely on designing and delivering messages that benefited the subscribers.

Many employees are still rewarded for behavior designed to keep channels organized and managed separately when there's no longer any benefit (and likely a disadvantage) to doing so. We worked with a company that wanted to have the branch network educate customers about what they could do online. To make this possible, we had to rebuild the branch metrics so they stopped encouraging staff to contain all business within the branch. If staff were to do things differently, actively promoting and supporting the Internet channel, they had to be rewarded for that behavior. We also had to review other existing targets and measures, such as branch sales volume, to be sure they didn't work at cross-purposes to the new objective.

Ultimately, a technology bridge was needed to influence branch and call center staff to advocate self-service online. With siloed systems, they couldn't get credit for leads they successfully moved to online channels, where the sales were closed. Integrated systems would allow the bank to track the customer through a multi-channel sales process and credit staff appropriately along the way.

Scale, scope, and specialization pose further challenges to breaking down organizational silos. The knowledge and disciplines for a contact center are different from those in a branch or in a back office. Some skills and disciplines are the same, but the devil is in the detail. Therefore channel integration has to be more than one person's responsibility, and some form of teaming approach is needed to get consistency across channels. Dedicated design or process improvement teams can help, but they also need expertise in how to exploit the capabilities of each channel and work within the limitations. Another mechanism is to have a group of system architects who knit things together. These glue-type groups might report through to an executive who has responsibility across the related channels.

Finally, progressive organizations including DIRECTV and T-Mobile have succeeded at knocking down organizational barriers by creating central "Customer Experience" groups that cover the customer experience end to end. Far from keeping channels separate, these groups bring together all the internal owners to ensure that messages and processes are consistently designed and applied across the board.

Foundation Four: Energized People

Frontline employees have a huge impact on delivering all seven of the Me2B customer needs, even the needs that technology and process appear to have baked in to the organization. For example, the organization may have made data available to staff to help them know and remember customers, but do staff even look at it? There may be a process to offer choices, but staff can always choose whether they want to bother. Maybe if it's close to the lunch break or they don't like the look of the customer, they take a pass. They could make the customer's life easier by performing their job with excellence and making smart judgment calls, but that doesn't mean they will! Energized employees invest time to solve problems and make customers feel valued. They listen carefully and evaluate correctly when to trust a customer. They go to the effort of creating surprising experiences and sometimes even invest their own time and energy in helping the customer do more. Table 10.2 outlines the ways employee attitude interacts with the Me2B needs.

Table 10.2 How Employee Engagement Impacts Customer Experience

Driver	Energized Behavior	Lackluster Behavior
You know me, you remember me.	Take time to read previous notes, check customer purchase history; ask questions of the customer and don't assume; greet guests with "welcome back!" if they've stayed with you before.	Start call with desultory "How can I help you?" but without recognizing customer history or importance; ask everyone "Is this your first time you've stayed with us?"
You give me choices.	Skip the script and offer more generous refunds or alternatives.	Stick to the script and offer precisely what some automaton thought is best for the customer.
You make it easy for me.	Finish the interaction (on the phone or in the retail store) with tips how to self-serve the next time; listen for key words like "you're hard to work with" and probe for ways to make customer's life easier.	Ask the customer a battery of questions that were already answered online or in the IVR in order to qualify someone for help.
You value me.	Listen for key words like "I'd like to get this from your company" or "this is broken" and note and circulate what customer is saying (we call this WOCAS).	Move briskly to the close and take the next call or next customer in line.
You trust me.	Take the customer's word for what has happened when appropriate.	Hide behind the company policy shield.
You surprise me with stuff that I can't imagine.	Listen to background noise on the call (such as a crying baby or barking dog) and then offer something meaningful (for the child or pooch). Provide a free drink in coach for loyal customers without their asking for anything.	Boringly read the script.
You help me be better and do more.	Look ahead for the customer, explaining what to expect next.	Get done and move on.

Me2B Leaders work to create the kind of workforce that customers like dealing with. The following sections explore five of their key approaches.

Recruit for Attitude

For any business that deals directly with the customer, the attitude of staff really matters. What some companies have realized is that it's much easier to teach skills than it is to change attitude. Earlier we shared the story of the Nordstrom employee who brought different shoes to a customer late at night before a big presentation in Dallas. You can't train for that level of enthusiasm; people need to bring it in with them when they sign on.

Identifying candidates with that kind of attitude—and weeding out the lazy or disaffected ones—requires rigor and savvy in the recruiting process. Today there are psychological tests and assessment processes that add some science to that process. Well-structured behavioral interviews also help. Assessment centers where recruits are put in real-world situations, such as handling a complaint, are also interesting. Most important is to focus on finding people with the right attitude as the goal of recruitment.

Of course, maintaining an energized workforce doesn't stop with recruitment. At Yamato Transport, the company's experienced drivers take newly hired staff under their wings for up to six months to ensure that the new folks have a customer-focused attitude. Employees with poor attitudes are bad for morale and need to be weeded out. Customer-friendly attitudes need to be measured and encouraged over and over again in the workplace. Unfortunately, most quality-checking systems aren't set up to do this. They can penalize someone for getting a process wrong, but they do not recognize the person who has done something inventive for a customer or handled a difficult situation with aplomb.

Give People Opportunity

Giving people opportunity requires two things. First, it requires empowering them, a notion that deserves more attention than it usually gets. Second, it requires giving the most capable people opportunities to help improve the broader processes that affect their work.

Empowerment gets talked about a great deal as the antidote to command-and-control regimes where the staff don't feel free to do the right things for customers. But as discussed in the section on culture, many elements of a business can inhibit employee freedom—measures and procedural controls being the most common examples. If frontline staff think productivity and speed are the metrics their performance will be measured against, they cannot feel empowered to resolve problems or offer unusual solutions. In other situations, limitations on their control are built into systems. This can be through authority limits, access to certain functions, or other types of system controls. The Complaints Department of a large telecom wasn't allowed to send customers e-mail messages even in cases in which customers simply wanted a note to confirm something that had been agreed.

If people are to be empowered, they need more than encouragement or permission from management. Existing barriers to getting things done need to be examined—and systems, measures, structures, and processes all play a part.

A great example of this occurred at egg.plc, a leader in online financial services and transactions. When egg was planning to launch into new markets from its U.K. base, it was trying to sort through a maze of metrics for its frontline agents, including handle time, quality scores, customer feedback, and more. Instead of copying its U.K. metrics stew, which added up to an oppressive quality control system, egg listened to its outside advisers and decided to try something quite radical. It dropped all metrics, reporting them to center management but not to each agent. Some thought this madness, but the results after the first month alone changed all disbelievers' minds. Once agents were freed from the metric yoke, not only did handle time drop but customer satisfaction rose!

Another way to give staff an opportunity is to involve them in improvement projects from inception. At Australian utility AGL, a team of frontline staff was brought together with a group of external consultants to design better ways of working. This group included two team members who were known for making frequent suggestions about what could be different and for e-mailing message after message to the customer service manager on what was broken and how to fix it. In some organizations these people might have been labeled as troublemakers or squeaky wheels. But the manager in this case recognized an energized employee who needed to be given an opportunity to help. The business improvement project gave the agents a chance to put suggestions into action, and the results were remarkable. The revised process designs produced cheers and rounds of applause when they were demonstrated to other team members. They raised rates of resolution by 20 percent and reduced the end-to-end effort for the customer by more than a minute on most contacts.

Don't Invest in Basket Cases; Do Invest in Potential

In any frontline crew, some staff members will outperform others. Managers and supervisors have to choose where to invest their limited time to improve overall team performance. The most successful companies quickly spot poor performers who have been hired incorrectly and waste no time on those who cannot succeed. That can seem unfair at times, but if some team members simply shouldn't be there or would take far too much effort to turn around, it doesn't make sense to invest in them. Management will get far more return from those who have the potential to excel but are sitting below or around average performance.

To spot those with potential, management needs to know what to look for. Attitude again becomes an important criterion. If team members are keen to succeed but lack certain skills and knowledge, they can be trained to perform at a higher level. These are the people with potential to deliver good experiences.

We recommend that companies profile their best performers and find more employees like them (we call this agent performance management or APM). Companies such as Apple and JP Morgan Chase have adopted this approach. Instead of coaching your worst performers and abandoning your best performers, pay close attention to your best performers. Learn what makes them so good, profile them to improve recruitment, and nurture them so that they don't leave. As for the weaker performers, let them leave of their own accord—or show them the door.

Use More Carrots

Positive reinforcement plays a critical role in behavior change. As seen in the story about egg, onerous quality systems in many contact centers lead to caution and conservative behavior. One center we visited invested far more time in arguing about quality scores and outcomes than in discussing things people had done well.

In contrast is the very successful Me2B leader FlightCentre. In an era when all customers are supposed to want to make their own bookings online, FlightCentre's storefront travel agencies have grown continuously in Australia, the United Kingdom, and the United States. Its measurement system focuses on positive rewards. A big part of staff remuneration is sales commission, but the rewards system goes well beyond that. Every year FlightCentre takes a planeload of top performers to an exotic destination for a massive concert and party—now that's one big carrot! It also offers branch managers a financial stake in their branch's success, like a franchise model but without the financial risks. These are just a few examples of the unusual mechanisms that encourage staff to offer customers really great experiences, such as check-in calls just before a passenger is due to fly and even queries after a trip to ensure all went to plan. These little touches and examples of "Surprise Me" bring people back into the FlightCentre stores. FlightCentre also makes sure to hire people who love to travel and bring their passion into their work. That means all employees are also keen travelers, so they really do want to help people do more.

Be Visible as Leaders

In some organizations, leaders constantly put themselves on the front line. Getting out and about lets everyone know that they're committed to the process and care how customers are treated. We've worked with the CEO of a major bank who visited a branch every single month and with executives who insist on delivering any news about changes facing the customer to staff. When Bill was running customer service at Amazon, he spent more than ten hours per month with the front line, double-jacking and listening to calls, observing e-mail interactions, or sitting in on agent roundtables (and sending many e-mail messages to other VPs after spotting ways to improve the customer experience). Putting forward that level of care and personalized attention set the tone for how customers were to be treated, and emphasized how important that was to the organization.

Integrating the Foundations of Me2B Excellence

While it is tempting to think about each foundation in isolation, we find that their integration delivers the best business results. Each foundation alone may offset weaknesses in the others, but it's hard to get benefits from one or two of the foundations if the rest are faulty. It's a bit like a rowing four. If two of the rowers are synchronized but the other two are out of time or ineffective, the boat hardly moves; it rocks from side to side or goes round in circles. But when the four rowers are in sync the boat stays balanced and powers along. These four foundations are just like those four rowers: The more they are aligned, the better the outcomes. With multifaceted design techniques and processes, integration *is* possible.

DON'T WAIT TO ACT

The great French Marshal Lyautey once asked his gardener to plant a tree. The gardener objected that the tree was slow-growing and would not reach maturity for over a hundred years. The marshal replied, "In that case, there is no time to lose. Plant it this afternoon."

—JOHN F. KENNEDY

This book offers an in-depth look at how today's leading organizations are satisfying seven fundamental customer needs and delivering exceptional experiences in the process, providing a tool for our readers to transform their own organizations.

So, how do you get started?

To kick off this journey, companies need to analyze and articulate their strengths and weaknesses across the four foundations of success. They then need a full-scale review of customer interactions and experience through the lens of all seven customer needs. Every interaction and contact that customers make should be assessed: "Was the customer known and identified where it mattered?" "How many choices were available?" "Was the interaction easy—and could we find a way to make it require even less effort?"

Managers and staff need to understand what is wrong and what success looks like. When communicating priorities, it helps to be as specific and fact-based as possible. Saying "our processes are broken" becomes more persuasive when presented as "25 percent of our processes don't get the resolution our customers have requested."

The risk of self-diagnosis is that everyone within the company may be too close to the way things work to see opportunities for change. There may also be some unwillingness to be as self-critical as necessary. Finally, leaders, managers, and staff who have only worked in a single industry may also not be familiar with the range of possible solutions.

And yet the biggest challenge for existing businesses is that it is hard to launch a complete renovation when you're still living in the building. It's not impossible, but it requires sacrifices and willingness to make fundamental changes—and it is critical that companies find a way. We are seeing major disruption to old business models at an unprecedented rate across all business sectors, in all countries. Organizations stuck thinking in terms of B2C or B2B rather than Me2B are vulnerable and need to act now rather than wait for one of those near-death experiences we describe in Chapter Nine. Many companies in industries such as telecommunications, insurance, retail, airlines, computing, and professional services have failed to act and either went bankrupt or were purchased at bargain prices. The foundations for Me2B success can't be built overnight, but once they're in place, the benefits multiply quickly.

We urge you to start your Me2B journey sooner rather than later. We're convinced that the organizations that cultivate true relationships with customers and consistently satisfy these unchanging seven needs will be those that survive and prosper in the years to come.

Notes

Chapter One

1. Fox, Jeremy. 2012. "Complaint-to-Compliment Ratio of MBTA Tweets Remains High." Boston.com, February 24. Accessed May 20, 2014. http://www.boston.com /yourtown/news/downtown/2012/02/complaint-to-compliment_ratio.html.

2. Poulter, Sean. 2014. "Npower Ranks Top for Moans: Customer Complaints Against Energy Giant Soar 25%." *Mail Online*, January 14. Accessed February 12, 2014. http://www.dailymail.co.uk/news/article-2539614/Npower-ranks-moans-Customer -complaints-against-energy-giant-soar-25.html—ixzz2xknP6ayY.

3. Baer, Jay. 2011. "70% of Companies Ignore Customer Complaints on Twitter." *Convince & Convert*, October 12. Accessed May 20, 2014. http://www.convinceandconvert .com/social-media-monitoring/70-of-companies-ignore-customer-complaints-on -twitter/.

4. ACSI, Inc. 2014. "National Customer Satisfaction Index." Accessed May 20, 2014. http://www.theacsi.org/national-economic-indicator/national-customer-satisfaction -index.

5. Picoult, John. 2013. "The Watermark Consulting 2013 Customer Experience ROI Study." *Watermark*, April 2. Accessed May 20, 2014. http://www.watermarkconsult .net/blog/2013/04/02/the-watermark-consulting-2013-customer-experience-roi -study/.

6. Accenture. 2013. "Accenture 2013 Global Consumer Pulse Survey: Global & U.S. Key Findings." Accessed May 20, 2014. http://www.accenture.com/SiteCollectionDocu ments/PDF/Accenture-Global-Consumer-Pulse-Research-Study-2013-Key-Findings .pdf.

7. Cullum, Philip. 2006. *The Stupid Company: How British Businesses Throw Away Money by Alienating Customers*. National Consumer Council, p. 9.

8. Marketing Charts. 2014. "Millennials and Brand-Marketing: A Complicated Affair." March 25. Accessed May 17, 2014. http://www.marketingcharts.com/wp/traditional /millennials-and-brand-loyalty-a-complicated-affair-41522/.

9. Morrison, Kimberlee. 2013. "[Infographic] Peer Recommendations Are More Influential Than Any Other Form of Advertising." *SocialTimes*, November 7. Accessed May 20, 2014. http://socialtimes.com/90-percent-consumers-trust-earned-media

-form-advertising_b137463. See also Peppers, Don, and Martha Rogers. 2012 *Extreme Trust: Honesty as a Competitive Advantage*. New York: Penguin.

10. Temkin Group. 2014. "Top 10 in 2014 Temkin Experience Ratings" (cycling entry; requires JavaScript). Accessed May 20, 2014. http://www.temkinratings.com. See also Beyond Philosophy. 2014. "Global Customer Experience Survey 2012–2013, Executive Summary." Accessed May 20, 2014. Copy can be requested at http://www .beyondphilosophy.com/thought-leadership/global-leaders-survey/.

Chapter Two

1. J.D. Power & Associates. 2005. "J.D. Power and Associates Reports." March 23. Accessed June 6, 2014. http://businesscenter.jdpower.com/news/pressrelease.aspx?ID= 2005051.

2. Bain & Company. 2013. "Customer Loyalty in Retail Banking: Global Edition 2013." November 6. Accessed May 20, 2014. http://www.bain.com/Images/BAIN_REPORT _Loyalty_in_Retail_Banking_2013.pdf.

3. Hill, Kashmir. 2012. "How Target Figured Out a Teen Girl Was Pregnant Before Her Father Did." *Forbes*, February 16. Accessed May 20, 2014. http://www.forbes.com /sites/kashmirhill/2012/02/16/how-target-figured-out-a-teen-girl-was-pregnant-before -her-father-did/.

Chapter Three

1. BRW magazine. 2013. "Fast 100." Accessed July 29, 2014. http://www.brw.com.au/lists /fast-100/2013.

2. Peppers, Don, and Martha Rogers. 1996. *The One to One Future: Building Relationships One Customer at a Time*. New York: Doubleday.

3. Griffin, Jill, and Robert T. Herres. 2002. *Customer Loyalty: How to Earn It, How to Keep It*. San Francisco: Jossey-Bass.

4. Fox, Jodie. 2014. Presentation at Chief Customer Officer Forum, Sydney, Australia.

Chapter Four

1. Gabb, Jacqui, Martina Klett-Davies, Janet Fink, and Manuela Thomae. "Enduring Love? Couple Relationships in the 21st Century." Open University Enduring Love Research Project. 2014. Accessed May 20, 2014. http://www.open.ac.uk/researchprojects /enduringlove/files/enduringlove/file/ecms/web-content/Final-Enduring-Love-Survey -Report.pdf.

2. Customer Contact Leadership Council. 2009. "Shifting the Loyalty Curve." Accessed May 20, 2014. https://ccc.executiveboard.com/public/Shifting_the_Loyalty_Curve (B2C).pdf.

3. Jardon Bouska, former president of CheckFree Division. 2011. E-mail to Bill Price.
4. Dixon, Matthew, Karen Freeman, and Nicholas Toman. "Stop Trying to Delight Your Customers." *Harvard Business Review* 88, no. 7/8 (2010): 116–122.

Chapter Five

1. Binkovitz, Leah. 2013. "A Nike Shoe, Now a Part of the Smithsonian." *Smithsonian*, February, 2013. Accessed May 20, 2014. http://www.smithsonianmag.com/smithsonian -institution/a-nike-shoe-now-a-part-of-the-smithsonian-4378596/.
2. Peters, Tom, and Nancy Austin. 1985. "Doing MBWA." In *A Passion for Excellence: The Leadership Difference*. New York: Random House.

Chapter Six

1. "3 Honor System Farm Stands." YouTube video, 10:42. Posted by Paul Wheaton. February 12, 2012. http://www.youtube.com/watch?v=Gy_H-eQf6Ng.
2. "Heinz." 2013. *In Superbrands Annual 2013: An Insight into Some of Britain's Strongest Brands*. Accessed May 20, 2014. d3iixjhp5u37hr.cloudfront.net/files/2013/02/Heinz -89pY4Z.pdf.
3. Peppers, Don, and Martha Rogers. 2012. *Extreme Trust: Honesty as a Competitive Advantage*. New York: Penguin.

Chapter Seven

1. Prakash, Neha. 2013. "WestJet Christmas Surprise Will Make You Believe in Santa." *Mashable*, December 9. Accessed May 20, 2014. http://mashable.com/2013/12/09 /westjet-christmas-miracle-ad/.
2. Nordstrom customer letter sent to Bill Price May 16, 2014, by Nordstrom Corporate Communications.

Chapter Eight

1. Prabhakar, Pinoy. 2013. "Virgin Atlantic Is One of My Long-Standing Business Affairs: Richard Branson." *Economic Times*, November 17. Accessed May 20, 2014. http://economictimes.indiatimes.com/opinion/interviews/virgin-atlantic-is-one-of-my -long-standing-business-affairs-richard-branson/articleshow/25902725.cms.
2. Wang, Jennifer. 2014. "Grabbing Attention Is Retailers' Focus." *Orange County Reporter*, January 22.
3. Connelly, Sheryl. 2013. "Looking Further with Ford: 13 Trends for 2013." http://i .usatoday.net/money/_pdfs/ford-consumer-trend-report.pdf.
4. Colvin, Jeff. 2012. "How Can American Express Help You?" *Fortune*, April 19. Accessed May 20, 2014. http://management.fortune.cnn.com/2012/04/19/american-express -customer-service/.

Chapter Nine

1. Amazon.com. "1997 Letter to Shareholders (Reprinted from the 1997 Annual Report)." Accessed May 20, 2014. http://benhorowitz.files.wordpress.com/2010/05/amzn _shareholder-letter-20072.pdf.

2. Bill Price's notes from attending his first meeting at Amazon.com led by Jeff Bezos. Spring 1999.

3. *Economist*. 1999. "When the Bubble Bursts." January 28. Accessed May 20, 2014. http://www.economist.com/node/183857.

4. Yamato Transport Europe B.V. "About Us." 2014. Accessed June 7, 2014. http://www .yamatoeurope.com/about-us/.

5. first direct. 2014. "first direct Awards." Accessed May 20, 2014. http://discover.firstdirect .com/awards.

6. ACSI. 2014. Benchmarks by Company. Accessed May 20, 2014. http://www.theacsi.org /index.php?option=com_content&view=article&id=149&catid=&Itemid=214&c= Home+Depot.

7. Schultz, Howard. 2012. *Onward: How Starbucks Fought for Its Life Without Losing Its Soul*. New York: Rodale.

8. Nemcick-Cruz, Margie. 2013. "Deteriorating Morale and Stock Price at Hewlett-Packard." Motley Fool, May 8. Accessed May 20, 2014. http://beta.fool.com/margiecfl /2013/05/08/deteriorating-morale-and-stock-price-at-hewlett-pa/33356/.

Chapter Ten

1. Phelps, Stan. 2013. "Celebrating Super Human Customer Service." *9 Inch Marketing*. January 13. Accessed May 20, 2014. http://9inchmarketing.com/2013/01/13/heroes -wanted-and-rewarded-zappos/.

2. Interview with Yamato Transport top managers, conducted by Bill Price and LimeBridge Japan partner Osamu Taniguchi, August 25, 2011.

3. "Vente-privee.com au Zénith: Relation Client," 2013. Stratégies, February 14. Accessed June 24, 2014. http://www.strategies.fr/actualites/marques/205965W/vente-privee -com-au-zenith.html.

Glossary

We tend to use terms familiar to those who operate in customer-facing roles. Nonetheless, we thought we should add a glossary for those who might need it.

360-Degree View of Customer   A system or group of systems that provides a view of every interaction and product for a given customer. Such systems capture all products and all contacts that customers make regardless of how they make contact.

ACSI: American Customer Satisfaction Index   The ACSI is a national survey of seventy thousand customers that occurs each month in the United States. It is used as a benchmark of attitudes toward companies across forty-three industries and is the most commonly quoted of such surveys.

ANI: Automatic Number Identification—See CLI

APM: Agent Performance Management   A systemic process to assess, manage, and improve the performance of frontline staff. Developed by coauthor Bill Price, typically this consists of a balanced scorecard of measures, a process of ranking, and then associated coaching and training processes that help frontline staff improve their performance.

B2B: Business to Business   Businesses whose primary relationship is directly with other businesses.

B2B2C: Business to Business to Customer   Businesses that use intermediary businesses to sell to end consumers. For example, companies in this group may sell products through brokers or financial advisers, or may franchise operations.

B2C: Business to Customer   Businesses whose primary relationship is directly with end consumers.

Big Data Customer Analytics   IT systems used to aggregate all the interactions, purchases, and behaviors of customers in order to predict future behaviors, likelihood to purchase, and potential return to the business.

BPOs: Business Process Outsourcers   Specialized suppliers of outsourced services for complex or repetitive business processes, such as statement printing, mailing, insurance claims processing, and mortgage application processing. Many businesses have used such suppliers because they offer scale, low cost, specialization, or access to low-cost countries such as India or the Philippines.

C2C: Customer to Customer   Interactions in which the customer assists or advises other customers. Shared help sites, blogs, forums, and new waves of social media are examples.

CES: Customer Effort Score   A customer's rating of investment in a given interaction, typically scoring from very low effort (1) to very high effort (5).

CLI: Caller Line Identification   Same as ANI in North America; identifies the number from which the customer is calling, often matched automatically in the contact center with customer data so that the agent does not have to ask for basic account data.

CLV: Customer Lifetime Value   A process to calculate the total revenue and profit return that a company can obtain from a given customer over the entire span of their relationship. This process is often used in segmenting customers so that business can work out how to attract the most valuable customers and invest appropriately in the relationship.

CRM: Customer Relationship Management   Either the process by which companies attempt to get closer to their customers by combining contact and purchase history with other details, or the hardware and software systems that combine and present these data; we prefer the first definition because the second gets us too wrapped up in system integration language instead of VOC.

Customer Effort   The amount of time and energy that customers have to invest to use the products and services of a company. This also includes measuring how much effort the customer perceives having invested.

FCR: First Contact Resolution   Usually expressed as a percentage, indicating the proportion of customer contacts that are resolved without follow-up by the customer or by the agent to the customer, but including all the agents involved before the customer hangs up—for example, transfers to other agents through escalation or to seek a specialist to resolve the issue (see FPR).

FPR: First Point Resolution Usually expressed as a percentage, indicating the proportion of customer contacts that are resolved without follow-up by the customer or by the agent to the customer, without resorting to internal transfers, escalations, or support by anyone other than that first agent the customer dealt with.

IVR: Interactive Voice Response Phone-based system that enables the customer to enter digits onto the touch-tone pad or speak plain or natural language in order to obtain automated information (such as account balance or order status) or provide information to the company.

Last Contact Benchmarking As developed by co-author Bill Price, comparing your operations with the best experiences that your customers have had recently, not necessarily with your direct competitors or those in the industry.

Me2B The emerging business model in which customers are taking control of their relationship with business. They are dictating the products and services they want, the way they want interactions to work, and the price they are prepared to pay.

Multi-Channel The ability to offer sales and service via multiple interaction mechanisms such as call center, the Internet, face to face, social media. A multi-channel business is one involving more than one such channel (see also Omni-Channel).

NPS: Net Promoter Score A survey technique to measure a customer's likely loyalty to a business. It asks the customer how likely they are to recommend the company to a friend or colleague on a ten-point scale where 10 is very likely and 0 not likely. The score counts those who score 9 or 10 as promoters and these are then netted against those who score 0–6, who are seen as detractors. By subtracting promoters from detractors you obtain a Net Promoter Score as a percentage of respondents. This can range from negative 100 percent if all are detractors to positive 100 percent if all are promoters.

Omni-Channel A business in which sales and service are offered by multiple channels but in which the channels are integrated. So a customer can start an interaction in one channel and complete it in another.

RFM: Recency, Frequency, and Monetary Value   RFM is a method used for analyzing customer value based on how recently they have purchased, how often they purchase, and how much they purchase. It is commonly used in database marketing and direct marketing to assess the value and potential of customers and to help segment customers.

Share of Wallet   A technique used by companies to assess what percentage of a customer's expenditure in their industry or for related items is spent on their company. In financial services, a bank might assess what percentage of a customer's overall loans, deposits, and insurance is spent with it as a bank.

Snowballs   Repeat contacts, or 100 percent minus FCR or FPR; calculated using input-output ratios per team, center, and enterprise.

Tier 1 and Tier 2   Most organizations staff their customer-facing teams as Tier 1, with escalation or follow-up provided by Tier 2 personnel.

Virtual Agents   A form of online automation in which help and support on websites or kiosks are provided by automated help figures or avatars. These figures are made available to answer questions or guide a customer through an interaction. Not to be confused with customer service agents working from home who are sometimes also called "virtual agents."

VOC: Voice of the Customer   The art and science of listening to what the customer is telling the company, either directly (for example, verbatim comments) or indirectly (for example, via customer service); see also WOCAS.

WOCAS: What Our Customers Are Saying   Process of collecting VOC from frontline employees with whom the customers interact on a regular basis; now, a formal product that collects, codes, scores, routes, and reports VOC through the frontline employees. Coined by coauthor Bill Price and now commercialized by our LimeBridge partner in Germany, Stephan Pucker.

WOM: Word of Mouth   How customers tell other customers about a product or service. Word-of-mouth marketing is where an organization hopes or encourages customers to promote a product to other customers. A precursor of NPS.

Recommended Reading

Don Peppers and Martha Rogers, *Extreme Trust: Honesty as a Competitive Advantage*. Penguin, 2012.

James L. Heskett, W. Earl Sasser Jr., and Leonard A. Schlesinger, *The Service Profit Chain: How Leading Companies Link Profit and Growth to Loyalty, Satisfaction, and Value*. Free Press, 1997.

Tony Hsieh, *Delivering Happiness: A Path to Profits, Passion, and Purpose*. Hachette, 2010.

Chip Conley, *Emotional Equations: Simple Steps for Creating Happiness + Success in Business + Life*. Atria, 2012.

Hanson Hosein, *Storyteller Uprising: Trust and Persuasion in the Digital Age*. HRH Media, 2012.

Clotaire Rapaille, *The Culture Code: An Ingenious Way to Understand Why People Around the World Live and Buy as They Do*. Crown, 2006.

Robert Spector and Patrick McCarthy, *The Nordstrom Way to Customer Service Excellence*. Wiley, 2012.

John H. Fleming and Jim Asplund, *Human Sigma: Managing the Employee-Customer Encounter*. Gallup, 2007.

Christopher Morace and Sara Gaviser Leslie, *Transform: How Leading Companies Are Winning with Disruptive Social Technology*. McGraw-Hill, 2014.

Adam Bryant, *The Corner Office: Indispensable and Unexpected Lessons from CEOs on How to Lead and Succeed*. Henry Holt, 2011.

Steve Krug, *Don't Make Me Think: A Common Sense Approach to Web Usability*. New Riders, 2006.

Glenn L. Gardiner, *Foremanship*. Shaw, 1927.

Claudia Gabler, editor, *Best Customer InterACTion: Creating Exceptional Customer Experiences in the Contact Center*. Competence Call Center, 2012.

Hap Klopp with Brian Tarcy, *Conquering the North Face: An Adventure in Leadership*. iUniverse, 2013.

Libby Sartain and Mark Schumann, *Brand from the Inside: Eight Essentials to Emotionally Connect Your Employees to Your Business*. Jossey-Bass, 2006.

Robert J. Serling, *Characters & Characters: The Spirit of Alaska Airlines*. Documentary Media, 2008.

ACKNOWLEDGMENTS

The authors would like to thank our LimeBridge colleagues across the world for their support, bad and good stories, and active deployment of our first book on Best Service, particularly Peter Massey in the United Kingdom for his continued passion for Fast + Simple processes; Osama Taniguchi in Japan for sharing with us Yamato Transport and other Me2B Leaders; Stephan Pucker in Germany for his passion for the WOCAS program; Joseph Kort in France for inspiring us with French wine and success stories; MD Ramaswami and Vinit Singhal in India for their tireless enthusiasm for new business ideas; and Toby Detter in Sweden for his strategic and marketing perspectives.

David would also like to thank Peter Morrison and Graham Howard, his business partners in Australia, for supporting the idea of the book and acting as a sounding board. They also agreed to use of the cartoons. He also needs to thank the core LimeBridge Australia team—Caroline Loughrey, Probal das Gupta, Michael Hazel, Luke Hannemann, Synth Senthi, John Spooner, Karen Witty, and Helen Moses—for their continued good work that has freed him for Skype calls and book writing.

Bill would like to thank his U.S.-based colleagues past and present—Cass Nevada, David Morad, Doug Cassell, Jamie Erze, Jim Bartz, Jim Folk, John Rushing, Linda Chidester, Pat Larson, Paul Davis, Phil Vandecar, Wes Pitman, and Zulma Pereira—for their continued dedication with our clients, editorial advice, and loyalty to the relentless pursuit of Best Service and Me2B, and to the implications of Me2B leadership. Bill learned from and thanks the Best Service and Me2B enthusiasts, too many to name, who have shared their stories with us, in particular Cate Hardy, Starbucks;

Gary Qualls, DIRECTV; Gibbs Jones, Suddenlink; Harvey Trager, Danaher/Fluke; Jardon Bouska, CheckFree/Fiserv; Laurent Tupin, Vente-Privee; Mike Baker, First Data and UHG; Philippe Tisserand, Owi; Sara Kearney, Hyatt; Scott Maxwell, OpenView Venture Partners; and Scott Tweedy, T-Mobile.

We would also like to thank professional colleagues Daniel Ziv from Verint, Keith Fiveson from ITESA, Sarah Beardsley from Accenture, and Michelle Watson from Match.com (now Walmart .com) for challenging our thinking and contributing key ingredients for Me2B.

The authors could not have brought our book to life without the incredible partnership with Karen Murphy and John Maas at Jossey-Bass; Sara Grace who helped us greatly to reshape our manuscript; and production editors Mary Garrett and Mark Karmendy and copyeditor Hilary Powers who brought the book into this final crisp and clear form.

We both need to thank Jon Kudelka for his amazing cartoons. David and Jon have been producing fifteen of these a year for the last ten years and they are admired all over the world. Jon has won many Australian journalism awards and we thank him for his unique contribution.

In particular we must thank our families: Erika and Rachel, and Rebecca and Patrick, for putting up with the periodic absence of their dads and their apparent preference for laptops and PCs over their children; Rebecca in particular took up driving at an ideal time to let David type away in the back of the car. Last but probably most, we need to thank Sue and Lori for their love, encouragement, and inspiration, as well as crucial edits and suggestions to strengthen our arguments.

David needs to thank Bill for his vision and ideas and for agreeing to team on this. If anything I think we've gotten better as a team and I'm always pleasantly surprised by Bill's willingness to listen to my thoughts and share his. I may have thrown up two hundred–odd titles, but Bill came up with the ones that mattered. Similarly, we've never diverted from the ideas at the core of the book (which were all Bill's), but he had the flexibility to let me flesh those out and refine them. It's also a pleasure to work with a partner who listens, reflects, and improves. So thanks again, Bill, for agreeing to this international collaboration and the joys of American spelling and grammar.

Last, Bill needs to acknowledge that without David's tireless focus and desire to produce this second book together; his good humor and pithy phrases; his numerous additions and refinements to Bill's original musings about "customer happiness," "back to the customer future," and "wooly mammoths and artichokes"; and his amazing ability to craft tables, create titles, and synthesize complex and varied stories into concise needs and success factors, Me2B would never have happened—good on you once again, mate!

About the Authors

Bill Price, coauthor of *The Best Service Is No Service*, founded Driva Solutions, LLC, in September 2001 to help build clients' customer service strategies and improve operational performance, after serving as Amazon's first global VP of customer service. In 2002 he co-founded the ten-country LimeBridge Global Alliance and the now thirty-nine-organization Global Operations Council that shares "best practices and worst experiences"; he also chairs the Chief Customer Officer Forum, Americas. He is a Partner with Antuit, a Big Data analytics company based in Singapore, building its customer and marketing programs.

Price started his career with McKinsey & Company in its San Francisco and Stockholm offices, serving global clients and working on what turned into *In Search of Excellence*. He then became CFO and COO at an early IVR service bureau, Automated Call Processing Corporation, whose network routing division MCI acquired; he built MCI Call Center Services' automation, consulting, and agent outsourcing divisions, and was named one of the first Call Center Pioneers by *CRM Magazine*'s editors in 1997.

Price is a frequent keynote speaker, graduate school instructor in marketing and global business management, and advisory board member. He graduated from Dartmouth College and the Stanford Graduate School of Business, and lives with his wife in Bellevue and Vashon, Washington, where he maintains his weekly running regimen and summertime kayaking. One of his two daughters is applying her master's degree in primate behavior and his other daughter will soon be applying her degree in mechanical engineering.

For more information, please visit www.drivasolutions.com.

David Jaffe, coauthor of *The Best Service Is No Service*, lives in Melbourne, Australia, and is the consulting director and founder of LimeBridge Australia, a specialist customer experience business. He grew up in England and studied philosophy, politics, and economics at Oxford University before starting a consulting career and then migrating to Australia.

Jaffe has been a consultant for twenty-eight years in Britain, Ireland, and Australia, and has also consulted in India, New Zealand, Hong Kong, the Philippines, Singapore, and the United States. He has worked across many industries in customer-facing sales and service areas, such as branches, call centers, self-service, and administration. He began his career with Accenture, where he became a national partner with responsibility for the Customer Practice for Financial Services in Asia-Pacific. He then joined AT Kearney as a principal in its Financial Institutions Group. He left AT Kearney to help found LimeBridge Australia.

Within LimeBridge Australia Jaffe leads major client development, research, and marketing. He has spoken at numerous conferences in Australia, Asia, and North America. He created the Chief Customer Officer Forum in Australia and is a sought-after speaker at events across the world.

He has a wife and two children and is also a keen chorale singer, orienteer, and after-dinner entertainer.

For more information, please visit www.limebridge.com.au.

INDEX

Page numbers in italics refer to figures, tables, and other illustrative material.

THE BOOK OF
TERRIFYINGLY
AWESOME
TECHNOLOGY

SEAN CONNOLLY

WORKMAN PUBLISHING · NEW YORK

Library of Congress Cataloging-in-Publication Data is available.

ISBN 978-1-5235-0494-7

Design by Claire Torres
Interior and cover illustrations by Kristyna Baczynski
Editing by Danny Cooper
Production editing by Beth Levy
Photo research by Angela Cherry
Production manager Julie Primavera
Photo credits: Adobe Stock: p. 219; Alamy Images: NG Images p. 164;
Getty Images: Archive Photos p. 138, Bloomberg pp. 19, 79, 85,
ferrantraite/iStock Unreleased p. 147, Catrina Genovese/WireImage
p. 72, Koichi Kamoshida p. 207, Picture Alliance p. 62, Rick_Jo p. 29,
Science & Society Picture Library p. 36, Universal Images Group p. 122;
Science Source: Peter Menzel p. 27; Shutterstock.com: pp. ix, 3, 13, 20, 43,
55, 63, 67, 71, 80, 89, 97, 104, 117 (all), 124, 125, 133, 139, 141 (all),
155, 172, 173, 179, 181, 188, 189, 190, 197.

Workman Publishing Co., Inc.
225 Varick Street
New York, NY 10014-4381
workman.com

Printed in the United States

First printing August 2019

10 9 8 7 6 5 4 3 2 1

★ ★

*To the memory of my uncle, Patrick Connolly,
and the team of linotype operators at the
Cuneo Press of New England.*

★ ★

Those linotype operators were experts in a type of technology that has been replaced several times over, but they embodied some timeless values. Two of the most important are teamwork and professionalism. Their books, like mine, developed and blossomed thanks to diligence and attention to detail of a dedicated team.

Each member of my "team" deserves recognition for delivering this book to you. Their enthusiasm, patience, and dedication to excellence inspired me. My wife, Frederika, and family have been steadfast and supportive throughout. Members of my wider family include my agent, Jim Levine of the Levine Greenberg Rostan Literary Agency, illustrator Kristyna Baczynski, Workman editor and guru Danny Cooper, and the Workman team responsible for helping the words and images take shape on the page—production editor Beth Levy, production manager Julie Primavera, typesetter Annie O'Donnell, designer Claire Torres, and photo researcher Angela Cherry.

The following individuals and organizations provided invaluable assistance and inspiration: the Bath Royal Literary and Scientific Institution, Berkshire Film & Video, the Boston Public Library, Frank Ciccotti, Rick Desira, Gregory Etter, Dr. Gary Hoffman, Dr. Peter Lydon, William Matthiesen, MIT's Educational Studies Program, Peter Rielly, Jennifer Spohn, Elizabeth Stell, Williams College, and Woods Hole Oceanographic Institution.

CONTENTS

INTRODUCTION

You've probably come across the abbreviation STEM a lot at school. It stands for **S**cience, **T**echnology, **E**ngineering, and **M**ath, and schools around the country—and the world—are eager that we all learn more about those subjects. This book looks closely at the "T" of that abbreviation, finding out how it's improving our lives . . . while somehow carrying a whiff of danger.

Here's a pretty standard definition of technology: "science or knowledge put into practical use to solve problems or invent useful tools." Okay, hold up. That's a pretty wide-ranging definition, and it means that the "T" of STEM probably ties in neatly with the "S," "E," and "M." After all, a reusable rocket (see page 33) is a pretty cool form of modern technology. But designers must be up to speed with their science to know how that rocket can escape Earth's gravity (going up) and not burn apart in the atmosphere (coming back down). It takes advanced engineering skills to build a rocket to these specifications. And to provide the calculations needed for those specifications? That sure sounds like a job for math!

BACK IN TIME

It's human nature, almost an instinct, to be curious, resourceful, and inventive. STEM might be a new term, but human beings have been using those four fields of science for thousands—and possibly millions—of years, whether they know it or not. "Putting science or knowledge into practical use" doesn't sound very exciting, but consider all of the thinking that led to the development of steam engines, the printing press, the bow and arrow, and even that all-purpose bit of technology— the wheel.

Sometimes, however, even inventions with the best intentions can go awry. Steam power lay behind the great advances of the Industrial Revolution in the 18th and 19th centuries: Just think of clothing factories, the earliest trains, and electrical generation. But steam could also power warships. Meanwhile, printing presses could spread hatred, and the bow and arrow could be used against human enemies as well as to hunt for food.

All of that is the background to this book. It explains and celebrates awesome technological ideas while keeping in mind how those ideas could go wrong or be twisted into something . . . terrifying.

WHAT YOU'LL FIND

You don't need to look into the past to find terrifyingly awesome tech. It's all around you! And there's always more in the pipeline. *The Book of Terrifyingly Awesome Technology* examines these latest breakthroughs. It takes a good look at what makes them tick (hmm . . . does modern tech stuff even tick anymore?) before finding out how they might scare the heck out of us.

Each of the 26 chapters concerns a type of technology that's either very recent but already familiar, like the World Wide Web (page 69) or that's not yet in use but might arrive in the near future, like air-conditioned clothing (page 129). You've probably had loads of contact with the first group (the stuff that's already around you), but maybe you're doubtful that the other ("near future") stuff will ever get off the drawing board. Well, you might be surprised, because some of them have pretty convincing backing—either from one of the world's richest people (see Reusable Rockets, page 33) or from a leading group of international scientists with a detailed plan (see Space Elevator, page 211).

HOW THIS BOOK WORKS

Each chapter presents information in an easy-to-follow format. An introduction sets the scene and gives you a taste of what the technology's all about. You'll get a hint of what makes this tech tick, as well as a few ideas about how it sneaked into a book with the word "terrifying" in its title.

Then there's a section on "How Life Is Better" because, after all, isn't that what new technology is all about? You might call this the "nuts and bolts" of the chapter: It gives you the real lowdown on how the technology works, how and why it was developed, and how the world is (or could be) a better place because of it.

The chapter then fills you in on "Related Technology" so you can see how it fits in with, or maybe improves on, stuff that's already in use. You'll see how even ground-breaking, cutting-edge technological ideas have links to earlier versions and other forms of tech. You'll see why GPS (page 121), for instance, plays a big part in driver-less automobiles (page 77), drones (page 169), and many other modern technological marvels.

Then it's time to think back to the title of the book and to see how the technology is "Terrifyingly Awesome." It's fascinating—and possibly scary—to consider how bad guys can sometimes derail good ideas, or how those good ideas might have some pretty scary unexpected consequences. Cool illustrations, quick definitions, and neat panels run through all of these sections, helping you get a fuller idea of these fascinating, awe-inspiring technological breakthroughs.

To round off each chapter, you can do an experiment that links directly to the chapter's technology. Each of these comes with easy, step-by-step instructions and a Time Factor to tell you how long you'll need to do it—ranging from something to fill a few minutes, right up to two weeks. You may not wind up performing laser surgery directly or battling a forest fire with a sound disrupter, but you'll get a fun, hands-on look into the scientific ideas that make those things possible . . . or even dream-up-able.

There you have it. It's time to push on and test the boundaries of technology. Try not to be too terrified!

CHAPTER 1

PLANT SPEED BREEDING

→ − +   X

Talk about a serious subject—here's one so serious that it might just save the planet! And sometimes thinking about things beyond our planet can make a big difference down here on Earth.

Ever since the space program got cooking in the 1960s, critics have complained that all those millions of dollars should be spent helping to tackle huge Earthbound problems. One of those problems, of course, is being able to provide enough food for the world's growing population.

Well, it turns out that some of the research from NASA space missions has a direct bearing on agriculture. Think how hard it must be to pack food for a months-long mission (or years-long, if we go to Mars). Scientists have found a way to grow bountiful food plants quickly right on board a spaceship. That's a real breakthrough!

Could this be a miracle in the making? Or possibly a nightmare, if things go wrong?

HOW LIFE IS BETTER

It's no surprise that things are pretty tight on the food front here on Earth. Even if the richer countries were to cut down on food consumption—or switch to food choices that were less of a drain on the environment—we'd still be running low. We need a way of increasing food supply to feed all 7.5 billion hungry humans on Earth—along with the extra 2 billion expected by 2050.

And that's just feeding the people living on Earth. Some scientists believe that humanity's future lies in space travel, orbiting space stations, and even permanent colonies on Mars . . . and possibly beyond. Producing food in these inhospitable, cramped surroundings is a huge challenge, but finding ways to do it would also be a huge breakthrough in the food crisis on our own planet.

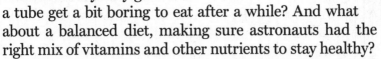

Imagine providing food for a space mission that could take months or even years. Where would you store it? Would dry crackers or mystery goo from a tube get a bit boring to eat after a while? And what about a balanced diet, making sure astronauts had the right mix of vitamins and other nutrients to stay healthy?

The answer is to find a way to grow food fast on board the small, enclosed spacecraft. That's where the whole idea of "speed breeding" comes in. It means raising crops under special conditions in a laboratory to make them grow faster. But how?

The breakthrough came when Australian scientists and NASA decided to mimic space-travel conditions in greenhouses on Earth. Astronaut plant breeders would have the advantage of constant, direct sunlight and no clouds to obscure the light. The scientists also considered the light that plants need to grow and wondered whether a particular type of light would work better than others. Remember how you can see different colors, ranging from red to violet, in a rainbow? Well, that range is called a spectrum. Each color in that spectrum has its own level of energy. The scientists discovered that isolating light from certain parts of the spectrum adds oomph to the photosynthesis process.

PHOTOSYNTHESIS

The chemical process that plants use to convert sunlight, carbon dioxide, and water into nutrients that fuel their growth and maintain their health.

The results were astounding—you might say "out of this world"—when the scientists directed a beam of red light on the experimental plants. They produced six generations of wheat, chickpea, and barley plants in a single year—as opposed to two in normal greenhouse conditions and one in plants grown outside in a field.

RELATED TECHNOLOGY

Genetically modified (GM) food has already become widespread in an effort to increase the yield (the amount harvested) of many crops. It uses the science of genetics (see page 113) to alter the basic makeup of an organism (plant or animal). The DNA of an organism with a desirable trait, such as resistance to disease, is incorporated into another organism. As this organism breeds, it passes on the desired traits to offspring.

So just as speed breeding gets results faster, GM techniques also boost yields by making sure that the plants are stronger, healthier, and better able to breed.

TERRIFYINGLY AWESOME?

There's something a bit creepy about weeds and other plants just "springing up" overnight. What if they get out of control and grow *too* fast? Well, people have already found a lot to fear with the development of GM technology. Some of the weirdest, absolutely real results are bizarre or even a little scary: How do you feel about a pig that glows in the dark or a chicken bred to have no feathers?

The changes made to plants might not be as dramatic, but they are potentially just as worrying. Also, if we've already developed the technology to modify organisms that benefit humanity, could organisms be modified for evil purposes? And with a technique like speed breeding available to pick up the pace . . . then who knows what might replace familiar crops before anyone knew that something fishy was going on?

Triffids

Come on! What do plants have to do with being terrified? Well, you might think differently if you read the book *The Day of the Triffids*, written in 1951 by John Wyndham. The triffids, you see, are killer plants that are capable of moving around. Cities and towns are terrorized and taken over by these roving killers. Psychologists had a field day studying why readers were so scared by this prospect. One theory is that it seems like a nightmarish account of the plant kingdom seeking revenge on the world's animals . . . including humans. Maybe you'll think about it the next time you trim the hedges or eat a salad!

EXPERIMENT
GARDENER'S GREEN THUMB— OR IS IT YELLOW OR VIOLET?

Here's a hands-on home version of what those speed-breeding scientists did in greenhouses. But you'll be testing something similar: Which color of light produces the best growing results?

Light moves in wave patterns, and each color has its own unique wavelength (distance from one wave to another). What we see as "light," or "white light," is really a mixture of different colors with different wavelengths. Shone through a prism or seen in a rainbow (in which raindrops act as tiny prisms), white light shows its "true colors," ranging from red on one side to violet on the other. Your experiment will test results from three of those colors.

YOU WILL NEED

- Paper tissues (like Kleenex)
- Water
- 3 plastic or paper cups (5 fl. oz./150 ml size)
- Radish seeds
- Ruler
- See-through cellophane sheets: red, yellow, and violet
- Windowsill or shelf that gets sunlight

METHOD

(1) Moisten three tissues with a little water and place one in each cup.

2 Spread about 10 radish seeds on each tissue.

3 Cover each cup with a different color of cellophane.

4 Place the cups on a windowsill or shelf so that each receives the same amount of light.

5 Measure and record the height of the radish seedlings each day for five days.

6 Remember to replace the cellophane on each cup after measuring and to keep each tissue moist (using the same amount of water for each cup).

DATA ANALYSIS

The longest wavelength of light is red, which also carries the least energy. Violet—at the other end of the spectrum—has the shortest wavelength and packs the most energy. Yellow is in the middle between them. Did you notice any connection between the amount of energy that a color carries and the growth of the radishes getting that color's light?

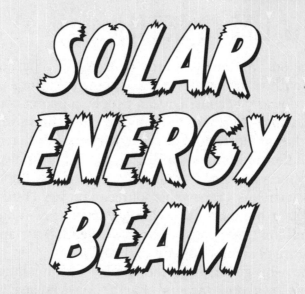

CHAPTER 2

SOLAR ENERGY BEAM

→ − +   X

"What will happen when the oil (or coal, or natural gas, or shale) runs out?" We hear this alarming question more and more often as people consider how to deal with "the energy crisis."

Crisis? You bet it is! With a growing population (about 7.5 billion at the last count), planet Earth is feeding, housing, educating, transporting, heating, cooling, and entertaining more and more people. And all of that uses energy, which has to be found somewhere or somehow.

Solar (Sun-related) power is one of the most attractive and exciting of these methods, and it's not just limited to panels on house roofs. Huge fields of panels are already appearing, and a logical next step is to send them into space. Imagine harnessing the Sun's power high above the clouds. And beaming all of that energy down would be great . . . or would it?

HOW LIFE IS BETTER

Come on, wouldn't you breathe a sigh of relief to know that with solar power, we're not going to suffer a permanent power blackout? Or that people in poorer countries would have inexpensive power to help improve living standards? How about clean, efficient power that doesn't harm the environment with pollution? It looks as though everyone would be a winner. Perhaps most important, solar energy is a renewable source of power. Think of the Sun as a humongous, rechargeable battery—one that's 1.3 million times bigger than Earth, with a surface temperature of about 11,000°F (6,000°C).

So why go through the trouble of launching solar panels into orbit around Earth? Well, space has no

clouds, rain, or darkness. (Space may seem black, but that's because there are no objects out there to reflect light—except for planets, asteroids, and other stuff floating around.) If the panels are in the right orbit, there's no night, so they are converting sunlight into electricity 24/7. Not bad!

Scientists are still at the drawing board on how best to get solar panels into space, but back here on Earth, solar power is very advanced. Here's how it works. The panels are made of smaller units called photovoltaic cells. You already know the "photo" part, which means "light" (photons are tiny particles containing energy, including light). "Volt" reminds us that we're talking about electricity. The photovoltaic cells are the key to catching light and converting it to electricity.

The cells absorb sunlight, and that light knocks loose each cell's electrons (negatively charged particles orbiting atoms). The electrons "migrate" (flow) from the inside of the cells to the surface, creating an electric current. And I bet you already know a common name for the flow of electrons—yes, electricity.

So what would a humongous solar panel in space look like? One idea is to launch a satellite, and once free of the Earth's atmosphere (which could burn up the sensitive equipment because of friction), a panel would unfurl until it looked like a huge flying carpet. It would be like watching one of those paper party horns uncurl when you blow into them—except the panel is about two-thirds as long as a football field.

Another plan takes the idea even further, sending 2,500 such satellites into space to orbit in close formation. Together they can build a solar-panel "field" that covers 3.5 square miles (9 km^2). The 12 gigawatts (12 billion watts) of power supplied by the satellites would be about the same as 40 million solar panels back on Earth. This seems better and better—or crazier and crazier.

RELATED TECHNOLOGY

Solar power isn't the only source of energy that doesn't rely on fossil fuels. Any energy source that doesn't drain resources is considered renewable. Wind is free and plentiful in many parts of the world. That explains why massive wind turbines (like huge windmills) have begun lining windswept hills. Here's another one: tidal power. Ocean tides come in and out like clockwork, drawn back and forth by the Moon's gravitational pull. Think of the power locked into the movement of all that water.

FOSSIL FUELS

Oil, coal, and natural gas are called fossil fuels because (like fossils) they come from old life-forms that have decomposed (broken down) over long periods, often millions of years. The Earth contains a limited amount of such fuel, and once it has been extracted, it cannot be replaced. That's why fossil fuels are also called nonrenewable resources.

TERRIFYINGLY AWESOME?

Have you ever seen someone use a magnifying glass to focus the Sun's rays into a bright light that burns a hole in a piece of paper? That's another way of harnessing solar power. Now imagine each of those huge orbiting solar panels focusing enormous amounts of solar power to a receiver back on Earth. One method of sending it down is using powerful beams of light we call lasers.

Okay, that makes sense. All of that energy is being focused and stored so lights can stay on in New York or London or Rio de Janeiro. Now imagine that something quite small but traveling really fast—like a meteor or an asteroid—bumps into that orbiting panel. Instead of focusing the beam of energy onto an electrical transmitter, it focuses directly onto the Earth's surface. Uh-oh.

That's all pretty terrifying, and luckily lasers aren't the only option. After all, the light in lasers is just one part of the electromagnetic spectrum. Maybe we could use another form of energy? The latest idea is to convert the electricity into radio waves. Those would be focused on a receiver on Earth, where the process could be reversed. Don't forget: Alexander Graham Bell had a similar idea when he invented the telephone—transferring sound energy into electrical energy and back again.

Whew! Looks like we'll be using radio waves, then. That is, unless someone finds out that a super-powerful flow of radio waves (like from an orbiting solar panel) has damaging effects that we haven't predicted.

The Alternative?

We get hints of the problems that lie in store by looking at the way things are going—increased gasoline costs, occasional blackouts—but one day we might flick a switch and find that nothing happens. Then we'll know that the needle really does point to "E." And that's "E" for Empty, not Energy.

Feel like tapping into some solar power in your own kitchen or living room? This experiment is a quick way to see just how effective the Sun is at providing energy. You won't be turning that solar power into electricity, but you'll have a cool (well, more likely warm) demonstration of the electromagnetic spectrum.

That's a mouthful, but it really boils down to the way we describe and measure different types of energy. A wavelength is one of the things that sets a particular type of energy apart from others. The colors we see are simply different wavelengths of light (a form of energy). Confused? You won't be after performing this experiment. It's a matter of black and white—literally!

YOU WILL NEED

- 2 paintbrushes
- 2 empty plastic milk jugs (preferably white)
- Black craft paint
- White craft paint (if jugs aren't white)
- 2 party balloons (one black, one white)
- Wide windowsill or table near a sunny window

METHOD

1 Use one of the brushes to paint one jug completely black and let it dry.

2 If the other plastic jug is clear or not quite white already, paint it white and let it dry.

3 Take the black balloon and stretch its opening over the mouth of the black-painted jug.

4 Do the same with the white balloon on the white jug.

5 Set the jugs side by side on the windowsill or table, making sure it's sunny and that neither jug is at all shaded.

6 Make a prediction about whether either balloon will begin to inflate—and if so, which one.

7 Wait 15 minutes and observe both balloons.

DATA ANALYSIS

You'll probably have noticed that the black balloon has begun to inflate. That's because darker colors absorb visible light, and black absorbs the most. Solar panels usually appear dark for this reason. Lighter colors, on the other hand, reflect light. And light is a form of energy, which can transform into heat energy (or into electrical energy, if you're beaming it down from space). The extra heat inside the black jug warms the air, which then expands and fills the balloon.

CHAPTER 3

ROBOTS AND ANDROIDS

How many times have you wished that you had a robot to make your bed? Or to help you empty the dishwasher? Or to mow the lawn? Or even better—*to do your homework!*

Okay, it's easy to see why inventors and engineers are constantly improving designs for "machines that are capable of carrying out a complex series of actions automatically," as one dictionary describes robots. But why do they concentrate on getting robots to do all that boring stuff like building automobiles or assembling computer circuits? Don't inventors have beds to make or dishes to wash?

Think again. The tasks that robots and androids (robots with a human shape) can perform go way beyond all that simple back-and-forth stuff along factory assembly lines. How about a robot that can fly to a dangerous oil spill and start the rescue operation? Or a robot with living tissue that can heal itself, just like human skin?

The sky's the limit, or so it seems. Robots and androids will soon be able to think for themselves . . . and some experts predict that they might even be able to read our thoughts. Yikes!

HOW LIFE IS BETTER

At the most basic levels, robots are machines programmed to carry out tasks, and androids are simply robots designed to look more like humans. One of the main uses of robots is taking over some of the "3-D" jobs—the ones that are **D**ull, **D**irty, or **D**angerous. Would you want to screw 7,344 bolts into car fenders each day on a production line? (Sounds pretty Dull.) How about traveling a few hundred yards through a smelly sewer to find a blockage? (Sounds pretty Dirty.) Or perhaps creep along mile after mile of roads to see whether deadly bombs are hidden beneath? (Sounds really, *really* Dangerous.)

Nope, didn't think so, and that's where our automated friends can lend a hand. Robots are already hard at work moving poisonous substances in warehouses, disinfecting science labs, and moving cargo this way and that in factories. They even load and unload cargo in the International Space Station. Some of this business is dull, and most of it is repetitive, but all of it is stuff that humans don't want to—or can't—do.

They seem to handle those three D's pretty darn well. What about the modern, futuristic stuff? Well, how about the work of specialist robots called "Tugs" that work in hospitals in and around San Francisco? These little fellows don't look too much like sci-fi movie robots (in fact, they look more like coffee machines on wheels), but they can roll up to 500 miles along hospital corridors. In the course of a day, a Tug will deliver food to patients, empty trash, take equipment to labs, and even use high-tech security checks to make sure that the right patients get the right medicines. Doesn't sound *too* complicated, but it really helps make life better. If doctors, nurses, and other hospital staff are freed from those routine tasks, then they have more time to spend with patients.

Other robots—and some androids—are already helping elderly patients in Singapore and patients in remote parts of New Zealand. These robots can be like helpful caregivers, reminding patients about medication, appointments, and even when to eat. "Patients even feel that they're interacting when they see the robot light up," said one New Zealand doctor. That's interesting—would an elderly patient, living alone in a remote cabin, feel a little less lonely with a mechanical companion that acted like a nurse?

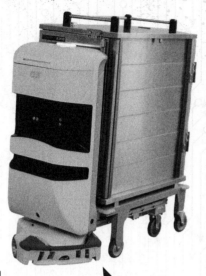

TUG

It probably all boils down to where we draw the line between humans and machines—especially androids that look, behave, and maybe even think like humans.

RELATED TECHNOLOGY

All this talk about robots and androids often leads to a real hot topic—artificial intelligence (see page 59). If we think of robots and androids as the "hardware," then the "software" of the future would be the brains in these human-made constructions. And that's where things can also get scary. It's one thing for a robot to look into your eyes for symptoms of disease, but what if it could also detect your emotions . . . and even read your

HARDWARE AND SOFTWARE

Hardware refers to the physical parts of a computer. Software describes the programs that operate the computer.

mind? Computer scientists are already developing methods for robots to interpret human facial expressions, eye movement, and gestures so the robots can read approval, disapproval, or even lying. So be careful next time a robot comes up to you and says, "Look into my eyes!"

TERRIFYINGLY AWESOME?

Here's where you, the reader, could probably take over and write this! Who hasn't had nightmares about all-powerful robots that turn against humans and take over the world? In fact, that's the name of the game in the play that gave the world the word *robot*.

Until—or unless—robots can be programmed to think completely for themselves (which some people find scary enough), they will always be subject to human control. But sometimes that control might not be quite right: Think of all the times when human error is blamed for accidents, for example. What if someone truly evil had control over an army of robots?

"Ah, that could never happen," you might hear people say. But people also claimed that dynamite would only be used in mining (its original use) and that no one would consider using atomic power to create powerful weapons.

What was that beeping behind you? Not an android with a grudge, I hope!

Roots of the Words

The word *robot* was invented in 1920 by the Czech playwright Karel Čapek for his play *Rossum's Universal Robot*s. Čapek based the name on the Czech word *robota*, which means "hard work" or "drudgery."

The word *android* (from the Greek words *andros*, meaning "man," and *oid*, meaning "likeness") goes back further. It might have been used as early as the Middle Ages. The first modern example can be seen in US patents for miniature windup toys from 1863.

EXPERIMENT
CAN YOU BEAT THAT?!
WARNING! ADULT SUPERVISION REQUIRED

Time
Factor:
20
mins

Want a good example of why people invented robots in the first place? Remember that they're machines designed to do our jobs faster, more efficiently, and maybe even better, all without getting tired or bored.

You're going to be having a "human versus machine" contest. It might remind you of the old legend of John Henry, an African American "steel-driving man" who had a contest with a machine to see who could drill into rock faster. He won, but his heart gave out and he died.

Note: You can use heavy cream or whipping cream instead of egg whites, but it might take a little longer to complete the experiment. Don't worry, no one should die—or even be hurt—in this experiment, but things could get messy!

YOU WILL NEED

- 2 egg separators (or an adult who can separate eggs)
- 4 eggs, at room temperature
- Small mixing bowl
- 2 large mixing bowls
- Wire whisk
- Electric hand mixer
- 1 pint heavy cream (optional)
- A friend to compete against you

METHOD

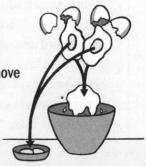

1. If you don't want to separate eggs, use the heavy cream instead, and move on to Step 4.

2. Use the separator to separate the yolks from the egg whites.

3 Set the yolks aside in the small bowl to use in another recipe and add two egg whites to each large mixing bowl.

4 Flip a coin to decide who'll have the wire whisk and who will use the electric hand mixer.

5 On the count of three, begin beating the eggs or cream.

6 Continue beating, and eventually the whites will begin to stiffen.

7 The winner is the first person who can turn their bowl upside down first without spilling any egg white.

DATA ANALYSIS

As you whisk, you're introducing bubbles into the egg whites (or cream). Egg whites are 90 percent water and 10 percent protein. Beating them causes the proteins to uncurl and form a sort of semisolid mesh (including water molecules) around all the bubbles.

The thing is, you need muscle power—and a lot of time—to do this by hand. But you don't need us to tell you that if you've just finished the experiment! The electric mixer performs the same task but faster and without getting tired or bored (or complaining). You can see why machines have replaced humans for so many tasks.

CHAPTER 4

MICRO-SATELLITES

→ ☐ − ╋   X

It was bound to happen, wasn't it? Two of the most exciting areas of new technology teaming up, that is.

First up, please welcome the wonderful world of nano-technology—the drive to make things smaller and smaller. And meet its new friend satellite technology, which sends objects into orbit around the Earth.

Most satellites weigh more than a ton (2,000 pounds/906 kg), so it's not surprising that it takes a giant rocket—and enormous amounts of fuel—to send them into orbit. Think of how much easier it would be if your satellite weighed just a 10th of that amount. Or a 100th. How about a 10,000th? Yep, that's how small some of these orbiting critters are.

Next question: Is all of this a good idea? I mean, how would you spot one in the rearview mirror of your spacecraft? And is it really wise to fill the sky with things that are too small to be detected?

HOW LIFE IS BETTER

By the middle of the 20th century, engineers had designed rockets powerful enough to send objects into orbit around our planet. Those objects balanced between traveling off into space (because of their speed) and falling back to Earth (because even a speed that high wasn't enough to let them escape Earth's gravity completely). The result is an orbit—the object is constantly moving forward and falling back to Earth as it travels around and around our planet.

Having these objects, called satellites, way up there has been a real breakthrough. Some satellites can relay radio and television signals to each other or bounce them back to Earth. Others can monitor weather conditions or the effects of climate change. Still others can be used as telescopes, high above the blurring effects of the Earth's atmosphere.

Since the Soviet Union (USSR) launched the first satellite, *Sputnik 1*, way back in 1957, things have come a long way. Space exploration began during the height of the Cold War, when the USA and USSR were trying to outdo each other by showing off their engineering, technology,

Sputnik 1

The first human-made satellite to orbit the Earth, launched by the Soviet Union in 1957, took its name from the Russian word meaning "traveler." It weighed 184 pounds (83 kg) and took 96 minutes to make each circuit around the planet.

and military might. The name of the game was "Look at us—we're the best!" rather than trying to make people's lives better.

Of course, satellites would eventually improve people's lives in areas as wide-ranging as weather forecasts, international phone and television communications, or just finding the way to that darned lake (thanks, GPS). But launching each of them has been a costly business—largely because of their weight. The Titan II rocket, used to launch many "traditional" satellites, burns up about 125 tons of fuel (113,398 kg, or the weight of 40 elephants) for each launch.

Enter the microsatellite. Using smaller (and lighter) satellite alternatives will mean that smaller rockets can propel them into orbit. That advance in miniaturization (making something smaller) will really help to make them less expensive to launch, maintain, and replace. The result is a whole new generation of "small fry" satellites, which are already helping scientists monitor the health of oceans, check on irrigation, and even keep watch on illegal fishing or tree cutting.

Before microsatellites came along in the early 1980s, space exploration had been pretty much sewn up by the United States and the Soviet Union. Those countries had the money to spend and enormous infrastructure (launching facilities, backup equipment, and much more) in place to launch the massive rockets for heavy spacecraft (including satellites). With the technology moving in

COLD WAR

A period from the end of World War II in 1945 until the breakup of the Soviet Union (known as Russia today) in 1991, when the United States and its main rival, the Soviet Union, faced a lengthy standoff. They never fought each other directly in a "hot war." Instead, they tried to outdo each other in building weapons that could give them the advantage if a real war broke out.

a more compact direction, there are now more opportunities for other countries or companies to go into orbit. And more participants mean that satellites can do more jobs once they're up in orbit. The big satellites—which weigh tens of thousands of pounds—still pull their weight with communications, weather forecasts, and defense, though.

RELATED TECHNOLOGY

Scientists and engineers just love bouncing ideas off one another, and "nano" has become a go-to prefix (start of a word) in many areas.

Any chance of using this new "nano" technology to help some of the big stuff that's orbiting our planet? You bet! The International Space Station (ISS) is a semipermanent home for astronauts from many countries. They're constantly performing experiments in the zero-gravity environment that's their home for 6- or even 12-month missions. It gets a little cramped on board the space station, so engineers are constantly replacing

Getting Those Terms Straight

Aiming for smaller and lighter satellites has led engineers to agree on terms to describe the different sizes. Small is small, after all, but how small is "micro," for example?

Engineers and scientists all work with the metric system, so the categories are all in kilograms (kg). Anything under 500 kg (1,100 pounds) is considered to be a small satellite.

The next step down is to microsatellites, which are less than 100 kg (220 pounds). Smaller and lighter still are the nanosatellites, topping out at less than 10 kg (22 pounds). The smallest are picosatellites, or "picosats." They come in at less than a kilo (2.2 pounds)—that's about what that half-gallon of ice cream in your freezer weighs.

heating, communications, or navigation equipment with updated—and smaller—versions. And that means extra room to stretch out and feel more human.

TERRIFYINGLY AWESOME?

People already talk about "space junk," the collection of disused (or inactive) satellites that are in constant orbit. The US Department of Defense has identified more than 17,500 of these human-made objects orbiting the Earth. Lots of NASA missions have had near misses as space debris came zooming past.

Think how much more terrifying things could get if those "traffic lanes" got even more crowded with pesky minisatellites that could punch a hole through a spacecraft before they could even be seen! Could one of these high-speed "mosquitoes" cause the precious air to leak out of a manned spacecraft? It's not that far-fetched—astronauts already swap stories about minimeteors that have knocked bits off their spacecraft.

International organizations take these risks seriously. Like all spacecraft, satellites eventually come to the end of their working life. That's when things could get hairy. International guidelines on "space debris" call for defunct satellites either to move into "graveyard orbits" (orbits away from heavy traffic) or to return through the Earth's atmosphere, where they will burn up—just like most meteors.

Want to see what it's like to launch a microsatellite into orbit? Time to make your own launchpad and learn a thing or two about mass (weight) and energy.

Does it seem like this is an outdoors experiment? You bet it is. Try to find an assortment of small "satellites" with different weights—for example, a tennis ball, baseball, Ping-Pong ball, a grape . . . use your imagination!

YOU WILL NEED

- Scrap paper
- Tape
- Piece of wood or plywood (about 4 feet long, 4 to 8 inches wide, and 1 inch thick (1.2 m long, 10 to 20 cm wide, and 2.5 cm thick)
- "Test flight" objects to be launched
- Baseball or softball bat
- Heavy book (like a dictionary)

METHOD

1. Scrunch up a piece of paper and form it into a basic bowl shape. Don't worry about making it neat—it's just going to be a basic holder.

2. Tape your "bowl" in place at one end of the piece of wood. (It's going to hold the "satellites" in place before launch.)

3. Lay the bat down away from any windows (on houses or cars).

4 Find a good target—to match its height, not to hit—like a clothesline, a branch, or even a grown-up (willing to stand still!).

5 Lay the board, bowl side up, across the bat so that the bat marks the halfway point. You've made a basic seesaw.

6 Place a "satellite" in the paper bowl and adjust the seesaw so that the bowl end is touching the ground.

7 Take the book and hold it over the other end of the seesaw at exactly shoulder height.

8 Drop the book onto the seesaw and observe the flight of the satellite.

9 Continue with all your satellites, noting which one flies the highest.

DATA ANALYSIS

You've been looking at the relationship between mass (the various "microsatellites") and energy (the force of the book hitting the board). If a given amount of energy lifts a less massive object higher than a more massive one, then you'll need less energy (or less rocket fuel) to reach the same height. So you've seen for yourself how a much smaller rocket can send a microsatellite into orbit. It's cheaper, too: $40,000 compared with $50–$100 million.

CHAPTER 5

REUSABLE ROCKETS

→ – +   X

We're getting better and better at recycling or reusing everyday items. All the bottles, cans, paper, and plastic we recycle help us save money, reduce litter, and make the planet healthier.

Imagine how much money you'd save if you could reuse something enormous and expensive . . . like a rocket! That's exactly where billionaires Elon Musk and Richard Branson are heading with their plans to send the same rockets into orbit again and again. And when those rockets return to Earth, they're nearly ready for another launch.

And it's not just wealthy space-lovers who are getting in on the act. Big companies and small countries are seeing that new reusable rocket technology offers almost limitless possibilities. From cheaply launching satellites to resupplying space stations, these rockets could have tons of uses . . . but are they safe?

HOW LIFE IS BETTER

Many rockets are made of different sections, called stages. When a rocket launches into space, it can discard one or more stages once it has used up the fuel they contain. But instead of just dumping those sections, imagine if you could recover them back on the ground and reuse them. The cost per launch would come way down. (After all, we don't throw away the family car's gas tank every time we run low on fuel!)

Researchers are experimenting with the possibilities. The Indian Space Research Organisation (ISRO) had a successful test launch of a reusable rocket, the RLV-TD, in 2012. Then Elon Musk's company SpaceX launched the Falcon 9 rocket, with a reusable first stage, in 2015.

We've already found a way to make it easier to launch satellites, because they can be built much smaller and lighter (see page 25). If keeping to a budget is important, why not make those launches even less expensive? One way, of course, is to reuse the rockets that send payloads (the cargo they carry) skyward rather than starting from scratch and having to keep building new ones.

Plus, think about the ways rockets already help us. If countries and companies are able to launch them for less money, then we should all benefit from lower phone charges, better communications, more precise weather and climate observation, and dozens of other awesome advantages.

The sky's the limit—or is it even a limit? SpaceX has already unveiled a design for its Interplanetary Transport System (ITS), which would use reusable rockets to send spacecraft carrying hundreds of passengers to Mars. Each rocket can be reused up to 1,000 times, the company says. Other plans for reusable rockets are more Earth-based. Feel like traveling from Buenos Aires

The Space Shuttle

NASA's Space Shuttle was a partly reusable spacecraft that could enter a low orbit around Earth and return to land safely. The bits that weren't reusable were related to the solid fuel tanks that helped power its vertical launch. Once it discarded those tanks, the Space Shuttle resembled a stout airplane with stubby wings. NASA produced six Shuttles, with the first launch in 1981.

The Space Shuttle Program had many scientific and engineering triumphs, including studies of the Earth's atmosphere and the launch and repair of the Hubble Space Telescope. Altogether more than 800 astronauts (in crews of seven) flew on it. But the Space Shuttle Program also had two deadly accidents. In 1986, the Space Shuttle *Challenger* broke apart just after takeoff. And in 2003, the *Columbia* burned apart while reentering the Earth's atmosphere. In each case, all seven crew members died.

In July 2011, the Space Shuttle *Atlantis* was the final launch in the program, which had outlasted its original 15-year mission.

to Beijing or Los Angeles to Sydney in less than an hour? Low-cost reusable rockets might be just the ticket.

The lower cost also means that countries with less money to spend on space exploration can now join the club, either by launching their own rockets (as India and China have already done) or having equipment "hitch a ride" on another country's mission. Is it too much to claim that this technology might make space exploration more democratic?

RELATED TECHNOLOGY

The NASA Space Shuttles, which flew 135 missions between 1981 and 2011, are probably the most famous reusable spacecraft. But they weren't the first: The US military launched the X-15 rocket-powered aircraft in 1959. That high-altitude aircraft, capable of reaching the edge of outer space, introduced a new term to the world of aeronautics: Reusable Launch System (RLS), sometimes called Reusable Launch Vehicle (RLV). The X-15 would be attached to the underside of a B-52 airplane (the "reusable" element) and flown to an altitude of 8.5 miles (13.7 km). Then, already traveling at a speed of 500 mph (800 kmh), it would be released, or "launched."
The X-15's speed record for a manned, powered aircraft—4,520 mph (7,274 kmh)—remains unbroken, despite being set more than 60 years ago.

Competition is strong as companies and countries aim to develop ways to reduce the weight of rockets while maximizing their power. At the same time, they must use materials that can withstand the stress of multiple launches and the enormous heat from reentering Earth's atmosphere.

TERRIFYINGLY AWESOME?

Have you noticed something of a chorus in this book? Just after reading about a cool new way that technology can make life better and more exciting, you hit the phrase: "But what if it fell into the hands of the wrong people?!"

Reusable rockets are a great idea for helping poorer countries engage in "out of this world" science, and they're probably paving the way for much faster world travel. But making rocket travel more available could lead to problems. What if, for example, a terrorist organization or even a super-wealthy criminal got hold of these rockets? They could cause all sorts of damage, wreaking havoc on communications satellites or launching terrible explosives high above antiaircraft defenses.

And, of course, there is the risk of traveling on *any* spacecraft, reusable or otherwise. Eleven years after the Space Shuttle *Columbia* accident, Richard Branson's reusable spacecraft broke up and crashed in California's Mojave Desert. The pilot of the Virgin Galactic Company's VSS *Enterprise* was killed and his copilot seriously injured. In 2019 a SpaceX capsule exploded on its Cape Canaveral launch pad during a test. Luckily no one was near it at the time. But 22 of the 543 astronauts (roughly 4 percent) who have gone into orbit have died—a pretty scary statistic. Reaching for the stars continues to have dangers attached to it.

EXPERIMENT
INSTANT REPLAY!

The first book in this series, *The Book of Totally Irresponsible Science*, has a great rocket-building experiment. It gives you the chance to be creative—cutting out and decorating fins, forming a nose cone, and sending the rocket sky-high.

It's super fun, and anyone who's built one of those rockets can proudly say, "Well, it really *is* rocket science." But like most real rockets, it takes time and a good deal of effort to make one. This experiment is all about rockets, too, but with some big differences. The journey from drawing board to liftoff is way shorter, and once the rocket comes down, it's nearly ready to be launched again!

Did someone mention reusable rockets? Well, you've got one right here. Oh, and this should be pretty obvious: Do this experiment outside!

YOU WILL NEED

- Mug (big enough to hold the drink bottle)
- Effervescent (fizzing) Alka-Seltzer or vitamin tablets
- Empty plastic 10 fl. oz. (300 ml) drink bottle with pop-top lid
- Water

METHOD

1. Put the mug on a table or level space.

2. Break an Alka-Seltzer or vitamin tablet in half so it will fit easily into the bottle.

3. Unscrew the cap and fill the bottle halfway with water.

4 Quickly put the pieces of tablet into the bottle, screw the lid back on, and press the pop-up bit down.

5 Give the bottle a good shake, then place it upside down in the mug.

6 Stand back—in a few seconds, you'll have liftoff!

7 Prove that it's reusable by repeating Steps 1 to 6 quickly.

DATA ANALYSIS

You've demonstrated some of the real advantages of a reusable rocket. It was easy to build, reliable, and ready to be used right away. Plus, you got an extra science lesson or two. The fuel for the rocket was the rapidly expanding carbon dioxide gas that was produced when the tablet reacted with the water. The pressure from the gas increased until it blew the lid off, propelling the rocket upward.

Like any good aerospace engineer, you're also going to make clear observations—and some predictions based on those observations. Did you notice any difference in how far a second or third launch traveled? How about the condition of your "rocket"? Can you detect wear and tear produced by each launch? Any idea of how many more launches you might get before retiring this old rocket?

CHAPTER 6

AUDIO SPOTLIGHTS

We all know why people like to wear headphones. Of course, part of it is that they want to "turn off" the outside world and to retreat into their own world of rap, heavy metal, country and western, you name it. But there's another reason: They just don't want to force everyone around them to listen to their choice of entertainment.

Now imagine the opposite. You could get someone to listen to—or at least hear—a sound. That's easy! Just talk to them or play some music. But how about getting just one person in a large crowd to hear you, sort of like a spotlight on a singer?

It'll never work. Or could it?

First things first. Just what *is* sound? Well, sound is really a series of invisible waves or vibrations traveling through the air (or something else like water or even metal). And the sounds we hear are linked to the size of those waves and their frequency, or the number of waves per second. A higher frequency (more waves) means a higher-pitched sound.

Remember this, too: Sound is usually omnidirectional. That is, the sound waves spread out in all directions from the source of the sound. It's like a stone thrown into a pond: The ripples (waves) spread out.

Here's where it starts to get really interesting. The "directivity" (ability to be aimed like a spotlight) depends on the size of the sound source compared with the size of the sound waves it produces. If the source is bigger than the wave, then the sound can be directed. Most audible ("hear-able") sound waves range from about a few inches to a few feet. That's roughly the size of radio speakers, for instance, so we hear the sounds that come out. But so could someone standing behind a radio, because its speakers aren't any bigger than the sound waves coming out.

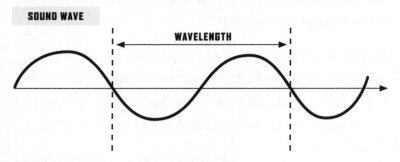

SOUND WAVE

WAVELENGTH

HOW LIFE IS BETTER

Can you see where this is leading? Audio engineers—the people who study and work with sound—know that humongous speakers can direct sound because they're bigger than the sound waves they emit. Or, it's probably easier to do it the other way around: Make the sound waves *smaller* than a normal-sized speaker.

That's where the audio spotlight comes in. Engineers have found a way of narrowing the wavelength of a sound so that it's much smaller than the source. They use a device called a transducer to combine audible sound waves with ultrasonic waves. Those waves are much too high for humans to hear. But mixed with regular sound waves, they narrow the audible sound into a directable beam, just as a spotlight falls on a singer but not the rest of the stage.

Just think about how many ways in which this technology can be—and is being—used. Audio spotlights now allow hospital patients to watch television or listen to the radio without disturbing fellow patients and without the need for headphones.

A teen center in a New York City library has an "audio corral." Inside it, young people can listen to loud music, play computer games, or even practice music. Outside the corral, other library users can read and browse shelves without having to cast a dirty look or say *Shhh!*

It doesn't take much imagination to think up dozens of other situations where one or just a few people should be able to hear something without disturbing those near them. Maybe it's a museum exhibition. Or in an air traffic control tower. Or even somewhere as ordinary as a local supermarket or toy store, where shoppers can learn about a specific breakfast cereal or Lego set.

WAVELENGTH

The distance between each peak (or trough) of energy being transmitted in waves. Audible sound waves have lengths ranging from several inches to a few feet. Light, on the other hand, has wavelengths that are hundreds of millions times shorter than an inch.

RELATED TECHNOLOGY

Audio engineers and sound scientists are also exploring other aspects of sound waves. It now appears that certain sound frequencies (and therefore wavelengths) have an effect on the human mind. Scientists have noted that humans have "natural frequencies" linked to the frequency of their own voice. Hearing an outside noise with the same frequency as the listener's voice can cause the body to release a type of endorphin (natural chemical) that creates a sense of pleasure or relaxation.

So when you think, "That song always makes me feel sad," you might be making a scientific observation. And it might even be possible—for better or worse—to change people's moods by altering what they hear.

TERRIFYINGLY AWESOME?

Come on! How can this be a bad thing, let alone terrifying? Well, can you imagine walking down a supermarket aisle and hearing a voice call you, "Hey! Over on aisle three—canned soups. Don't you think you really want to try the new Woodsman Beef Stew?"

You look around—you don't see anyone talking to you, and the other shoppers don't seem to have heard a thing. Then: "Yes, you! What's wrong, don't you like stew? Come on, think about it!"

This is perhaps taking the technology to absurd (and even funny) extremes, but it's not so far-fetched. In fact, companies are already using audio spotlighting in their advertising. Pedestrians walking through a New York City neighborhood in 2007 would have been startled to hear a woman's voice (coming from nowhere) saying, "It's not your imagination." It was all part of an ad campaign publicizing a TV program about unexplained events. The sound came from two large speakers on a rooftop above the seven-story billboard advertising the program. The woman's voice was focused on pedestrians using audio spotlight technology.

Is such advertising acceptable, or is it taking things too far? How do you think the public will react if it turns out that some people are making decisions about what stuff they read, watch, and buy because "they heard voices"?

EXPERIMENT
RIDING THE WAVES

Here's a great chance to learn more firsthand (or "first-ear") about how waves travel. Remember that the audio spotlight behaves a bit more like a visual spotlight than the way sound normally travels. That means it holds its narrow shape (like a flashlight's beam) because its wavelengths are so narrow.

This really simple experiment compares the waves of a light beam (which behaves like an audio beam) with sound waves. You'll be able to detect some real differences—but some surprising similarities!

YOU WILL NEED

- 2 friends
- 2 rooms, that share a wall and have a door connecting them
- Flashlight
- Whistle

METHOD

1 Have one friend stand in one room (holding the flashlight and whistle) and the other in the second room. Keep any connecting door open.

2 When both friends are ready, quietly ask the one with the flashlight to shine it five times at the wall between the rooms. (Make sure the other friend doesn't hear.)

3 Ask the friend in the other room to work out how many bursts of light came from the flashlight.

4 Now quietly ask the friend to blow the whistle seven times.

5 Ask the "other room" friend to work out how many times the whistle blew.

6 Ask the first friend to whisper four words and the other friend to figure out how many words were whispered.

DATA ANALYSIS

Although you've spent only a few minutes with this experiment, you've demonstrated some important features. First off, the fact that the whistle was audible shows that sound waves can bend around an object and then through an opening. The wall absorbed some of the sound energy, but not enough to stop the sound waves from diffracting (bending) their way through the doorway.

Meanwhile, the wall *is* able to absorb all of the energy from a weaker sound. Did your friend hear the other's whisper? Probably not. And the wall did the same with the light waves from the flashlight—the light energy was absorbed.

This is a really special chapter—two experiments! And although this is one of the simplest experiments in this book, it ties together two branches of science: acoustics (the study of sounds) and zoology (the study of animals). BUT you might not be able to do it at certain times of year.

"Wrong time of year?" Well, this experiment involves moths. That's right, moths flitting around an outside light. And that really means summer, or at least warm weather. So be patient. Wait for those nocturnal visitors to congregate, and then see what happens with your secret weapon—a bunch of keys!

YOU WILL NEED

- Moths flying around an outside light
- A bunch of keys (preferably a big bunch)

METHOD

1. Wait until you have a good view of the moths as they fly this way and that near the light.

2. Shake the bunch of keys to make a good jangling sound.

3. See how many moths stop flying and drop to the ground like stones.

We know that bats have exceptionally good hearing. They use echolocation to send out high-frequency sounds, called ultrasounds, and then analyze the echoes of those ultrasounds bouncing off stuff. Sort of like sonar on a submarine, it helps the bats to hunt or navigate past branches and buildings.

What's less well-known is that some moth species (let's hope you didn't find a dud!) can hear ultrasound, too. Okay, so what's this got to do with keys? Well, the jangling of keys produces not just sounds that we can hear but also ultrasound. That makes a moth think a bat's on its way to eat them! And when the moths hear it, the order is "Dive! Dive! Dive!" so they just plummet to the ground until the coast—or air—is clear.

CHAPTER 7

SOUND DISRUPTERS

→ − +   X

Imagine a firefighting training course with a tough old fire department captain trying to whip new recruits into shape.

"Okay, team. Let's have some fire-safety answers. Come up with the different ways that you can put out fires."

"Um, blowing them out?"

"Well, that's certainly true. Other ways?"

"With water."

"Yes, that's an important weapon in firefighting. More?"

"Special chemicals?"

"Good point. Certain electrical fires or fires involving other chemicals would get worse if you sprayed water on them. But I'm thinking of something else. I said, I'M THINKING OF SOMETHING ELSE!"

"Why shout? What's with the noise?"

"Great—you've got it. Noise. You can put out fires with sound. Just be sure not to get burned. . . ."

HOW LIFE IS BETTER

Let's start by getting one thing straight. We're not going to be able to extinguish a wide-ranging forest fire by blasting out heavy metal music until the flames back away. A sound disrupter will be more of a close-range tool, but one that could prove incredibly useful. The basic design being developed has a portable audio generator and amplifier. It sends sound down a tube to a handheld "gun" that can be aimed at a flame. The sound is at a low frequency, at the border between what we hear as deep bass sounds and what we actually feel as vibrations.

Why develop this new form of firefighting? Well, for a start, audio firefighting technology doesn't contain water, which is a precious resource and can ruin furniture and electrical appliances. Water also reacts dangerously with some chemicals—even producing explosions more damaging than the original fire. Ditto with the foam or chemicals sometimes used to fight fires. The audio approach doesn't involve making *any* physical contact with a burning object.

It works because of the basic link between sound and air. Most of us are aware that a sudden gust of wind—like the sort you make just before your birthday wish—can extinguish a flame. The wind (moving air) moves the candle flame away from its fuel source (the wax).

The sound disrupter also aims to separate the flame from its fuel source. That's because sound travels in waves through the air, moving the air with it. And depending on the size of those waves, the moved air might be enough to draw a flame away from its fuel.

So where and how could people battle fearsome flames with the power of noise? One example is a cockpit fire on a commercial flight. Airplane cockpits are jammed full of sensitive equipment, which could be damaged permanently or even destroyed if it got hit by a spray of water. A blast from a handheld sound disrupter could avoid that risk. Similarly, using conventional extinguishers to put out a fire in an even more enclosed—and zero-gravity—space (like on a spacecraft) would be disastrous. Foam and water would be floating inside the spacecraft for who knows how long.

Chemical and electrical fires can be extinguished with the same audio equipment, too. Up to now, firefighters had to know which extinguisher to use with each type of fire—often a problem when time is running out. With a sonic fire extinguisher, firefighters could have a powerful all-in-one tool.

RELATED TECHNOLOGY

Sonic disruption has already made its way into science fiction. Marvel supervillain Klaw uses a sonic cannon to blast opponents, and small-time crook Joe Chill invents a similar weapon in *Batman*. But it also figures in the real world. Blasts of high-intensity sounds that are too high (or low) to be heard can be used to cause dizziness, extreme headaches, hearing loss, and even brain damage (see below).

Luckily, sound technology can be put to more beneficial uses, too. Engineers and inventors working with sound disrupters are proposing a way of harnessing other cutting-edge technology to control much larger fires. Fleets, or "swarms," of drones (see page 169) could carry sonic disrupters into the heart of a forest fire, for example, able to combat flames well past the point where human firefighters could pass safely.

TERRIFYINGLY AWESOME?

High-volume sound has long been understood to be physically harmful, which is why many construction workers, airport ground mechanics, and stagehands at loud music concerts wear ear protection.

Normal-frequency sounds can be cranked up to torturous levels, too, and even innocent music can become unbearable if the listener can't turn it down or stop it. Sound disruption has a specific risk linked to it. The low frequencies that are most disruptive are often "felt more than they're heard," which means that these inaudible waves could be physically harming people without their realizing it.

Extremely high-volume sounds, often emitted through a sound cannon, can damage eardrums at levels above 130 decibels (dB). They can even leave people powerless to move (above 140 dB). Any damage to the ears upsets a person's sense of physical balance, so a sudden disruption caused by intense sound is unsettling. Police have used sound weapons to disrupt riots and other civil disturbances.

> **DECIBEL**
>
> A unit used to measure the power or intensity of sound.

Airport Sound Cannons

Airports, airlines, and passengers have become very concerned about a major threat to safe air travel: birds. That's right. Birds! Flocks of birds can fly directly into a plane's flight path and get sucked into the engines, which then conk out. The most famous example was the US Airways flight that had to make an emergency landing on the Hudson River in New York City in 2009.

Billions of dollars—not to mention many lives—could be saved if birds were driven away from these high-traffic air routes. With modern technology we can detect approaching birds and then switch on sound cannons to broadcast a range of directional sounds to disrupt and drive them away.

EXPERIMENT
BIRTHDAY BLAST
WARNING! ADULT SUPERVISION REQUIRED

People used to joke that the late, great singer Barry White, with his famous booming bass voice, could shake tables and rattle china plates when he sang those low notes. Well, Barry never caused any damage (that we know of) with his singing, but there is some testable science behind the power of sound.

This experiment is a cool way to learn more about something very hot—fire—and the part that sound can play in controlling it. And major bonus points if you can find an old Barry White CD or vinyl record!

YOU WILL NEED

- Large speaker connected to a stereo unit
- Table
- 6 votive candles (sometimes called tea lights)
- About 6 books
- Matches, with an adult to assist

METHOD

1 Position the speaker at one end of the table so it's aimed in toward the table.

2 Set the candles in a line leading out from the speaker.

3 You want the candles to be level with the actual sound source, so set them on the books if they need to be higher.

4 Have the adult light the candles.

5 Turn on the stereo so it's playing music.

6 Adjust the output so the bass is turned all the way up.

7 The candles should start to flicker and, depending on the strength of the bass, some of them will be extinguished.

8 You might need to turn the volume up a bit to get the best results, but make sure you're not disturbing anyone else.

DATA ANALYSIS

The simple explanation here is that the flame has been moved away from its fuel (the candle wax). A steady flame heats up the wax, causing it to melt and boil. And just like boiling water, the wax then becomes a vapor (the gas form of a material that is heated to its boiling point), which burns. The action of the sound makes the air turbulent, and just like a kid blowing out birthday candles, the disrupted air moves the flame away from the wax.

Low frequencies—like Barry White's deep bass voice—disrupt the air more than high frequencies. And speaking of low, we've suggested votive candles because they're short. The chances are your speaker will be low down (at about table level). It's the best way to keep the flame as close as possible to the source of the sound.

CHAPTER 8

ARTIFICIAL INTELLIGENCE

→ − + X

You've hit the heart of the book with this chapter. We're talking about a series of technologies that lie behind almost everything else you'll read about in these pages. Yep, artificial intelligence (or "AI" for short) really is the foundation of so much in the wide world of tech.

All the stuff you hear and learn about coding (devising instructions for a computer) is a stepping-stone to understanding just how far computing can go. "Artificial intelligence" goes even further—it refers to seeing whether computers can break down the barriers that people have always believed separated humans from computers. Those are things like translating, speech recognition, and—most importantly—independent thinking.

AI is already making life better for humans. But with each marvelous advance along the road toward "truly intelligent computers," we sometimes feel a little shiver of fear. Maybe things have gone a little too far, and too fast. A smartphone, after all, is one thing, but a super-intelligent computer with "a mind of its own"? Hmm . . .

HOW LIFE IS BETTER

The basic definition of AI is the ability of a machine or computer program to think, act, and learn like a human being. A computer engineer would probably rephrase that slightly—to them, AI machines interact with their environment and then act in a way that we'd consider to be intelligent.

Here are some examples. Online music-streaming services such as Spotify and Apple Music scan what you listen to so they can recommend what you should listen to next. Characters in video games react to your movements and decisions in real time as you play. Other AI applications have been around for decades. For example, Deep Blue (an IBM computer) beat world chess grandmaster Garry Kasparov in a match back in 1997. Something more down to earth? How about asking Siri or Alexa how many eggs you need to make pancakes? Now *there's* a practical and yummy way to use AI.

Computer experts realize that many people are worried by AI's growing power and presence in our lives. With that in mind, a number of projects planned or underway are loosely grouped as "AI for Good." These projects aim to help study, and maybe even solve, some

So What Is "Intelligence," Anyway?

Most people consider intelligence to be the ability to retain information and solve problems accurately and quickly. But many education and computer experts would say that true intelligence has more to do with adapting and building on what you've already learned and remembered.

Imagine reaching for a delicious-smelling hot dog grilling on a barbecue. It's too hot to touch, so you pull your fingers back in a hurry. You're be acting on instinct (which is unconscious action). But if you walked by another barbecue with an even more delicious-smelling weenie and kept both hands well away, you'd be demonstrating intelligence. You remembered that a hot barbecue burns, so you didn't let it happen again.

Artificial intelligence experts are interested in that type of intelligence. The burning barbecue is a basic example, but think of how much learning and remembering is needed for software in a driverless car (see page 77). For one thing, it would have to remember the saying you might hear one day in driving school: "A rolling ball is often followed by a running child." Then it would have to think about how rain affects braking, whether sunlight is in other drivers' eyes, whether there's enough gas in the tank to drive past the next gas station, and on and on.

of society's toughest problems using AI. For example, one group at Stanford University is using satellite images to focus on areas where poverty is highest. The computers receive a constant stream of data and make accurate predictions to help aid organizations decide which regions are experiencing drought, flooding, or warfare.

Artificial intelligence really comes into its own in the field of education. You've perhaps experienced some elements of education AI already, with online virtual tutors and even holograms (see page 153) that resemble historical figures. Higher education also benefits from AI, something that the US government and military have understood for a long time. DARPA (the Defense Advanced Research Projects Agency) has used a digital AI tutor to instruct new naval recruits on how to operate technical equipment. AI is able to sift through learners' data quickly to identify students' individual needs, just as a teacher can do with pupils in a classroom.

That use of AI has helped trigger a remarkable rise in large-group learning over the internet. Massive Online Open Courses (MOOCs) have allowed students from around the world to take university courses at the same time. So a student in Manila or Mexico City can "attend Harvard or Stanford" while never leaving home.

RELATED TECHNOLOGY

Here's something interesting. Just about every other chapter in this book deals with a technology that's related to—or depends on—artificial intelligence. Want some examples? Perhaps you already have audio spotlight (see page 41) technology but you need to know exactly when

Space Station Helper

An experimental AI robot with an animated cartoon face has been sent to the International Space Station (ISS). Called CIMON (Crew Interactive Mobile Companion), it's designed to instruct astronauts on how to carry out experiments and to answer questions about those experiments. Cimon weighs around 11 pounds (5 kg), but in the zero-gravity surroundings of the ISS, the head-shaped robot floats around like a balloon.

and where to use it. AI can trace patterns of shopping or library use to help you put that to the best use.

"Virtual nurses" could perform many repetitive tasks, such as taking patients' temperatures, blood pressure, and so forth, freeing up time for "real" nurses to interact with the patients. Overall, AI advances are predicted to save the US health industry $150 billion by 2026.

How about global positioning systems (see page 121)? That's already a great example of artificial intelligence being used constantly. A GPS system can remember which roads get crowded at school times, which are likely to get flooded in a downpour, and even which route has the most donut shops along the way.

TERRIFYINGLY AWESOME?

AI is one of the most terrifyingly awesome technologies that you'll come across in this book. The stakes are high, of course, because AI also has the chance to make life better on so many levels. But here's where the "what-ifs?" really hit home. What if, for example, AI becomes so advanced that computers really do become self-aware? What if a human couldn't tell AI and another human apart? Would super-advanced AI see humans as a threat, like an enemy to be destroyed? Uh-oh.

It's somewhere around this point where the discussion of artificial intelligence draws in experts from fields outside of science and technology. Philosophers wonder whether AI will be left behind as technology leads to something more advanced (and humanlike): something that's often called *artificial consciousness*. And things get even more complicated and serious when the debate asks, "Are such advanced computers really alive?"

Here's what seems to be a simple memory test, but it goes a lot further. By staging this contest with three of your friends, you can learn a lot about learning . . . or at least about *how* our memories work. Plus, you'll be doing the sort of activity that computer engineers do constantly with their computer programs as they aim to develop and improve artificial intelligence.

Make sure you have two rooms available, because you don't want any of the contestants accidentally getting a peek at the objects being viewed in the contest.

YOU WILL NEED

- 3 friends
- 20 photographs (cut from newspapers or magazines, or printed from the internet); they should be of familiar people or recognizable objects
- 3 sheets of paper
- 4 pens or pencils
- Scissors
- Tape
- Table or desk
- Clock or timer

METHOD

1. Ask your friends to wait in another room until you call them in one by one.

2. Before asking your first friend to join you, divide the photographs into two piles of 10 each—Pile A and Pile B.

3. Leave Pile A to the side, then, on a sheet of paper, write a one- or two-word description of each photograph in Pile B: for example, "Abraham Lincoln," "apple," or "cloud."

4 Cut out those descriptions and tape each to its photograph, making sure you don't block the picture.

5 On another piece of paper, write a list of things not related to any of the photos in Pile B. Again, keep it to one or two words each.

6 Ask your first friend to come in and sit at the table or desk.

7 Spread out the photos in Pile A (without labels) in front of them for 30 seconds.

8 Take the photos away, then hand your friend a blank piece of paper and a pen. Ask them to write down the names of as many of the images as they can in 30 seconds.

9 Take the paper away and replace it with the sheet of paper that you made in Step 5. Remember: That's the list of things unrelated to any of the photos.

10 Repeat Steps 7 and 8, having your friend look at the "unrelated" list for 30 seconds and then trying to remember the words when the sheet is removed.

11 Now lay out the 10 labeled photographs from Pile B that you made in Step 4.

12 Repeat Steps 7 and 8.

13 Do the same test (all three versions) with each of your other two friends.

14 You and your friends can "correct" the test papers to see which version got the highest score.

DATA ANALYSIS

The chances are that the sheet of paper from Step 4 (labeled photographs in Pile B) will have received the best results. That's because your friends' brains were able to use two different inputs (words and pictures) to help their memories. Teachers sometimes use a similar technique, called *multisensory instruction*, to help children learn. For example, pupils might learn how to spell "apple" more easily if they smell an apple while they look at the printed word.

IT (information technology) engineers also create software so that computers can "learn" in the same way, to help build artificial intelligence. It's a big feature in driverless cars (see page 77), too. The computers can assess road directions, slope, and traffic flows visually, teaching themselves in real time.

CHAPTER 9

THE WORLD WIDE WEB

→ ‒ + X

Here's something that most people use nearly all the time, and although it's a recent invention (well, compared to something like television, or the printing press, or hieroglyphics), we can't imagine life without it.

There's something else odd about the way we think of the World Wide Web (or "web," for short). Lots of us think it's the same thing as the internet. Well, it's not. Sure, the internet's important, and without it we couldn't really have the web. But when you come right down to it, the internet is really only the *way* that stuff travels all over the place.

The web is the stuff that's *doing* all that traveling—sound files, uploaded photos, lengthy documents about the composition of fertilizer. In other words, information of all kinds: fascinating, goofy, edgy, or maybe even a little bit boring. What could possibly be bad about such an explosion of information? Well . . . think about some of the nasty ways that information can be passed on, from unpleasant gossip to misleading magazine articles to instructions on how to make bombs. Then imagine a way of transmitting that kind of thing around the world in an instant.

How does that sound?

HOW LIFE IS BETTER

Anyone reading this book could probably write this section. Where to start? Whether you're using social media, writing a blog, playing games, or getting a head start on your homework, you're using the web. And just as most drivers don't know the ins and outs of carburetors, oil filters, and crankshafts inside their car engines, most internet users don't really know how the web works, either. Even though they rely on it constantly.

Since the terms "web" and "internet" are mentioned so often in the same breath, it's worth looking at what each of them really is and seeing what sets the web apart. The internet is a way of transporting content (information) to and from computers around the world. It acts as the underlying network connection for the World Wide Web to run on. The internet has sometimes been called the "information superhighway," because it involves things moving along it at high speed, like cars on a highway.

The web, on the other hand, is the software that allows you to use that content or contribute your own. It's just one of the many things that can run along the internet,

but it's by far the most widely used. For the web to work, our computers need to speak the same language. One of the most common sets of agreed-upon instructions is known as HTTP (hypertext transfer protocol).

Your computer, known as a "client," runs a program called a "web browser" to start the linking process. The browser uses HTTP to set up a series of exchanges with another computer (a "web server," or simply "server") to ask for information. These exchanges continue as the server sends information (picture files, text, sound files, and so on) to your computer. Eventually your computer has a full set of information, known as a web page—and that's what you see using your browser.

It's this wonderful ability to exchange information (academic articles, photos, funny videos of cats) that has made the web so exciting. Want to post a vacation photo on social media? Look for the best Italian restaurant in Tokyo? Find out who led the National League in stolen bases in 1948? The information is usually just a few clicks away.

The web was developed by British scientist Sir Tim Berners-Lee in 1989 as a way of helping scientists exchange ideas. In August 1991, it became available to the public and ushered in what many people describe as the New Information Age. The web now lets us shop online, chat with friends, learn about the weather (on Earth or on Mars), and even build our own websites to spread the word about our softball team or school trip to Mexico.

RELATED TECHNOLOGY

The first internet (and therefore web) connections for the public relied on signals transmitted along phone lines into a house or office. That form of link is still common, although more modern fiber-optic cables offer a much faster internet connection than normal phone lines. But nowadays, many people have no "landline" and their web connection comes through a Wi-Fi setup.

Wi-Fi (an abbreviation of "wireless fidelity"), like cell phones, uses radio waves to transmit information across a network. To do so, the wireless adapter on your computer (or phone) encodes data into a radio signal and transmits it using an antenna. A wireless router receives the signal, decodes it, and sends it on to the internet using a wired connection. From there it goes to another router (at the destination), which reverses the process: The information is converted back into a radio signal, which is then beamed to the computer's wireless adapter.

TERRIFYINGLY AWESOME?

Sir Tim Berners-Lee, who invented the World Wide Web, has often spoken about the risks posed by his world-changing invention. He had foreseen a technology that would provide a flow of information, free of either harsh government control or greedy profit-making users.

SIR TIM BERNERS-LEE

Unfortunately, both of those problems are part of the web, and people need to use care as they access information. The idea of a "limitless library" where information can be exchanged still exists because the web is so extensive. But some governments have found ways of blocking websites as a form of censorship so that information about their cruel

The Arab Spring

In the spring of 2011, demonstrators in Tunisia, Egypt, Morocco, Syria, and Bahrain began protesting the lack of political freedoms and poor living conditions in their countries. Many of the protests were organized through Facebook and other social media outlets so that people were able to gather quickly for their demonstrations. Word also spread from country to country in the same way, and the protests became known as the "Arab Spring." Several of the governments responded by blocking certain websites or even blocking Internet service entirely.

policies can't reach the wider world, and so that their own citizens can't learn the full truth either.

Why do some governments view the web as a threat? It's the same reason that political rulers 500 years ago feared the printing press: They lose complete power over what people can learn or say. The experience of the Arab Spring proves what a positive force the web can be ... but also how it can be seen as threatening.

Some government involvement, however, can be positive: Just think of the sorts of hateful things that people *can't* say on television or radio because of government broadcast regulations. But being free of control can also mean being free to promote racial or religious hatred, or even to plan attacks on people.

The web also allows people to create fake online profiles to take advantage of innocent users. This form of deception, known as "catfishing," can also happen to young people. It's a worrying modern twist on the traditional advice about not accepting rides from strangers.

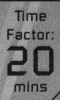

This experiment will help you understand how your browser is able to "translate" the information on a website and turn it into pictures, music, messages . . . all the things you see and hear when you open a web page. It's a really simple experiment to help you get a hang of some pretty complicated stuff.

You'll be called on to use your imagination as you do this experiment, which is really a neat demonstration. And like the web itself, the possibilities are limitless—your "secret message" can be different each time.

YOU WILL NEED

- Pencil or pen
- Piece of graph paper
- Friend
- Magic Marker

METHOD

1 With the pencil or pen, draw a dot outline of an image—a cat, a clown's face, or something simple like a circle—on the graph paper.

2 Now turn every dot into a number "1" by lengthening it a bit.

3 You should have an image made up of lots of ones.

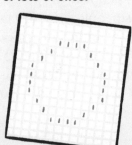

4 Fill as much of the paper as you can with zeroes about the same size as the ones.

5 With luck, your image will be a bit hidden in the mixture of ones and zeroes.

6 Now show it to your friend and ask them to use the marker to connect all the ones. The image should be revealed.

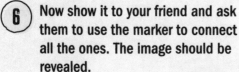

Well, we said it would be simple. But it's really demonstrating what a web browser does when it comes to a web page. The information on the web page is in a computer code that's made up of—you guessed it—lots of ones and zeroes. And that's it. It's called *binary code*, from the Latin word *binarius* ("consisting of two"). The patterns of ones and zeroes can be presented and understood in infinite ways, and computer images, text, programming instructions, and other data can be expressed in binary code. Of course, "decoding" a web page reveals a lot more than just a simple drawing, but the main point is the same.

CHAPTER 10

DRIVERLESS CARS

→ − +   X

For years, Americans arriving at British airports have been startled by signs advertising "self-drive cars."

"Just think of it—a car that drives itself! I get it. Must be that famous English sense of humor. Pretty funny."

Well, years ago you would probably agree that it was a weird idea. (In fact, the British still use that term to mean rental cars that you drive yourself—without paying for a chauffeur.) So it would be something to chuckle about when you had a cup of tea with your British friends.

Today it's not so strange or futuristic. Cars that drive themselves (or "driverless cars") have not only been thought about, they're already out there on the roads . . . at least as test versions.

Come on. There's got to be a catch! Can we really trust a car that has no human being in the driver's seat? The engineers say yes. But would *you* feel happy going for a spin?

HOW LIFE IS BETTER

Here's a new technology that divides the public like perhaps no other in this book. Some folks are convinced that driverless cars are a logical advance to a more modern, safer world. Others take the opposite view. They're convinced that driving is a job strictly for humans. No mere computer can possibly predict what or who might be coming around the next bend. And what about the pure fun of revving that engine and making some crisp turns?

What do you think? Would you sit behind the wheel of a driverless car zooming down the high-speed lane of an expressway? Or would you be absolutely terrified?

Apart from some highly publicized accidents in the testing stage, many automotive engineers and traffic-safety experts believe that driverless cars will reduce the number of accidents on the roads. Why? Well, for one thing, they don't get distracted by arguments in the back seat or fidgeting with the car radio. Instead, they rely on a variety of sensors to constantly judge and update their surroundings—things like radar, sonar, GPS, lidar, and other systems. Then they use computer vision to process that information.

Just like any powerful computer, the car's computer "brain" is constantly monitoring and reacting to data coming from different systems. Radar sensors placed along

Lidar

One of the most advanced tools in driverless car technology is called lidar, which stands for Light Detection and Ranging. This is the "next generation" beyond radar and sonar: Instead of using radio waves (like radar) or sound waves (like sonar) to "map" the surroundings, it uses laser light pulses. That means it can map a car's surroundings at the speed of light.

the edge of the car monitor the position of nearby pedestrians and vehicles. Video cameras read road signs and detect traffic lights. Light sensors detect the edge of the road as well as lane markers. Remember that the car itself—plus much of what it's monitoring—is moving, so

the data must be processed in a way that predicts movement. The constant processing of data sends signals to the steering column, brakes, and accelerator so that the car can make minor adjustments as it cruises (just like your mom's slight touches of the wheel or the gas pedal even when the road's straight and clear).

Can a human driver match that high-tech bag of tricks and be switched "on" full-time once the car starts? Supporters say "absolutely not" and that the roads will be safer once more driverless cars really take over. Reckless or drunk driving will be a thing of the past, and traffic will even be able to flow more smoothly because of fewer accidents.

Engineers are specific when describing cars with some or all of the new technology. For one thing, they refer to a wider term—automated driving. And within that you find five levels, ranging from Level 1 (Driver Assistance, which includes the cruise control most new cars have) right up to Level 4 (High Automation) and Level 5 (Complete Automation). It's those last two levels that really count as "driverless cars."

RELATED TECHNOLOGY

You may already have ridden in an "autonomous vehicle" without realizing it. Lots of airports have driverless trains to take passengers to and from terminals. The trains arrive punctually and travel smoothly, with barely anyone even wondering whether there's a driver in charge.

The French automaker Renault has designed a weird relative of the driverless car. It's called the EZ-PRO, and its designers were inspired by . . . a lunch box. Yes, a lunch box. The EZ-PRO is really a giant robot pod riding around on square-looking wheels. Measuring 16 feet by 7 feet (4.8 m by 2.1 m), it has a huge capacity and panels that open to the sides (that's the bit like the lunch box). Its job is to deliver food to city dwellers or packages to offices. But wait, it gets even stranger.

Setting out from a delivery center will be groups of these automated pods, with only the lead pod containing a human (called a "concierge," whose job is to check deliveries rather than to drive). Once the group enters a town or city, the concierge will organize which pods travel where, and the rest is automatic.

TERRIFYINGLY AWESOME?

Let's get one thing clear. For many people, the terrifying angle is absolutely real and not hypothetical. Since automated vehicles first appeared on public roads, four people have died in four separate accidents, to date.

Perhaps the answer about safety will only come once we get much more evidence. So far, the accident rate remains much lower than regular cars, despite these tragic deaths. But because the technology is brand-new, even a single death feels like one too many.

Driverless cars have stirred up fears and worries on other fronts besides safety. How

would you feel, for example, if your job disappeared almost overnight? And not just your job for a particular company—the actual work you'd been trained to do and had been using to support your family for years? That's probably what a whole range of drivers wake up worrying about—taxi drivers, bus drivers, long-distance truck drivers, or local delivery drivers.

Also, the whole ability for driverless cars to work depends on artificial intelligence (see page 59). That's the ability of computers to make independent decisions based on the data they receive. Complex programming feeds AI systems with commands based on stuff happening in real time: for example, "If a child runs out from between two parked cars, apply the brakes." But can human programmers ever design computers to anticipate *every* possible risk that a driver faces, each of which calls for a snap decision? Or say your family is driving on a highway and something big and round is about to roll off the back of a flatbed truck ahead of you. Is it a stone garden ornament (you'd better swerve) or just a beach ball (safer to keep going straight)?

EXPERIMENT
GOING FOR A SPIN

Time Factor:

30 mins

The lidar system lies at the heart of how driverless cars work—constantly gathering information and updating their assessments of what's happening around them. The systems used in cars have laser beams that are continually being sent out and reflected back.

And rather than having to spin the lasers around and around to get a 360-degree view, the lasers remain still and the beam is reflected onto a rotating mirror. In this experiment, you're going to use foil instead of mirrors to reflect light and send it out for your own 360-degree scan of the room. It's a hands-on version of the high-tech core of driverless driving.

YOU WILL NEED

- Aluminum foil
- 2 index cards
- Tape
- Poster putty
- A lazy Susan or record player
- 2 friends
- Small flashlight (with a narrow beam)

METHOD

1. Cut two pieces of foil, each slightly larger than an index card.

2. Place the pieces of foil on a table, shinier side down, and put a card on each piece.

3 Fold the excess bits of foil over the index cards and tape them in place (the foil on the other side of the card should be tight and flat).

4 Form a piece of poster putty into a ball about the size of a Ping-Pong ball.

5 Press the poster-putty ball into the back of one card, halfway across and not quite in the center of its length.

6 Press this card, shiny side up, in the center of the lazy Susan or record turntable. Press it down just hard enough to hold it in place. But it should be tilting because of the poster putty beneath it.

7 Have one friend shine the flashlight straight out at about chest height.

8 Another friend holds the second card so the shiny side is like a mirror, reflecting the flashlight beam.

9 That friend can practice moving the "mirror" around until they can get it to shine down.

10 Begin turning the lazy Susan or switch the turntable on at its slowest setting. The "mirror" on it should now be rotating.

11 Have your friends adjust the flashlight and second "mirror" so that the beam is pointing downward, onto the rotating mirror.

12 You should now see the beam rotating across the room at a full 360 degrees because the light has been reflected, and it's changed direction twice: once reflecting down from the handheld mirror and then angled out again from the rotating mirror.

DATA ANALYSIS

One of the best, and funniest, things about this experiment is the way you used either basic (lazy Susan) or old-fashioned (record player) technology to demonstrate something modern and futuristic. And although a driverless car's lidar system uses spinning laser beams to observe and assess, it's the same principle as using that household flashlight. After all, light reflects—whether it's visible light from a flashlight or the concentrated beam of a laser.

CHAPTER 11

VIRTUAL REALITY

→ − +   X

When many of us see 3-D movies, we shudder when dinosaurs seem to leap out from the screen or when spaceships from the Evil Empire scream up from behind and zoom on beyond. But we know that these are special effects, tricks of the moviemaking trade.

Virtual reality (VR) goes beyond that. It's not just sights and sounds that we see and hear—from Amazonian jungles or the Wild West or ancient Rome—it's the touch and smell of those experiences, too. We feel that we really *are* playing in the Super Bowl or walking on the Moon.

It's technology, all right, but technology that hovers on the border between imaginary and real-life experiences. And we all know that some real-life experiences can be pretty scary.

The technology behind a VR headset is advanced but it can be explained relatively simply. It taps into some of the ways in which our brains interpret sight and sound. One of those ways is stereoscopic vision, which gives us the impression of viewing depth. VR headsets use a pair of screens to display two images side by side. Our brains interpret the slight difference between the images as being caused by depth, so the image seems three-dimensional. (Those 3-D glasses at the movies do something similar.) The goggles have built-in sensors to monitor head movement—and change the images accordingly. That strengthens the 3-D illusion while we make out the VR images.

VR uses a technique called spatialized audio to create the impression of 3-D sound. By placing a sound "source" close to the visual image of, say, a pirate or gladiator, the technology allows our brains to believe that the image is real. The deception is strengthened because of something called the McGurk effect—another way in which the brain interprets input from the senses. It describes the way the brain can be tricked into merging unrelated "inputs"—we seem to "hear" the audio input from one source coming from something completely different (which isn't making that sound).

Virtual Reality Beginnings

The first VR plans were developed in the late 1950s. The "Sensorama" was described as an "experience theater" by its inventor, Morton Heilig. It combined a stereoscopic color display with sounds, movement, and even smells blown from the machine. The first head-mounted display (HMD) was developed in 1968. By the 1990s, companies such as Sega were producing headsets for home entertainment use. The launch of the Oculus Rift in 2016 opened the market for VR devices, and today there are dozens of suppliers.

On one level, virtual reality is part of a long line of ways the public can be tricked by "smoke and mirrors"—images that deceive the brain. Don't forget that motion pictures, or movies, aren't moving: They're a series of still images run past the eyes so fast that they seem to be moving.

The experience of using VR, however, goes way beyond watching movies or television. It combines advanced computer graphics and sound files to create an artificial—but totally believable—environment. It does this first of all by being immersive, meaning that you really feel part of its world (whether it's the Taj Mahal, one of Saturn's moons, or a bobsled run). And that in turn requires the VR experience to be interactive: What you see and hear with your VR device depends on your own movement and input. And what's more, you need to be able to explore. You want to get inside that shipwreck or open the door leading to the castle's dungeon.

HOW LIFE IS BETTER

It's easy to see how VR will make entertainment and gaming much more exciting. Imagine that you've just stepped onto a Viking raiding ship or a tightrope stretched across Niagara Falls. VR entertainment is already a major industry and looks set to continue growing.

Virtual reality also has thousands of other ways of helping us. VR simulators can help pilots train to fly aircraft or teenagers learn to drive cars. Medical students can learn how to perform operations without having to practice on dead bodies (a traditional med school practice—yikes). Medical scientists from Oxford University found that conquering height challenges with VR can help three out of four patients overcome their fear of heights (by far the most common phobia).

Virtual reality can also be a great tool for medical breakthroughs on a microscopic level. Scientists at Benaroya Research Institute in Seattle used VR to study lysosomes. Those are structures in cells that help clean up the insides of the cells. The research team was puzzled that these lysosomes seemed to be inside the nucleus of each cell they were studying—because that's not where they're supposed to be.

The researchers developed a special VR viewer to see the cells in three dimensions. With the aid of the viewer, they could see that the lysosome was not just outside the nucleus, but above it. The two-dimensional view couldn't make that clear, but the 3-D version solved the mystery.

RELATED TECHNOLOGY

Augmented reality (AR) is sort of a compromise between the virtual and real worlds. It uses a live image of the real world—say, seen through a smartphone screen—as its basis. Then it places layers of other information over it. Unlike VR, which provides an alternative reality, AR allows viewers to experience the real world, but "augmented" (added to) by computer-generated information.

For example, you might be standing in Miami Beach, pointing a smartphone or tablet at the buildings and palm trees and colorful cars. Then, appearing over that main image, you could see smaller images or text saying "good ice cream shop" or "best entrance to the beach." Or maybe you were swept up in the Pokémon Go craze. Players used their smartphones to capture and battle Pokémon who appeared to be out on the street, inside buildings, and even in players' homes.

Google Glass (see page 145) uses similar technology to overlay images on the eyeglass view. AR is also an incredibly useful tool in industry. Engineers can hold up tablets to complicated machinery, revealing which elements need replacing or are due for a tune-up.

TERRIFYINGLY AWESOME?

Like some of the other tech in this book, virtual reality has a moral dimension. It makes us think a lot about whether it's right or wrong, helpful or harmful.

Many people feel thrilled at first, then a little uneasy, then genuinely terrified by a technology that can make the unreal and imaginary seem real. How do we feel about VR games, for instance, where "bad guys" or simply "enemies" can be killed realistically? How might that effect the ways we think about other people in the real world? Some scientific evidence suggests that certain people become violent after watching violent movies or playing violent games. Researchers sharply disagree over the effects of such entertainment, but super-realistic VR may up the ante even more.

Okay, this one is going to call on your acting skills. Maybe you've seen foreign movies that have been dubbed into English where the actor says something but his lips keep moving for a second or two afterward. You've got to make sure you don't wind up looking (or sounding) like him.

Why? Because you're going to be heading right into the heart of virtual reality—the way in which it seems to trick our senses. You've probably heard the expression "Things aren't always what they seem." This experiment will prove the truth in that saying. It's pretty simple, but it sheds light on some pretty complicated ideas.

YOU WILL NEED

- Recording device (most smartphones will do the job well)
- An audience

METHOD

1. Use your phone or other device to record your voice.

2. Record yourself repeating the syllable "ba" over and over for 30 seconds.

3. Have the recording prepared to play.

4 Ask your audience to gather in front of you and ask them to repeat what they will hear you say (in the recording that you're about to play).

5 Here's where the timing comes in: Play the recording and silently say "ba" to match the syllables in the recording.

6 Ask the audience what they heard. They'll say that it was "ba."

7 Now get the recording ready to play for another 30 seconds.

8 Repeat Step 5, but this time silently say "fa" in time with the "ba" sounds in the recording.

9 Ask the audience what they heard. Most of them will probably say "fa."

DATA ANALYSIS

This is the McGurk Effect in action. The sense of sight can override "reality," just like in VR. You never made the "fa" sound, but the second time you played the recording, it looked as though you did. Even if they don't realize it, people often look at the shape of your mouth when you speak to determine what sounds you've made. We're all natural lip-readers! The way your lips looked made it seem as though you were saying "fa" . . . but you were saying "ba" all along.

CHAPTER 12

THE CLOUD

A lot of new technology seems hard to understand for people who like to be able to touch, see, or smell the things around them. Software and web designers respond to that by finding ways to use familiar, three-dimensional images to describe features or developments that are a bit . . . well, computer-y.

Think of a computer "file," "folder," or the trash can icon that shows what happens to deleted files. Those are images that make sense even to someone who's never used a computer. Here's another term to add to those: the cloud.

It's where tons of data can be stored away from your computer (so it doesn't use up memory), but you can retrieve in an instant. It's all up there somewhere in the cloud, after all.

But some people's concerns about the cloud—or even computers themselves—reflect basic fears that just won't go away. "Don't put all your eggs in one basket" and "always keep a spare" have always been sound advice. With so many people relying solely on the cloud, maybe these sayings are even more fitting than ever?

HOW LIFE IS BETTER

You may already know that cloud computing gives us some awesome, cutting-edge benefits like storing all your songs, photos, and more. Even computer haters could come to appreciate a technology that lets them keep track of (and retrieve instantly) just about every file they can think of, from important medical documents to silly pet videos. But what is it, really?

For something so wide-ranging, the cloud is pretty simple to explain. It's a way of storing and accessing applications and data on the internet instead of local servers or computers. Think of the arrangement as having a front end (the user's computer and the software needed to link to the cloud) and a back end (the server). Linking them is a network, which is usually the internet. The system works by letting the cloud's powerful array of computers and data-storage systems do all the "heavy lifting" (like running just about any type of computer program).

Because of the cloud's power and capacity, these programs run quickly—far more efficiently than on most personal computers. In practice, it means that lots of your software and files are sent via the internet to be stored. You pay a company to do all this storing, but it means you can get that stuff whenever or as often as you need it. Then back it goes to the cloud.

Another main attraction is that the cloud frees up memory on all your devices—whether they're PCs, laptops, tablets, or phones. And having more memory "down here" means

SERVER

A server is any combination of software and hardware that provides services such as file storage and programs to clients (computer users). If it's part of the client's computer, then it's called a local server. Remote servers, on the other hand, are much more powerful. They're located somewhere else, and clients access them through a network. Cloud computing uses remote servers to provide services and information to clients.

that those devices can work more smoothly. The cloud isn't just for storage, either. People can use its power to share files—such as lengthy videos—quickly with their friends and family.

One great way to understand a concept like the cloud is to hear from kids themselves. One technology website interviewed some slightly older children and asked them to explain it. The website pointed out that these preteens have never known a world without iTunes or Amazon, so it's no surprise to see how confident they are about how computing (and especially the cloud) can help.

Here's one take on the subject: "In cloud computing, information's not stored on my computer, it's stored in the cloud. And this cloud can be accessed by any computer anywhere in the world."

Would a 9-year-old in 1980 have understood any of that? Would a 9-year-old in 1980 even have understood the word *accessed*? It's a fast-changing world, and the cloud is just part of it.

RELATED TECHNOLOGY

The sky's the limit with how the cloud can tie in with other technologies. One obvious use is through cloud-based "Software as a Service" (SaaS). Rather than having to pay a tech company a large sum to use its software (which an individual might need only once or twice), clients can use a pay-as-you-go or on-demand method of paying only for what they need to use.

Improved broadband connections (as well as much faster Wi-Fi technology) have already allowed more people to use the cloud. Both types of connection are getting faster all the time.

Grid computing is another way of linking computers through a network. This technology allows a large number of computers to work together as a "virtual supercomputer" that can tap an enormous database. Teaming up allows scientists and researchers to perform calculations that would take years to complete on individual computers.

How to Tell the Kids

The bosses of some tech companies were asked how they would explain the cloud (or cloud computing) to a 5-year-old. Some of the answers were full of advanced computer terms, making you wonder whether they'd ever met—or been—a 5-year-old. Other answers hit the nail on the head. Which one makes the most sense to you?

"Cloud computing is IT delivered as a service rather than as a product, like watching movies on Netflix . . . rather than buying them all on DVD or Blu-ray."

—Paul Evans

"Cloud computing is the stuff that makes Google and Facebook work. It's having lots of computers working together when you need them, shared between everyone."

—Ashley Unitt

"Think of the cloud as a big imaginary box in the sky which can hold all of your important things so that you can get to them whenever you like."

—Annrai O'Toole

TERRIFYINGLY AWESOME?

The cloud can help many of us to get more clutter-free. But what would happen if the remote server (operated by the cloud-computing company) that's holding on to your information crashes—just as we've all experienced with computers or laptops, or even with internet service providers? That really would be pretty terrifying—a virtual version of accidentally throwing away your birth certificate or entire baseball card collection.

The big cloud companies are aware of those potential emergencies and of people's fears. They go out of their way to reassure the public that their enormous system of backups will preserve all the information. Many companies even have backup servers on different continents and are prepared for the worst, from earthquakes to hackers to dinosaur attacks. (Well, maybe not that last one.)

So in the end, it's up to the public to decide how terrified or reassured they feel about this development in file storage and sharing. As the experts tell potential investors in the stock market, "Don't invest more than you're prepared to lose." Can you adapt that advice to storing data on the cloud? It's your call.

It's time for a bit of teamwork. There's nothing like getting those competitive juices flowing to understand some complex computer science.

At its heart, though, cloud technology is all about finding the fastest, most efficient way of storing information. Ever wonder why computer "files" got their name? It's because computer experts didn't want their work to seem too weird and different from what people were familiar with. And most people were familiar with paper files that were put in cardboard "folders" (hmm, another computer term).

So we're getting back to basics with this experiment. We're showing how "files" (or playing cards, in this experiment) can be stored quickly and efficiently. A bit like the cloud, really.

YOU WILL NEED

- 9 people (to form 3 teams of 3)
- A shoebox
- 3 decks of playing cards (no jokers)

METHOD

1. This experiment can be done inside or out, but the bigger the space, the better the payoff will be.

2. Ask everyone to form three teams of three: Team A (floppy disk), Team B (USB stick), and Team C (cloud). You'll be the umpire.

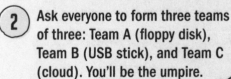

3 Place the open shoebox about 6 feet from where the teams are standing.

4 Shuffle each deck of cards carefully and hand one to each team.

5 Tell each team that they must sort the cards into four piles (clubs, diamonds, hearts, spades) and take them to their team's "target"—the far side of the room (for Teams A and B) or the shoebox nearby (Team C).

6 Explain another rule: Team A can take only one card at a time to their target; Team B can take as many as a whole suit (13 cards); and Team C has no limits at all.

7 Ask the teams to start on your cue. See who finishes first.

DATA ANALYSIS

What you've seen (and produced) is a demonstration of how and why the cloud is so attractive. Think of those playing cards as data (such as files), and you'll get the idea. You're "saving" or transferring these files just as you would with a computer. The experiment demonstrates how each advance—up to and including the cloud—has allowed more data to be stored, and also how much faster each can perform those tasks.

You have probably never heard of floppy disks (Team A), but compared to today's technology they were really primitive, with 1.44MB of memory. USB sticks (Team B) can hold up to 512GB of memory (more than 500,000 times that of a floppy disk), but that's nothing compared to the potential of the cloud. One study estimates that the cloud can hold one exabyte—or 1,152,921,504,606,846,976 bytes—of data.

CHAPTER 13

THE INTERNET OF THINGS

→ − +   X

What does your garage door have to do with your kitchen lights? Maybe you heard your dirty laundry basket talking to the family car? Or perhaps it was a broken water pipe under your street crying out, "I'm about to leak—fix me!"

These random things are all examples of the Internet of Things (or IoT). It's a network of everyday gadgets that communicate with one another and their owners via the internet to make sure that they work as they should and when they should. Forget for a minute about using cutting-edge software to send spacecraft to Mars and think of how all that instant-communication stuff can help us in our daily lives.

It's all pretty cool, turning normal life into a web of activity using the internet. But what if some of those signals go astray, so that the neighbor's lights keep going on and off or you get 10 pizzas delivered when you haven't ordered any? Sounds like a comedy? Could be more of a disaster movie!

HOW LIFE IS BETTER

Just when people were beginning to understand the internet in the early 1990s (even if they didn't use it very much), the World Wide Web (see page 69) came along. People began to realize that it was the internet that connected things and that computers were the things being connected via the web. Then along came laptops, and people realized that they too could be connected via the internet, even outside the house. Then smartphones, some smartwatches . . . where does it end?

Well, that's just the point. The Internet of Things is a connection between "things" that we never before thought could be internet-enabled computers—stuff like oven doors or sewage pipes or washing machines. But all of these can be built or modified to connect with each other and you to create a "smart home."

That "connectivity" provided by Wi-Fi is one of the technologies that your smartphone or laptop uses to go online. A Wi-Fi network, like a cellphone network, uses radio signals to send and receive information. A computer (in this case, it could be a household thermostat)

uses a wireless adapter to translate data into a radio signal and transmit it using an antenna. A wireless router receives the signal and decodes it, sending it on to the internet. The opposite process takes place at the other end: A router receives the internet data and converts it into a radio signal that's sent to the wireless adapter of the other computer (such as a smartphone controlling your home's temperature). Another conversion turns the radio signal back into data.

In many ways, the Internet of Things is easier for newcomers to grasp than some other IT (information technology) concepts that make people's eyes glaze over. Let's think of something that's pretty familiar to all of us—you're on the way home and can't wait to chow down your favorite snacks. With the Internet of Things, you'd be able to connect your smartphone with the refrigerator and get a live view of what's in there. Or you could turn up the heat remotely, have a kettle for hot chocolate timed to receive a signal from your alarm clock, and program the blinds to open and close depending on the level of light outside.

RELATED TECHNOLOGY

Like so many of the other technologies in this book, you've probably experienced a version of this one already. Here are a few examples of how it's already in operation, even if you didn't realize it was the Internet of Things at work. Maybe you've used a virtual assistant device like Google Home or Amazon Alexa. Or driven into a city with your parents and gotten real-time information about where to park. Or wondered how the heat at your friend's house went on just when that icy wind hit unexpectedly.

You could probably think of more. In fact, reading through these pages, you'll find it hard to find a technology that *isn't* somehow tied in with the IoT. "Everything connects," as they say.

TERRIFYINGLY AWESOME?

At first it might seem almost funny, rather than terrifying, to imagine the Internet of Things going wrong. What's the worst that could happen—your garage door opening and closing all night? Your toaster asking you whether you want another slice of bread over and over? But think again—having "things" linked ever more closely carries a lot of risks with it. For example, what if the Wi-Fi—which does all the linking—fails? Would you even remember how to turn on the washing machine? What if the garage door closes and there's no handle to open it "in person"? Speaking of doors—or speaking doors—how do you get in if your door is voice-activated and there's no knob?

Recent years have seen a number of highly publicized attacks on computer networks owned by both governments and private companies. These cyberattacks aren't just hypothetically terrifying; they're already happening, and they are a serious threat to international security.

Just as individual computer users have software to protect them against computer viruses and malware, larger networks at national and international levels constantly try to upgrade their protection against cyberattacks. Sweden, for example, has always been an early adopter of new technologies, including the IoT. Now some Swedish security experts are concerned about the safety of their country's computer network.

Many of Sweden's government departments, right down to the local level, are connected in a system that could be described as an Internet of Things. Like so many things in Sweden, it works efficiently, making sure that different national regions have enough natural resources, police protection, snowy roads plowed, and so on. The network can even monitor things like when garbage trucks need

CYBERATTACK

An attack on a computer network or system by an individual (a "hacker") or organization that has been able to get past security barriers.

a tune-up. Any link in this complicated chain could become an entry point for an attack that could affect the entire system—and the security of the country.

Another feature of the IoT—in fact, one of its big selling points—has raised alarm bells. Being "always connected" to your house keys, the thermostat at home, your email account, and more means that information about you is going back and forth the whole time. In a way, everyone is being watched—where they go, what they buy, how late they arrive home. Many people think that sort of snooping is a price worth paying in return for all the advantages of the IoT. But imagine if a president or a general could be monitored by an enemy because of all the "personal" information going back and forth.

> **MALWARE**
>
> A shortened form of the term "malicious software." It refers to a broad range of software that is harmful to a computer user. Computer viruses are just one type of malware—it also includes other software that can "infect" computers and either harm them or copy sensitive information.

EXPERIMENT
HOW ARE "THINGS"?

A smart home is probably the best example of the Internet of Things in action. After all, it's a way of getting familiar objects and machines (like garage doors, thermostats, ovens, and locks) to speak to you—and each other.

The key to all this chatting is, of course, the Wi-Fi connection. The same signals that keep your smartphone, laptop, or tablet connected also link these silent objects and let them communicate.

Don't worry—we're not going to imbed microchips in you to get you connected. But using smartphones, you can team up with your friends to demonstrate how a home can "smarten up." You can have some fun along the way, surprising a grown-up on his or her way home. Just make sure you know when they're likely to return—from work, or a run, or a visit to the dentist. It doesn't matter whether you live in an apartment or a house—you can adapt the experiment to see what works best. Plus, you can make it even more impressive by adding more actions.

YOU WILL NEED

- 2 friends (or more if you want to beef up the experiment)
- Cell phones (or walkie-talkies turned down low) for you and all your friends
- Front door (to apartment or house)
- Coffee maker
- Portable radio (preferably one that can be turned on with a remote) placed in the kitchen
- Unsuspecting adult (whose routines you know)

METHOD

1. Each volunteer should have their phone on silent but also a text message ("to all") waiting to be quickly sent.

2. Hide somewhere just within sight of the front door (possibly on the porch, or down the hall for an apartment).

3. Volunteer A is inside the front door.

4. Volunteer B is in the kitchen.

5. When the adult is three steps from the front door, text "approaching."

6 That is the cue for A to open the door and hide nearby and for B to turn on the coffee maker.

7 As the adult enters, A texts "entered."

8 That's the cue for B to turn on the radio and hide.

9 If you pull it off, you'll have demonstrated how a smart home would welcome its owner after a hard day's work or a morning workout.

10 Of course, with more friends to help, you could make this even more involved. Just don't scare the adult too much!

Although you could make this experiment far more complicated by using your imagination to add more "payoffs," it would still remain very focused on what makes smart homes (and the Internet of Things) work. And that's the idea of connectedness and communication.

Even the earliest computers had programs that used the terms "if" and "then." So, if you were running a calculation, you could write "*If* x (representing a number) is less than 10, *then* multiply it by 3." And "*If* x is greater than 10, *then* multiply it by 5." Those commands are called conditional statements. Of course, modern computers don't just do arithmetic—they can perform or trigger a wide range of actions using conditional statements. That's at the heart of the Internet of Things, and now you'll see how the popular Internet of Things web service (IFTTT) got its name. It stands for "If This, Then That."

IFTTT uses applets (internet-based programs) to link devices so that actions can be performed. A "trigger" (such as a car entering a driveway) starts an applet, which sends a signal to perform an "action" (opening the garage door). In this experiment, you and your friends are doing the work of applets, signaling to each other and performing the actions.

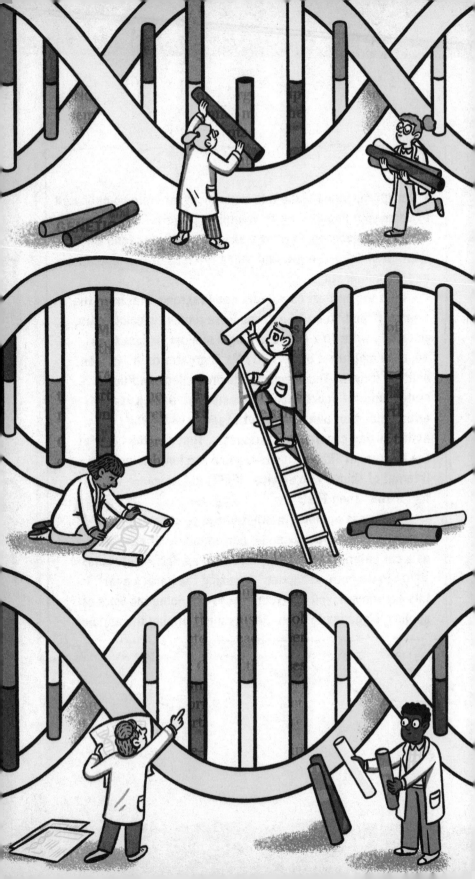

CHAPTER 14

GENOME TECHNOLOGY

→ − +   X

We've all heard people say things like, "Oh, look—she's got her mother's eyes," or "Twins run in our family," or "What a messy room—he takes after his father" (well, your author heard that a lot). And even if we're not scientists, we figure it all has to do with what we've inherited from our parents, and their parents before them.

If we look a little further, we come across the words *gene* and *genetics*. For more than 150 years the world has known that genes are how those qualities (or traits) are passed on, but it's only in the last 60 years that scientists have figured out how they work.

That's where another word comes in: *genome*. It refers to the complete set of genes in every cell of a living thing. And what's more, scientists have begun finding ways to alter those "blueprints" so that the change sweeps through every cell.

Great! A scientific way to eliminate the messiness gene or to make it harder for diseases to be passed on. Yep, except it's also a way to create . . . well, who knows what in the next generation.

Okay, hold on tight, because you have about 4 million years' worth of human development to understand in the next couple of pages. By the end, you'll work out what we mean by genetic engineering.

"Deoxyribonucleic acid" is a bit of a mouthful, so most people refer to it by its abbreviation: DNA. It's a molecule, or collection of atoms, and that collection is shaped like a long chain in the shape of a twisting ladder. Scientists refer to that shape as a "double helix." DNA is often described as a blueprint for an organism (living thing)—anything ranging from bacteria to blue whales to human beings.

Organisms may be very different from one another, but we all rely on DNA to keep things right. Here's how:

1. DNA helps amino acids line up accurately to form proteins;
2. Proteins group together to form cells;
3. Cells group together to form tissue;
4. Tissues form together to form organs; and
5. Organs, once they're all in place, add up to an organism. Presto!

Remember that DNA is shaped like a ladder with "rungs." A DNA molecule might have millions of "rungs," each holding a pair of chemicals. Scientists have worked out that only four different kinds of chemicals (called nucleotides) appear on this lengthy strand.

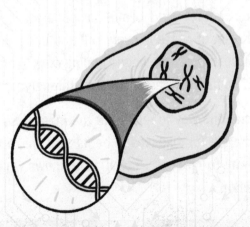

They have identified those nucleotides by letter: A (adenine), C (cytosine), G (guanine), and T (thymine). If you imagine pulling the DNA rungs apart, you'd find how those same four nucleotides form an incredibly long series of letters. Here's where scientists figure they'd hit pay dirt. They can look at the long string of chemicals of just one half of the DNA to see its chemical sequence, or "genetic code."

Aha! Eureka! We've come across the word *gene*, sort of. That's familiar!

Let's tie things up now. A gene is a section of DNA that is responsible for developing the makeup of an organism—how it looks and also how it behaves. And genes are what get passed on from both of your parents, so you might have inherited your dad's curly hair, your mom's gift for singing, and a good sense of humor from both sides.

That's a big introduction to make it easier to understand an even newer development: genome technology.

HOW LIFE IS BETTER

The wider understanding of genes and inheritance (how genes are passed on to the next generation) has been a huge help to doctors and other medical professionals. Understanding a patient's "genetic makeup" helps to identify diseases or even the likelihood of acquiring certain diseases later on.

Long before genetics were fully understood, it was already observed that certain groups of people were more likely than others to contract particular diseases. For example, doctors were able to conclude that a blood disease called sickle cell anemia was most common among people with African or southern European ancestry.

That type of "early warning" has served doctors well. The much more detailed information from recent advances such as the Human Genome Project (more on that soon) will help them identify and treat far more diseases.

All of which leads to the subject of "genome editing." This is a way of targeting specific genes (possibly disease-causing) and modifying them so that the risk is reduced. In one technique called CRISPR, for instance, scientists can "cut" a sequence in an organism's DNA using a chemical. It's called "editing" the genome to remove or alter a sequence. When the cell repairs the cut, the DNA remains in the new, "edited" form with the changes in place. This technique can treat diseases such as leukemia, a form of cancer that affects the blood. It could also help prevent future generations inheriting a disease trait.

GENOME

An organism's complete set of DNA, including all of its genes. Each genome contains all the information needed to build and maintain that organism.

All of this might seem to be concentrating on humans, but since DNA is present in all organisms, we can use genome editing for other purposes. Genome editing of mosquitoes can eliminate their ability to transmit malaria, a disease that's often deadly for humans. Scientists can also edit the genome of crops to make them more disease-resistant, or they can help livestock to cope better with changing environmental conditions.

RELATED TECHNOLOGY

The Human Genome Project was an international effort, led by the United States, to map out the sequence of the human genome and to identify all of the roughly 25,000 genes. (Yes, that's a whole lot of genes.) It began in 1990 and finished its task two years early, in 2003.

The project opened up many lines of important research into DNA, proteins, genes, and exactly what it is to be a human being. The most immediate benefit is to medicine. The new information will help medical scientists identify and treat diseases that are passed on genetically.

Some results of this research also wind up closer to home. Companies now offer DNA ancestry tests, based on a tube of spit (yuck!) that customers send off for analysis. A typical result might tell the customer that she's 30.2% European, 4.1% Western Asian, 0.1% North African and Sub-Saharan African, and so on . . . maybe even including a dash of Neanderthal!

TERRIFYINGLY AWESOME?

Ever seen *Jurassic Park* or any of its sequels? Those movies took a bit of real science—the bit about DNA containing all the building blocks for an organism—and turned it into something really scary. T. rexes and velociraptors, extinct for more than 65 million years, were brought back to life because traces of their DNA had miraculously been preserved in fossils.

On a more realistic—but still terrifying—level, it's easy to imagine what might happen if some of this genome editing goes wrong. Instead of treating diseases or other medical conditions, altering the genetic code could lead to terrible mutations, with patients suffering terribly. Genome editing also has a moral dimension. If the genetic code can be modified, then some parents might choose to have "designer babies," editing out genes for features they didn't like. No more freckles? Green eyes only? Not too serious, it might seem, but think of where that editing could lead.

In this experiment you'll practice being a genetic specialist. Don't worry: You won't have to wear a white lab coat or find a gigantic, super-powerful microscope. But you will be performing a "home version" of one method of modifying genes to help them fight disease.

Scientists can use a small number of cells to modify genes in a patient's entire body. One way of doing that is to harness the power of viruses. We know that viruses can be very harmful, leading to all sorts of illnesses from the common cold to deadly diseases. And it's pretty obvious that they spread quickly through the body—think how fast you can "come down with a cold." But some viruses are "good guys," and it's these viruses—and that ability to speed through the body—that come to the rescue in genetic modification.

YOU WILL NEED

- 3 1-pint glass mixing bowls (but could be larger or smaller)
- Water
- Red food coloring
- Yellow food coloring
- Green food coloring
- Blue food coloring
- 3 teaspoons
- 3 tablespoons
- A friend

METHOD

1. Fill each bowl with water and add one or two drops of red food coloring to one of the bowls to give it a slight blush.

2. Add one or two drops of yellow food coloring to the second bowl and the same amount of green food coloring to the third bowl.

3 Stir each mixture with a clean teaspoon to get the color even.

4 Dip a tablespoon into the red mixture and hold the spoon steady above the liquid.

5 Ask your friend to mix 4 drops of blue food coloring into the spoon. There should be enough to give it a strong blue look.

6 Now pour the contents of the tablespoon back into the bowl and stir.

7 It will change color, taking on a much bluer look.

8 Repeat Step 5 with the red and yellow bowls. At the end, each bowl will have the same color.

DATA ANALYSIS

Genetic scientists can remove human body cells, treat them with a helpful virus, and then place the cells back in the patient's body, where the modified cells can launch the "good" virus into the entire system. Eventually the body's genes wind up just as modified—for the good.

Your experiment was a visual version of that same process. Each bowl represented the total number of cells in an organism, like your own body, and the bowl's color (red, yellow, or green) represented a particular gene present in each cell. The concentrated blue food coloring ("launched" from a tablespoon) represented the viruses traveling through the organism and editing the genes in each cell.

CHAPTER 15

GPS

→ − +   X

"Are you sure we're on the right road? We've been driving for hours."

"Slow down . . . no, stop. I'll get the map. Stormview Road, page 18, D-8. No, that's another Stormview Road, because it's by a lake and we're in the woods!"

Ah, yes. The days of fumbling over paper maps, before GPS could lead drivers right to their destination. Think of all the time this marvelous invention has saved—and all the family squabbles that are now a thing of the past.

"Terrifying" tech? Not likely. But horror stories are becoming more common, like the woman who drove 900 miles (1,450 km) out of her way in Europe, or tractor trailers that were led into lakes. What went wrong?

HOW LIFE IS BETTER

It's a great relief to have an expert give you the exact route to your destination, especially if you don't have a passenger to help you navigate unfamiliar territory. GPS, short for Global Positioning System, is the way that we in the 21st century can find those expert directions, no matter where in the world we are. (Well, almost.)

And although the system is modern and constantly being updated, it is in fact a link to the way people navigated thousands of years in the past. In the days of the ancient Chinese and Greeks, more than 3,000 years ago, people traveling in desert caravans or on ships at sea would look to the stars to guide them. They would set their course based on the position of those stars in the night sky.

GPS also relies on looking to the heavens, except the "guides" up there are much closer than stars. They're satellites, 12,550 miles (20,240 km) above us, forming just one part of a system that also includes ground stations and receivers. Of the 27 satellites orbiting the Earth, only 24 of them are "on duty" at any one time—three of them are spares in case there's an emergency. At any one time, four of these satellites will be above any place on Earth.

All of the satellites contain super-accurate clocks and monitors of their location. Even so, ground stations use radar to confirm those locations once every 24 hours. And here's where the third bit—the bit that's in your phone or car—comes in. It's the "receiver." The receiver uses a computer to work out its own location by getting the bearings

A

B

C

(detailed locations) of three of those four satellites. That system is called trilateration. And with your receiver and the satellites always moving, this information is constantly being recalculated so that your location is updated.

GPS has made life better in many, many ways. Of course, one of the most common ways is by simplifying directions. That can help drivers not only reach their destinations sooner but save fuel. Getting the right direction is even more important for ships, so GPS has made shipping safer and cheaper (for that same fuel-saving reason). And of course, if you fell and broke your ankle in the middle of nowhere, your GPS would guide rescuers to you easily—just make sure the batteries don't run out!

> **TRILATERATION**
>
> A method of determining the location of one point (in the case of GPS, the receiver) if the distances between that point and three other points (with exact locations) are known. It differs from triangulation, which uses angles (rather than distances) to determine locations.

RELATED TECHNOLOGY

People have found a way of turning GPS technology into an entertaining activity. It's called geocaching. The name is a combination of "geography" and "cache," which means "something hidden away." All players need is a GPS device (which could be a smartphone) and the right sort of clothing to hike through the countryside or city streets.

Players, known as geocachers, go to a listing website to learn the coordinates of caches (hidden containers) near them. They use their GPS device to track one down. Once they succeed, they open the waterproof container and write some comments in a logbook that's inside. Geocachers also post comments online about their finds. Often there's a treasure (known as "swag") inside the container, which is something small, like an unusual coin or book. The geocacher is free to take the swag as long as they replace it with something of the same (or greater) value. Then the geocachers replace the container at the exact coordinates where they found it so that others can also reach it.

TERRIFYINGLY AWESOME?

What could possibly be worrying about a technology that helps you find your way? Think about it a little. We've all complained about glitches and crashes and freezes with our computers or phones. It's a hassle, but you can often solve the problem by using that old favorite: Just turn it off then back on again.

Now imagine that your GPS software "glitched." Try pulling the old "off then back on again" routine while driving on a busy Los Angeles freeway or when

you're in Japan and can't read the road signs. That might not be terrifying, but it would certainly be stressful, especially if you didn't have a road map for the area (because you'd been relying on GPS).

That's just one possibility. Here's another: GPS might be wrong. That's right, wrong. All the high-tech stuff that sends information down from space might be working fine, as far as communications go. But when the voice in the car says "Take the second left," does the GPS system really know what that second left is?

Real-life stories about "GPS gone wrong" are scary. In 2008, drivers in Yorkshire, England, were sent on a winding lane along the edge of a 100-foot (30 m) cliff near the village of Crackpot. (Yes, that's a real town name.) And in 2013, an elderly Californian couple followed the GPS directions down a dirt road in rural Oregon. The road turned out to be a disused logging trail, and the couple wound up stranded inside their 23-foot (7.2 m) motor home, stuck in mud and hemmed in by fallen trees. Emergency services arrived two days later with chainsaws to free them.

Sometimes it's being found—not being lost—that's the scary part of GPS technology. Parents can now track their kids, and some husbands and wives even track each other. Companies can find your location and target you with messages about their nearest stores. And although the public elects the politicians who govern them, do people really want the government to be able to track their every move? Hmm. Maybe it would be nicer to "slip under the radar" and have some privacy?

You keep hearing the word *trilateration* when people talk about GPS, satellites, and finding the right coordinates. The subject is pretty complicated on one level—just think of all that nonstop high-speed math. But on another level, it can be demonstrated pretty easily in your own kitchen or out on a patio. Just remember that the word starts with the letters "tri," so you can think of the number three.

We've moved down a rung or two on the technology ladder. Instead of using satellites with high-speed computers, you'll be working with pieces of string and some chair legs. But don't forget: The basic principle is the same.

YOU WILL NEED

- A flat, open space (kitchen floor, patio)
- Scissors
- String
- 3 chairs
- 3 friends

METHOD

1 Use the scissors to cut three pieces of string, each about 5 feet (1.5 m) long. Tie one end of each of them to the top of a chair (one string for each chair).

2 Move two of the chairs so they're facing away from each other, with their backs about 2 feet (0.6 m) feet apart. The strings will be dangling loosely from them.

3 Take the free end of each string and hold them together, pinched between your fingers. Keep the ends of the strings touching the floor.

4 Have two of your friends pull the chairs back slowly until the strings become tight. Each string should look like a straight line heading from a chair to your pinched fingers.

5 Slide your hands back and forth, keeping the strings tight and their ends still touching the floor. (Read Data Analysis after you finish for an explanation of this step.)

6 Now ask your third friend to move their chair closer.

7 Take the free end of that string (still holding the first two) and ask the third friend to pull the chair back slowly.

8 With all three strings kept tight, there's only one spot where the three strings can touch the floor.

DATA ANALYSIS

You've used the strings to represent how GPS uses distances from three satellites to pinpoint a location. Imagine that the strings are beams being sent down from three satellites (the chairs), and you'll see how the GPS can work out the location. In the same way, knowing the distances up to two satellites would give a line of possible locations, but with no idea of where the exact location is along that line. Step 5 demonstrated that your position could have been anywhere along the line, but adding the third string gave you the precision you needed. In real life, the GPS software would calculate in the opposite direction. It would know the position of the three satellites and the distance up to each of them. Trilateration would help identify its own position based on that information.

CHAPTER 16

AIR-CONDITIONED CLOTHING

Ever felt like wearing a robot to school? Or wished that the shirt that's always been too big for you would automatically fit perfectly? What about deciding that your outfit will work well as an air conditioner?

Yes, technology really has seeped into every aspect of our lives. It's no longer confined to tablets and laptops, lasers and space exploration. Even food has become a booming area for tech. (Don't forget that microwaves once seemed like science fiction.) So why not clothing, too?

What could possibly go wrong? How about "Good, that's a snugger fit. Okay, that's fine. Ooh, a little too tight . . . Hey, enough's enough!"

HOW LIFE IS BETTER

Considering that we carry around clothes every day, it's surprising how long it's taken to get them to pay their way and not just tag along for a free ride. Sure, they keep us warm, protected from the blazing sun, and dry in rain and snow. But isn't there just a little bit *more* that they could do?

Well, the waiting seems to be over. Life really is getting better thanks to what might be called "clothing technology." Just take the air-conditioning . . . right in your shirt. What the heck? How's that work?

Scientists at Stanford University were considering the cost of keeping people comfortable—and possibly even cool—in places with hot climates. Many of the world's hottest countries are also among the poorest and least developed, so air-conditioning would be ruled out because of the cost and poor reliability of electricity supplies. Eventually the scientists had one of those "Eureka!" moments when a completely new solution to a problem suddenly appears from nowhere.

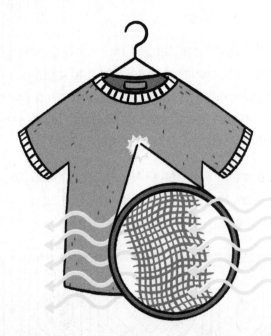

They turned the project on its head. Rather than spend lots of money (and use precious energy) cooling down large offices and other buildings, why not find a way to help each individual get a bit cooler? That was a start, but the next obvious question was "How?"

The team studied a range of fabrics to see which allowed heat to escape best. Cotton is the most common fabric in countries with hot climates, because it allows perspiration (that's "sweat" to nonscientists) to evaporate through the material. But the team developed a plastic-based textile that made the wearer feel nearly 4°F (2.2°C) cooler when they were wearing it. While cotton's evaporation is a good start, the Stanford fabric takes the cooling further, into the realm of electromagnetic radiation.

Let's consider something basic at this point: Cooling down means allowing heat to escape. That's what's happening with the evaporation. But somewhere between 40 percent and 60 percent of our body heat is released through infrared radiation. Most fabrics trap that radiation, so the body doesn't cool down so much. The Stanford research

Electromagnetic Radiation

This term describes the wide range of ways in which energy is radiated (sent out). All forms of radiation have both electric and magnetic qualities, and they travel in waves. The differences relate to their different wavelengths. Radio waves have the longest wavelengths and gamma rays the shortest. Visible light falls in between, with infrared having slightly longer wavelengths.

team developed a plastic-based fabric that allowed infrared radiation to pass through. It's a relative of the plastic wrap that we use for food, but it's not transparent (which definitely makes it a lot better for clothing).

This magic fabric is still in the final stages of production, with scientists working on the ideal combination of the plastic base (for the air-conditioning advantages) and some natural fabrics (for a comfortable feel). The latest advance is a three-ply version: two layers of plastic with a layer of cloth between them for comfort.

RELATED TECHNOLOGY

The movie *Back to the Future* imagined a teenager from the 1980s traveling back and forth through time. The "future" in these movies was 2015, a time of amazing advances. But rather than concentrate on the medical or engineering marvels of that far-off time, young Marty is intrigued by something even closer to his heart—a pair of self-lacing Nike sneakers!

Smart Clothing

Fabrics with woven-in solar batteries fall into a tech category called "smart clothing" or sometimes "e-textiles." The term refers generally to clothing that has some form of sensors built into it. This is a growing area of research, with a range of high-tech clothing that increases by the day.

You can buy "smart" running socks that judge your running style, or you might want to try yoga pants with built-in vibrating sensors to guide you into the right pose. There's a Levi's denim "commuter jacket" with sensors on the sleeves to let you take phone calls or read map apps. You can even wear a smart bikini that will tell you when you've been in the sun too long or need to use more sunblock.

Fast-forward one year in real life to 2016 to find Jayan Thomas, a researcher at the University of Central Florida, with an invention that he says was inspired by those self-lacing shoes. Thomas developed narrow filaments (slender fibers) that capture and store solar energy. They can be woven into cloth and other textiles to turn clothing into solar-powered batteries.

This all might be cutting-edge science developed by a professor with a list of credentials as long as your arm, but it was the film that inspired him: "That movie was the motivation. If you can develop self-charging clothes or textiles, you can realize those cinematic fantasies. That's the cool thing."

TERRIFYINGLY AWESOME?

We should be on reasonably safe ground with clothing-related technology, but some of the questions posed in other chapters still apply. Okay, maybe not the "But what if it were to fall into the wrong hands?" scenario. (What would happen? "Oh, no, the supervillain made the FBI agents' pants shrink!")

The "plastic air-conditioning" fabric uses the properties of the materials to do its work. But the real worries arise when clothing combines with electricity inside it. Is there any chance of an electric shock? What about burning, if things get overheated? What happens if it gets wet or sweaty? Does this stuff shrink? I don't want to get squeezed out!

EXPERIMENT
CHILL OUT!

Maybe you've heard your parents talk about improving the insulation in your house to keep it warmer and to save on fuel bills. And perhaps you've done some experiments or scientific investigations into how to keep things warm.

We're turning that on its head with this experiment. You're going to be assuming the role of "textile scientist," seeing which material allows heat to escape most effectively. That, after all, is what air-conditioned clothing is all about. So stay cool while you look into letting heat escape.

YOU WILL NEED

- Plastic food wrap
- 3 empty glass jars of the same size
- Piece of paper
- Tape
- Wool sock or mitten (large enough to cover the side of a jar)
- Rubber band
- Hot water
- Bulb thermometer (that can be submerged in water)
- Clock or timer

METHOD

1 Stretch a piece of food wrap around one jar so that it's wrapped up (not the base or opening).

2 Wrap a piece of paper around a second jar, taping it in place tightly.

3 Wrap the woolen sock or mitten around the third jar, using the rubber band to hold in place.

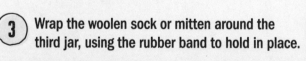

4 Run the hot water in the kitchen sink so that it's warm but not too hot, then fill each jar.

5 Take the temperature of the water in one of the jars and record it. (You don't need to do this with the others, because they start out at the same temperature.)

6 Wait 10 minutes and record each temperature.

7 Do the same 10 minutes later (20 minutes from the start).

8 Note which jar lost the most heat in those periods.

It will be clear that you were measuring heat loss rather than heat retention in this experiment. And if you were a materials scientist—an expert who conducts this sort of research—you'd be looking for the *worst* insulating material. Why? Because it's the one that allows heat to escape most. Remember, heat escaping means cooling down, which is the aim of the project.

Each of the materials you're testing is sometimes used as a heat insulator. Think of a woolen hat you might wear in the winter. Some people stretch a layer of plastic wrap across windows to keep heat in during the winter, and maybe you've had some hot chocolate in a paper cup that didn't burn your hand. So this might be a close call, unlike comparing any of these materials with copper, iron, or other metals that *conduct* heat far more. Looked at that way, you could say that an aluminum shirt would be a great air conditioner—but maybe a tad uncomfortable?

CHAPTER 17

3-D PRINTING

→ − +   X

How do you suppose they made that nuts-and-bolts combination that helps hold your desk together? Molding? Forging? Sculpting? How would you feel if you found out it was printed?

The "3-D" in the chapter title should be a clue that we're talking about solid (that is, three-dimensional) objects being printed. That's a pretty neat idea, and the way it's done—or at least finished up—looks a lot like a stack of pancakes getting higher and higher next to the stove.

The whole idea is to think of an object in layers, then print (and stack) layer upon layer of material upward. Each layer can change just a fraction wider or narrower so that the stack takes on its final shape by the last layer. The technique has already been used to "print" clothing, tools, and even body parts. (Oh, dear, here we go again!) Think a bit, then, about a world where deadly weapons could be printed at home by anyone. Are you terrified yet?

HOW LIFE IS BETTER

Most people's jaws seem to drop to the floor when they first come across 3-D printing. It's a head-scratching, hard-to-figure technology that seems to go against some things that we always thought were true. It used to be that printing was done on two dimensions: length and width. And although the images you print can wind up on solid objects like paper, cardboard, or even some forms of plastic, they're still finishing up on a flat (two-dimensional) surface.

But now, some people claim that three-dimensional printing is the biggest techno-logical breakthrough since, well, printing. And the arrival of printing in Europe turned out to be revolutionary—and, for some people, scary. Up until about 1500, most documents were written by hand. If you wanted a copy of something, you started from scratch and wrote out another one. So there weren't too many written things around, and not many people who were able to write or even read those documents.

In the Europe of the 1500s, things changed thanks to the invention of movable type, which is another way of describing printing presses. Now it was possible to create a document by moving solid letters around on a press until a page full of words was prepared. Then you could literally "press" out copy after copy, sheet by sheet.

The result was amazing. It helped trigger a religious revolution in the 1520s known as the Reformation. That terrified some opponents of the Reformation. Then political pamphlets began to appear with messages like "Down with the king!" "Give more land to the poor!" and "No more war!" Strong political messages—still printed in two dimensions—continue today. Just look at newspaper headlines. Imagine how revolutionary a move to another dimension (the third) would be for printing!

Printing has only just started to catch up with lots of the other super-cool technologies developing around it. So how in the world do you go from printing papers and posters to printing all kinds of tools, computer equipment, and even cars?

The process of 3-D printing begins with the real "tech" bit. Design software can turn a two-dimensional image into three dimensions, especially if the 2-D images show views (or "projections") from different angles. Traditional blueprints (technical plans) of houses, for example, have 2-D images of the house from east, west, north, south, and above. 3-D printing software uses similar views. Some software can take an ordinary drawing and "imagine" how it would look in three dimensions—kids have even designed toys this way.

The next bit looks a lot more familiar, especially if you've ever used molds with modeling clay. The printer uses the image (from the drawing) and imagines it as a pile of slices, like a stack of pancakes. Then it sends a soft, gooey material through the printer's nozzles, slice after slice, so that they pile up. The nozzle's opening changes with each slice, according to the computer program, and eventually the soft material hardens to create the finished printed object. The end result could be just about any shape, ranging from a complicated and delicate sculpture to a stout, rectangular storage box. Some engineers have half-seriously explored the idea of using a 3-D printer to print a 3-D printer!

As you can imagine, 3-D printers must be built and maintained to precise measurements.

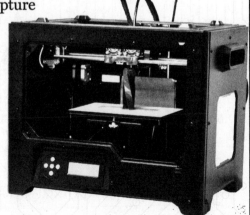

The pulleys, extruder, and printhead need to be aligned exactly because of the way the end result is built up layer by layer. You'll know the problem if you've ever gone a bit off center on one of the lowest layers of a stack of books or blocks.

EXTRUDER

A piece of equipment that squeezes out (extrudes) soft or melted material just like we might squeeze a tube of toothpaste.

Some 3-D printing technology is showing how schoolkids—some before they reach middle school—can build 3-D maps, cell-phone cases, and even prosthetic limbs, or at least learn the basics. Meanwhile, hospitals and medical centers are using similar technology to produce first-aid kits, emergency clothing and protective gear, and lab equipment, all with their own printers.

RELATED TECHNOLOGY

It's possible to link 3-D printing with other technologies. Using artificial intelligence (see page 59) or virtual reality (page 87), you can look at an object and scan it right there. The data could be sent automatically to a 3-D printer, which would transfer the data into a printable form. Then a printed version of the original would be produced. All of this could be done in minutes if, for example, a mechanic were to spot an automobile engine part that needed replacing. Send out to a warehouse for a spare? Nah, just print a replacement!

There's even a way of combining cells from a patient with biocompatible plastic (plastic that can coexist with living tissue) for medical 3-D printing. The cell–plastic combination builds up, layer by layer, just like "normal" 3-D printing would, until a new ear, nose, or other human organ is produced.

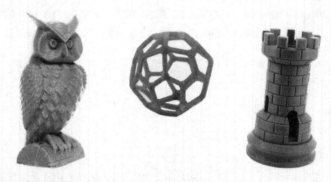

TERRIFYINGLY AWESOME?

Here's a technology that definitely makes life better *and* could cause a lot of danger. Once again, it's a case of limitless possibilities being used to help people . . . or to inflict terrible harm.

One of the most terrifying areas of 3-D printing concerns firearms. Some companies have already posted plans for 3-D handguns and shotguns on their websites. Many individuals and governments view this development with fear. Could a criminal or a terrorist simply download the software and print out a stack of weapons? What about children?

Many of the concerns that people have about the internet and the World Wide Web (see page 69) are strongest when people consider 3-D firearms. And there doesn't seem to be any reassuring answer . . . yet.

Here's an experiment that you could do just as easily with pancakes, and they'd probably taste better than a modeling-clay snowman!

One of the best ways to learn a technology's value is to look at what it can replace. So you've got the job of doing the old-fashioned stuff, waiting expectantly for a computer whiz in shining armor to rescue you and make life easier. Well, don't hold your breath—but you'll see what we mean in a few minutes.

YOU WILL NEED

- Modeling clay
- Wooden cutting board
- Rolling pin
- Sharp knife (with adult to supervise)
- One each of as many different coins as you can find: penny, nickel, dime, quarter, and (if you're lucky) half-dollar

METHOD

1 Place a bit of modeling clay (about the size of a small orange) on the cutting board.

2 Use the rolling pin to flatten it into a strip about ¼-inch thick.

3 Put a dime on the clay and use the knife to trace around it to create a disk shape.

4 Place that clay disk on a table or counter.

5 Now do the same thing with a penny and lay it carefully on the "clay dime."

6 Repeat this with a nickel, laying it on top.

7 Continue with a quarter and then with a half-dollar (if you can find one).

8 Now work back down in shape, cutting and laying a "quarter" on the half-dollar, then a "nickel" on the quarter, and so on.

9 By the end, you should have created a ball.

10 If you're patient enough, you can make a modeling-clay "snowman." Make a smaller ball (like the first without the largest "disk") and place it on the first ball. Then make an even smaller ball, placing it on the second ball.

DATA ANALYSIS

You've been doing, by hand and painstakingly, what a 3-D printer does really, really fast. It has a program that has "sliced" up an intended product, and then it produces layer after layer to build it up. Each layer is very thin—only about 0.1 mm (1/250 inch) thick. It gets wider or narrower as it grows (just like your "clay coin" disks) until it reaches the top. If you measure the height of your snowman in inches, then multiply that by 250, you'll get an idea of how many layers a 3-D printer would use for the same job.

CHAPTER 18

SMART GLASSES

Would you want to buy a "wearable Android device" that is voice-activated and projects images onto a pair of eyeglasses? That was a question the Google company wrestled with. They decided that a lot of people would say yes. What the Google folks didn't count on was how the rest of the world—the people who *didn't* buy the glasses—might feel about the idea.

Google tried out a few tests of its "smart glasses" in 2013 and 2015 but withdrew the product after getting some pretty angry feedback. Lots of the people who weren't wearing the glasses felt that they were being snooped on. In 2017, Google went back to the drawing board, and in 2018, Facebook decided to join in.

Will these two companies win big with this idea, or will they put both sets of glasses back in their cases for good?

HOW LIFE IS BETTER

Smartphone engineers have long been fascinated by the idea of the "ubiquitous computer." The big brains at Google and elsewhere aimed to achieve that goal with "smart glasses." That term describes any pair of eyeglasses with built-in computers to add information to—or next to—what the wearer can see.

The second version of Google Glass, from 2015, featured a touch pad on the bit extending back to the ear. That would activate the screen, which would be visible by looking through the glasses normally. Sliding a finger along the touchpad would be like using a mouse on a computer. Google Glass had many voice-activated features, as well. People could either tap the touchpad or tilt their heads back a bit and then say, "Okay, Glass." The built-in computer would then be ready to perform a range of cool tasks. The wearer might say, "Send a message to my brother" or "Google, how far is Baltimore from Philadelphia?" and then the glasses would carry out the task.

> **UBIQUITOUS COMPUTER**
>
> A term to describe how computing can be present at all times, and not just when the user accesses a device such as a laptop or phone. The term takes its name from the word ubiquitous, which means "present everywhere."

But perhaps the most troublesome feature concerned photos and videos. Someone wearing the earliest smart glasses in 2013 could simply do the magic head tilt and quietly say "Take a picture" or "Record a video." It would be very difficult for someone else to tell whether the wearer had been photographing them. And lots of people showed they were definitely not happy about that—in social media posts, TV interviews, and newspaper reports.

Google tackled one of the main complaints about the original Glass—privacy and photo taking—in its modified 2015 version. Wearers could use their hands to touch the side of the glasses to frame (aim) and crop (remove the outer parts of) photos they were taking. That made the final photos more professional-looking. Wearers *had to* use their hands to take the photo, however, so people on the outside would always know what was happening. It became no more an invasion of privacy than someone holding up a normal camera, just like your mom or dad trying to take your picture without permission!

But the company felt that the public might still feel uneasy about seeing people walking around wearing these futuristic "gadgets." So Google decided to move away from retail (personal-use buyers) and on to business customers with another product launch in 2018. This version is called Google Glass Enterprise Edition.

Oh, dear . . . "business customers" sounds a little boring, huh? Not at all! It's at the business level that smart glasses really can make life better. Instead of being considered a personal plaything or a form of entertainment, a pair of smart glasses could make work easier and possibly even save lives.

The new version aims to revolutionize how people can do their jobs better in all kinds of exciting ways. A technician wearing these "industrial" smart glasses could start work by asking, "Help me select equipment" or "Which areas need urgent attention?" The glasses could say, or even display images of, how best to approach the

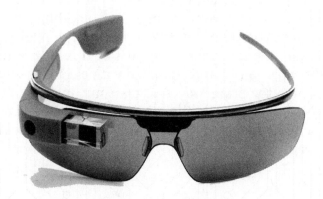

day. Or, while wearing the glasses during an operation, a surgeon could examine a patient and have the latest readings of the patient's organs displayed on the screen. (Okay, gross—but cool.)

Firefighters might be able to use smart glasses to guide them toward—or away from—dangerous fumes, or "hot spots." Emergency medical teams could benefit from hands-free assessments of injuries. Partially sighted people could have their vision perception improved dramatically by having shapes outlined, even as the people wearing the glasses move.

RELATED TECHNOLOGY

With the move into artificial intelligence (see page 59) and the cloud (page 95), smart glasses have bridged the gap to other technologies described in this book. Like some GPS watches, new models of smartphones have activity-tracking apps that are a boost for fitness and health. And the GPS (page 121) component can tie in with voice recognition software to make it seem as though a driver or pedestrian was talking to a local expert who could give them directions. Everything connects, or might be able to connect, with smart glasses—as long as the public will accept those connections.

Some experts predict that within a few years, people will be able to communicate with their devices directly from their brain. Forget about typing, nodding, or clicking—brain computer interface technology will allow people to interact with devices just by thinking. A lightweight cap or headband equipped with electrode sensors could monitor brain waves to transmit instructions to devices. Even that technology might not be the end of the line—chips implanted in our heads might be the obvious next step!

TERRIFYINGLY AWESOME?

Any new technology raises safety concerns, and smart glasses are no exception. For instance, how do you focus on what's in front of you when you're paying attention to something on the screen instead? But as we saw earlier in the book with virtual reality (page 87) and genetics (page 113), new tech can also have us wrestling with moral questions—in other words, not whether a technology works, but whether it is good or bad for people or the environment.

Now it looks like we've found another candidate. Even if it's a bit of a stretch to drag "terrifying" into the mix, people could easily find some other adjectives. Like "annoying" or "maddening" or "intrusive."

All of which leads back to the moral side of things. Is it right to wear something that others view as an invasion of their privacy? Should it be clearer (to the nonwearer) what exactly is going on behind those glasses? Will everyone just get used to it? Maybe these questions apply to other forms of technology, too, and if the engineers and manufacturers face up to those questions with glasses, then some happy solutions might be found.

If you're wearing smart glasses, the last thing you want is for the sound of music or voices to be blasting out for everyone else to hear. So Google Glass designers went back to basics, noting that sound travels through some materials better than it does through air.

Sound travels through lots of solid materials really, really fast—17 times faster through steel than through the air, for example. And there's another solid material that everyone has conveniently nearby: bone. Not sure what this is all about? Try this experiment, where you should find a spoon ringing like a bell . . . even though the folks around you might not hear a thing.

YOU WILL NEED
- Scissors
- String or yarn
- Metal teaspoon
- A friend to help
- Ruler

METHOD

1 Use the scissors to cut a length of string or yarn about 4 feet (1.2 m) long.

2 Make a loop in the middle and insert the handle of the spoon.

3 Tie the loop so that the spoon is midway along the length of string.

4 Loop each end of the string around one of your index fingers.

5 Hold the tips of your index fingers to your ears, taking care not to press too far in.

6 Lean forward so that the spoon is dangling freely.

7 Ask your friend to tap the spoon with the ruler. It should sound very loudly in your ears!

DATA ANALYSIS

Those earpieces in the Google Glass aren't broadcasting out into the air. They're sending the audio signals through a solid medium: your skull. Unlike headphones or earbuds, they don't have to be placed in your ears. Touching your skull near your ears does the trick.

You just saw (or heard) how that audio method, known as "bone conduction," works. With Google Glass, the audio vibrations pass through a single solid material (bone) to reach the brain. In this experiment, those audio vibrations are being sent along two solid mediums—the string and then the bones in your fingers. But the effect to other people is the same as it is for people standing near Google Glass wearers: They don't hear that otherwise clearly transmitted sound.

CHAPTER 19

HOLOGRAMS

→ − +   X

Sometimes the definition of something odd—or even terrifying—robs it of its "oomph" factor. Try this one for size. It's a definition of a hologram: "A three-dimensional image that has been projected and captured on a two-dimensional surface." Hmm. That sounds about as terrifying as watching your grandparents' collection of slides from their visit to the World's Largest Ball of Twine.

It's a shame, because holograms are some of the coolest, weirdest, funniest, and—yes—scariest technologies ever. A "projected three-dimensional image" is no way to describe a crazed pirate ready to slit your throat with a cutlass or the feeling that you're about to step out of a capsule onto the Moon's surface with no spacesuit!

Yeah, yeah—holograms perform useful functions in maintaining a free flow of information in the worlds of business and education and . . . *yawn*. Come on, we all know that they were invented to scare the heck out of us.

Holograms add a whole new dimension—literally—to the way that we can create and view images. Instead of looking at a flat (two-dimensional) surface, like the page you're on right now, you can look at something that has a third dimension: depth. That means you can look at it from all sides and it will look a little different, just as looking at a tree, skyscraper, or your sibling will give you a different image from each side.

Holograms manage to record these 3-D images using a special lens that splits one laser beam into two. The first, called the "reference beam," shines through a lens to spread the beam wider. Then it bounces off a mirror and onto film that's very similar to the type used in traditional, nondigital cameras. The second beam, or "object beam," does all that, too, but also reflects off the object that's being viewed.

It's what happens when these two beams intersect that makes holograms special. It's called an interference pattern. Remember that light travels in waves, so imagine dropping two stones in the same puddle. Each sends out ripples (waves), similar to how light waves are sent out. When the ripples from each splash meet, they create a pattern. That's like the interference pattern from the intersection of the hologram laser beams.

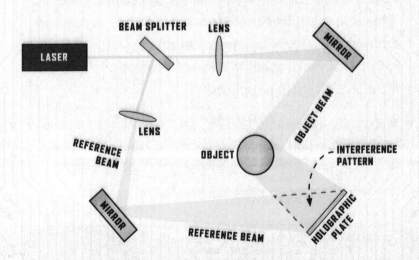

3-D Vision

Our sense of sight is based on a version of 3-D vision. We can see things as solid (and having length, width, and depth) because we have two eyes. If you close one eye and look at something and then close that eye and look through the other, you'll see slightly different images.

Your brain uses the difference in the two views to decide where in 3-D space that "something" is. The instant calculation gives us the full three-dimensional image—just like the calculation between the two laser beams of the hologram. If you don't think you need two eyes for "depth perception," try grabbing something with one eye shut and then with both eyes open. It should be a little easier with both eyes open.

If the two laser beams (the result of being split) bounced off different mirrors but were reflected onto the same destination, they'd appear the same. But because the object beam has reflected across all parts of the surface of the object, its path has changed somewhat. The interference pattern is really a record of that change—and a record of the three dimensions of the object. The result is an image showing all of the original object. You don't need special glasses or other equipment to see the 3-D image, which makes holograms very special.

HOW LIFE IS BETTER

Holograms are all around us, even if we're not always looking at spooky, thrilling, or mind-blowing versions. Bar code scanners at supermarket checkouts use hologram technology. So do Blu-rays, as a way of reading data with laser beams. And the medical world is constantly finding ways of using holograms to detect and treat illnesses by giving a 3-D view of "virtual" organs or growths to familiarize surgeons before they operate.

How about crime-fighting as a positive use of holograms? It's never been easy to produce counterfeit money, and governments have used all sorts of techniques to make banknotes harder to copy, like "watermarks" (a bit like tattoos). Holograms are *much* harder to copy, because the hologram is recorded on metallic film, which is then slotted into a gap in the paper money. Then, for even more security, a separate hologram strip is added over the first hologram. Not bad!

Apart from scaring the heck out of people at theme parks and spooky museums, holograms add real excitement to home entertainment. People can already watch prototype 3-D television thanks to holograms, and the world of gaming will be turned upside down when villains and explosions seem to be appearing in real life.

PROTOTYPE

A first version of a product or device that forms the basis for later (and possibly more advanced) versions.

RELATED TECHNOLOGY

GPS (see page 121) uses a similar method of looking at different images—satellites, placed in multiple locations—to work out your position. Luckily those are precise, useful measurements and not just a neat optical illusion.

Augmented reality (page 90), a variation of virtual reality, can use holograms to add interest or information to displays. Imagine using an iPad to read about the pyramids of Egypt and finding them pop up from the screen . . . and then the Sphinx . . . and then a pharaoh's brightly colored coffin. You can imagine the incredible ways that holograms might bring "boring old text" to life.

TERRIFYINGLY AWESOME?

It might seem cool to see a hologram of Abraham Lincoln delivering the Gettysburg Address or Alexander the Great leading his troops into battle about 2,300 years ago. But things look a bit different when we think about people who have died more recently. For example, there's lots of color film footage (with sound) of Nazi leader Adolf Hitler and Soviet dictator Josef Stalin—not to mention murderers, robbers, and other vicious criminals. That information could be used to create holograms of those real people. Imagine if they appeared before a willing audience, urging them to create havoc!

That possibility raises questions about the wider use of holograms. It's great that they're becoming more and more realistic, but could there be a problem with becoming *too* realistic? Could people be manipulated into confusing reality with a ghostly 3-D image? Perhaps they'd be persuaded to hand over money or even to take part in a dangerous or illegal activity.

EXPERIMENT
HOMEMADE HOLOGRAM
WARNING! ADULT SUPERVISION REQUIRED

Time
Factor:
40
mins

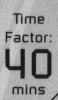

This experiment might take you a little longer than others, but it's absolutely worth the time and effort. So if it's a rainy afternoon—or you just have some time on your hands—go for it.

What you'll be producing is simple enough to explain: a hologram. It makes for a weird and awesome payoff. The ingredients call for an old CD or DVD case (with permission, of course), but any plastic that's clear and pretty firm should work just as well. Take care: You'll be designing (and cutting out) trapeziums, which are special geometric shapes.

YOU WILL NEED

- Ruler
- Sharpie or other permanent marker
- Hard sheet of transparent plastic (CD or DVD cases are ideal)
- Adult to help
- Scissors or X-Acto knife
- Scotch (clear) tape
- Smartphone

METHOD

1. Use the ruler and marker to trace a ½-inch (12 mm) line on the plastic sheet.

2. From the midway (¼-inch or 6 mm) mark of the line measure 1½ inches (38 mm) directly down. Mark that point with a dot.

3. Using that dot as a midpoint, trace a line 2½ inches (60 mm) along, parallel to the line that you've marked above it.

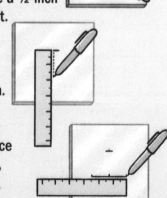

4 Connect the end points to create a four-sided object (trapezium) that has two parallel sides.

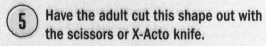

5 Have the adult cut this shape out with the scissors or X-Acto knife.

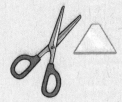

6 Use this shape as a pattern to trace and cut out three more trapezium shapes.

7 Use tape to join the angled sides (the sides that aren't parallel) of the four shapes to create a 3-D shape resembling a pyramid.

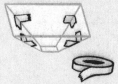

8 Use tape along the inside crease to make these connections permanent.

9 Place the shape that you've created (resting on the small side) on your smartphone and load up a "holographic video" site and you'll see a 3-D image!

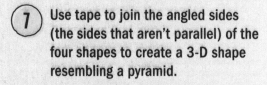

DATA ANALYSIS

Although you're learning about futuristic holograms, this experiment uses a centuries-old technique called "Pepper's Ghost," which used reflections off several sheets to create the 3-D effect. Your experiment used the inside of the four plastic sides, each reflecting the image from the smartphone. The four reflections combined to create the spooky 3-D image directly above the phone's screen.

CHAPTER 20

LASER SURGERY

→ − +   X

It was inevitable, wasn't it? Lasers, those cool sci-fi inventions that could cut through diamonds and shine a beam onto the Moon, were going to come down to Earth. We've already learned that auto factories use lasers, Blu-ray players rely on them, and they read the bar codes at supermarket checkouts.

In the mood for something a bit more "on the edge"? How about a laser burning its way through your flesh? Uh, no thanks! Well, in addition to being deadly sci-fi weapons, lasers can be turned to medical work and reach places where normal surgical equipment can't. Eye surgery, tumor removal, and even that once-common childhood operation (tonsil removal) can all be done more quickly and more safely than ever thanks to laser surgery.

Nevertheless, they can still be pretty scary, and if one of those "surgical aids" gets into the wrong hands, what then?

Okay, we've all heard about lasers and seen them used in dozens of sci-fi movies, but do we really know what they are? Something about light, right? Yep, but a very special type of light, which some people even call "human-made." The answer is right in the word laser, which is actually an abbreviation. It stands for **L**ight **A**mplification by **S**timulated **E**mission of **R**adiation. We'd use up way too many pages trying to explain "stimulated emission of radiation," so let's concentrate on the "light amplification" part.

Maybe you've played an electric guitar through an amplifier—you can get a huge sound out of it. So just remember that amplifying something usually makes it stronger. Let's also remember that light travels in vibrating waves, and each color matches one pattern of that vibration, known as wavelength. What we see as light (or "white light") is really a mixture of all the colors and wavelengths. But it's possible to break that up into the different colors if the light passes through a special type of glass (called a prism) or through fine droplets of water (as in a rainbow).

Machines can isolate a particular color and send it out as a concentrated beam: The concentration is the amplifying part. Because the beam (called a laser) is just the one color, it has a uniform wavelength. That's really important, and it's the reason why and how lasers can be so powerful and useful.

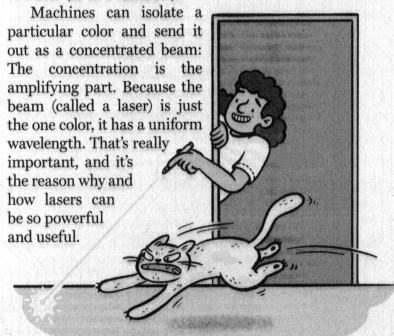

Laser Pointers

You've probably seen laser pointers (also called laser pens) before, shining a tiny, bright dot against a surface. These mini-lasers might be small, but they sure pack a punch.

Here's how they work. The battery powers a light, which shines on a crystal to amplify the light. This causes photons (tiny packets of light) to be emitted. Importantly, these bits of light are all of the same wavelength. They bounce back and forth off mirrors inside the pointer, causing more and more photons to join the process. The light then passes through a lens that focuses it, then out through the tiny hole at the end. Like the beam used in laser surgery, it is powerful enough to travel huge distances.

Having a uniform wavelength (because it's all one color) means that laser light is "coherent"—the beam remains concentrated, or "collimated." Just compare a laser's collimated beam (which would shine like a dot on something dozens of miles away) with the spread-out beam from the white light of a flashlight. It's a pretty big difference.

HOW LIFE IS BETTER

It's that concentration of light that makes lasers so well-suited to surgery. The powerful focus concentrates energy as well as visible light, and the tightness of the beam means they're extremely accurate and precise.

People often describe laser surgery as "burning away" tissue to remove obstacles or to make passages clearer. It's probably more accurate to say that lasers *vaporize* soft tissue. Since up to 60 percent of the human body is actually water, the laser is boiling away that water (turning it into vapor) because of its great heat.

Lasers are ideally suited to remove tumors (unwanted growths inside the body) and to seal small blood vessels to reduce blood loss. Laser surgery is particularly effective in eye operations. Surgeons also use lasers to deal with growths on the surface of the skin, often removing warts, moles, scars, and wrinkles. In recent years, doctors have seen many patients eager to have tattoos removed, too. (Hey, your SpongeBob tattoo may not have been such a bad idea after all.)

RELATED TECHNOLOGY

Lasers figure in so much modern technology that we'd probably fill another book if we tried to list all the related technology. For starters, industrial lasers can perform "surgery" on a wide range of metals and other materials, making precise, clean cuts. Computer-controlled lasers can cut fabric hundreds of layers thick, making it much more efficient and less expensive to produce clothing.

In 1969 and 1971, *Apollo 11* and *Apollo 14* astronauts installed reflectors on the Moon so the distance to Earth could be measured accurately. A measuring laser in Texas made a 4-mile-wide (6.4 km) image on the Moon, and the reflection was strong enough to calculate the distance to an accuracy of about 6 inches (15 cm).

Some scientists have even proposed using a huge array of orbiting mirrors to tap the Sun's energy and transform it into a powerful laser beam to destroy or deflect any comets and asteroids heading for Earth.

Vision Correction

One of the most successful and widespread forms of laser surgery involves the eyes. It is usually performed on patients who have had to wear glasses or contact lenses and want normal vision. This form of vision correction uses lasers instead of bladed surgical tools such as scalpels to reshape the front section (cornea) of the eye.

There are a few methods to choose from. The most common one actually uses two lasers: the first to open up a thin flap in the clear tissue covering the cornea and the second to reshape the cornea itself. The reshaping allows the eye to focus more accurately. The flap is then smoothed back over and remains in place without needing stitches. Grossed out yet?

TERRIFYING AWESOME?

Who hasn't been terrified by the thought of lasers? Luckily laser surgery has nothing to do with those same lasers that bank robbers use to burn holes in safes or that starship commanders use in combat. Surgeons are some of the most qualified and regulated professionals in the world, so there's no need for real fear about their use of lasers in surgery.

But dangers lurk whenever lasers are around. The United States military is developing lasers for all sorts of uses, from anti-missile defense to lasers mounted on helicopters. And it's not just the powerful ones that can be used as weapons. Even those handy laser pointers can damage the eyes of humans or pets. Pilots of commercial aircraft have been temporarily blinded by lasers pointed up from miles below.

EXPERIMENT
PREPARING FOR SURGERY?
WARNING! ADULT SUPERVISION REQUIRED

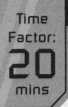

It would be a bit irresponsible (even *more* irresponsible than we normally are) to ask you to get your surgical outfit on and operate on anyone—even if it's your pesky brother or sister. But you *can* get to know a bit more about lasers, and perhaps also why they're so good as medical aids.

But first, a warning. For this experiment, you MUST have an adult with you at all times to handle the laser. That won't stop you and your friends from seeing the effects of the laser, though. And by learning more about a laser, you'll also be learning more about light itself.

You'll want to do this experiment inside, in a room where you can turn the light off and have it really dark.

YOU WILL NEED

- Clear glass
- Water
- An adult
- Clear bottle of tonic water (either glass or plastic)
- Blue-light laser pointer (These are widely available, but an adult must buy and operate it. Data Analysis explains why it must be blue.)

METHOD

1. Fill the glass with water and place it on a table or counter.

2. Predict what will happen when the beam passes through the water.

3 Turn the room lights off and ask the adult to shine the laser through the water.

4 Check your predictions against your observations.

5 Now place the bottle of tonic water on the table or counter. Do you think the result will be the same?

6 Repeat Step 3 and note the result. The whole bottle should be glowing a spooky blue.

DATA ANALYSIS

Our bodies contain lots of water, and in laser surgery, the beam passes through that water with no real change—just like in your experiment here. But when it reaches the "target tissue" in an operation, it reacts and does its work. The tonic water looks like normal water, but it contains a chemical called quinine. When laser photons (light particles) hit the quinine molecules, they become absorbed, just as target tissue does in a laser operation.

Soon afterward they are reemitted, but in a random direction. That's why you wind up seeing blue everywhere in the bottle. The process is called fluorescence, and it's similar to what happens in fluorescent lights. Longer wavelengths of light don't "excite" the quinine, which is why this experiment wouldn't work with a red or green laser.

CHAPTER 21

DRONES

Drone. What a great word! Talk about finding the right term to describe something. Think of those drone insects, like bees. Most of them have only one job to do: mate with a queen bee. Or help warm or cool down that queen. Take orders, basically. And buzz a lot.

That's pretty much what modern high-tech drones do, too. Yep, there's usually a lot of buzzing from their propellers, but beyond that they're pretty much airborne servants. And you—or some other human—are the boss. Spying, taking astonishing photos, rescuing swimmers . . . they seem to be able to do anything. That first word in the list (spying), though, gives you an idea that these innocent miniaircraft could turn nasty.

Want to know something even weirder? Some of the newest drones are about the size of insects. But when you get the flyswatter out, be careful—you might be about to destroy government property!

HOW LIFE IS BETTER

Drones, or unmanned aerial vehicles (UAVs), represent a maddening, uplifting, lifesaving, privacy-invading, noisy, and entertaining new technology. Sometimes they're all of those things at once.

So what exactly are drones, and how do they work? Drones come in many forms, but typically they are remote-controlled flying vehicles that are made from lightweight materials. A square or rectangular frame has rotors (propellers) at each corner, and a receiver is usually located in the center of the aircraft. The drone pilot, or controller, has a control box that acts as a radio transmitter. The receiver picks up those radio signals and converts them into electrical signals, which are sent to the flight controller (often called the "brains" of the drone). The flight controller gives orders to regulate motor speed and rotor angles (to steer and change altitude), and to trigger cameras. Some drones have more powerful engines, so they can carry a much heavier payload. These larger versions have proved to be extremely useful in emergencies.

Drone to the Rescue!

Two Australian teenagers, Monty Greenslade and Gabe Vidler, got into trouble while swimming at a beach in 2018. The strong current had swept them out to sea. Luckily the boys were near a group of lifeguards who were doing a drone-training course on the beach.

A friend sounded the alarm about the boys, and lifeguard Jai Sheridan immediately piloted a rescue drone (the type just used in the training session) out to them. It carried a flotation device, which dropped down to the boys and allowed them to get to shore safely.

"I was able to launch it, fly it to the location, and drop the pod all in about one to two minutes," Sheridan recalled. "On a normal day, that would have taken our lifeguards a few minutes longer to reach the members of the public." And a few minutes longer can mean the difference between life and death in many beach rescues.

The good and the bad about drone technology seem to be pretty well balanced. Let's start with some of the pretty stuff. If you go to a video-sharing website and type in "aerial view" or simply "drone" and then add just about any place in the world, you'll come up with loads of awesome choices: views over Paris, flying through the Grand Canyon, circling over a deserted Pacific island. Most of these would have been incredibly expensive or even impossible to film without a drone.

That same ability to set off from the Grand Canyon is an enormous advantage to emergency teams dealing with natural disasters. Drones can get past fallen trees in a landslide, buckled roads after an earthquake, or even red-hot lava flows if survivors need to be located. And if some of those survivors are stranded, drones can arrive with emergency food or medical supplies until first responders can reach the area in person.

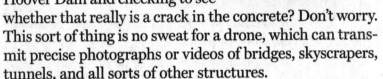

Feel like shinnying up one of the cables of the Golden Gate Bridge to make sure it's not too rusty at the top? Oh, and would you mind throwing a rope ladder down the side of the 726-foot-tall (221 m) Hoover Dam and checking to see whether that really is a crack in the concrete? Don't worry. This sort of thing is no sweat for a drone, which can transmit precise photographs or videos of bridges, skyscrapers, tunnels, and all sorts of other structures.

Drones have also helped farmers observe how well crops are responding to irrigation, fertilizer, or new planting arrangements. The drones can patrol fields and even get important details from individual plants. Cattle farmers use drones to keep track of their herds and flocks, too.

RELATED TECHNOLOGY

Drones are a natural progression from remote-control airplanes and cars, which have been around for decades. The difference, of course, is the ability of drones to slowly pass over—or even hover over—the land or sea below. No chance of that with a remote-control car, and planes could swoop, soar, and dive . . . but not stop to take photos or drop off parcels.

Drones are often teamed with other technologies, especially cameras and other data-gathering instruments. Military drones sometimes have packages of different equipment, with cameras able to use a form of night-vision or heat-sensitive image gathering. (Maybe that was the buzzing you heard above the barbecue last weekend.) GPS (see page 121) also ties in with drones to make sure that they stay on a direct (and fuel-saving) course to a destination or to guide them across agricultural fields that have to be monitored.

TERRIFYINGLY AWESOME?

Wow! Here's a chapter that could have been filled up with just the terrifying stuff. Where do we start? How about privacy: Would you welcome a buzzing intruder from above into your picnic or beach volleyball game? Or while you're just sitting in the backyard, practicing lines for a school play? That might not be terrifying, but it's part of the problem that society faces with drones. And that drone operators face with society.

Things became a little terrifying—and definitely infuriating—at Gatwick Airport (the UK's second largest) in December 2018. Drone sightings near busy runways caused the airport to cancel more than 1,000 flights over three days while authorities investigated. Officials had to be extra cautious, because a drone collision could cause a plane to crash.

News reports constantly tell us how drones have been used in spying and other military activities, including combat. Some sturdy drones can fire missiles. Many of us accept that type of use for this new technology, but at the same time we wonder what would happen if other armies or terrorists were able to use the same technology on our armed forces—or on us.

Any sort of powered aircraft has to find a way to master four basic forces: gravity (pulling it down), lift (pushing it upward), thrust (moving it forward), and drag (holding it back).

Engineers are constantly tinkering with aircraft and wing design to get the right mix of these four forces. Drone designers need to produce something that maneuvers well and can react to changing conditions. For example, a sudden gust of wind can provide either more thrust or more drag, depending on the wind direction. You can test these forces using a type of aircraft that you've probably created lots of times—a paper plane.

YOU WILL NEED
- Piece of paper (letter or computer size)
- Ruler
- Scissors

METHOD

1. Fold the piece of paper in half lengthwise, running your thumb down the crease; then unfold it.

2. Fold the two top corners inward so that one side of each meets the other. (They look like two triangles meeting.)

3. Fold the outside edges inward (as you did in Step 2 with the corners) so that their edges meet in the middle.

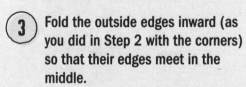

4. Lay the paper flat. Then fold the point back so that it meets where the two edges met.

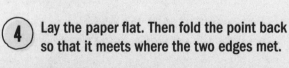

5) Fold the paper along the long crease and pinch the end where the point was folded in (in Step 4).

6) Still pinching the point, gently unfold the two long edges—which are now your plane's wings.

7) The plane is ready for takeoff. Pinch it near the front and launch it with a quick flick. Do several flights and judge the average distance.

8) Now make small folds at the back of the wings and judge the distance and direction of flight.

9) Return the wings to their normal position (undo the folds in Step 8) and use the scissors to cut a small flap just where each wing meets the ridge.

10) Fold the flaps so that each wing has a flap pointing upward, at a right angle to the wing. Do more test flights and record your findings.

DATA ANALYSIS

Believe it or not, aeronautical engineers do this sort of thing all the time! You provided the same amount of thrust in each test flight. The small folds in Step 8 provided more lift, and the flaps in Step 9 created drag. Drone designers also deal with lift, thrust, and drag by changing the speed of the four rotors (propellers). To move the drone horizontally, they need to tip it—and they do that by slowing two rotors on one side and revving up the other two. The slower two dip while the faster two rise, and the drone picks up more horizontal movement. And like your adjustments to the paper plane, the amount they angle the drone—and the power (thrust) they apply to the rotors—directs the drone.

CHAPTER 22

TEST-TUBE MEAT

In the 1960s, when everyone was absolutely riveted by the space race, you'd see TV commercials for foods and drinks "as used by NASA astronauts." Space food sure sounded exciting, but usually it meant something that you squeezed from a tube like toothpaste . . . and it didn't taste much better.

Fast-forward a few decades, and you find people talking about "test-tube meat" and other foods produced or grown in labs. There's no talk about astronauts munching this stuff, but the selling point usually still concerns Earth: saving it.

Many people are turning away from eating meat because of cruelty to animals. And even meat eaters agree that having all those cows around just to satisfy our taste for meat isn't good for the environment. Is it really worth cutting down forests to create enormous cattle fields? Why not create meat from almost nothing and grow it in science labs? Sounds ideal, doesn't it? That is, as long as you know exactly what's being grown!

HOW LIFE IS BETTER

Okay, admit it. You haven't been waiting years for someone to come up with a way of growing food in a science lab. Just think of the accidental science experiments in your refrigerator: ancient leftovers covered in mold and fungus. The mold and fungus were able to thrive because they grew in favorable conditions. You could even say that they were cultivated there. Scientists would probably describe them as "cultured" mold and fungus.

Your culturing process was probably a mistake, but the scientists developing "cultured meats" and other lab-produced foods have a pretty important reason for their work. They have been listening to warnings from climate scientists about how our food choices are harming the planet. Test-tube meat might just be one way of turning things around.

> **STEM CELLS**
>
> Cells in a living organism that can change into a different type of cell and then divide to produce more of the same type of cell.

The World's Most Expensive Burger

In August 2013, the most expensive burger in history was cooked and eaten in London. It had been created by Professor Mark Post of the University of Maastricht. Professor Post had taken muscle stem cells from cows and placed them in a medium (a gooey substance that provides a good environment for growing).

Once the cells had begun to divide and produce other muscle stem cells, Professor Post's team managed to mimic exercise by applying tension to the groups of muscle cells. This was to re-create what happens when real muscles exercise. Eventually, 20,000 strips of "test-tube muscle" were ready to be turned into a burger.

A professional formed the "beef" into a patty and pan-fried it up. Then it was time for the taste test: Two experts were called in. An Austrian nutritionist and an American food writer both found it a little dry and hard but still described it as meat.

It was all over in a matter of minutes, although the burger had taken three months and $335,000 to prepare. The price has come *way* down in recent years, however—Professor Post says it now costs just $11 to make.

We're all aware that dirty fossil fuels like oil and coal are extremely harmful to the environment and that we'll need new ways to produce energy and to get around. Electric cars (see page 195) are part of that search, along with alternative energy production such as wind, tidal, and solar power (page 9). These efforts are also well known and recognized for their long-term benefits.

Food production, though, is a little harder to portray as a danger to the planet. But think about how many forests have been cut down in the Amazon region and elsewhere to produce grazing land for cattle. And did you know that the world population of cows (most of which are bred for the food industry) accounts for nearly 15 percent of human-made greenhouse gas emissions? How's that?

GREENHOUSE GAS

A gas in the Earth's atmosphere (such as carbon dioxide or methane) that traps the Sun's energy inside the atmosphere without letting it escape. The result is dangerously high temperatures on Earth, just as a greenhouse keeps plants warm inside.

Try not to laugh, but cow burps and farts produce dangerous methane gas after digesting grass. Moving toward controlled, "cultured" production of meat—along with everyone eating less meat anyway—would be a step away from that dangerous and increasing threat to the world.

RELATED TECHNOLOGY

Fish farming, or pisciculture, is a way of raising fish or shellfish in enclosed ponds, pools, or other bodies of water. The fish are fed nutrients to make sure that the food supply is maintained and then are "harvested" for food consumption. Critics fear that unlike test-tube meat production, fish farming creates risks for the environment. Harmful pests and diseases can sweep quickly through the fish population and seep out into the wild. At present, though, as much as one third of fish and shellfish sold for food are farmed.

TERRIFYINGLY AWESOME?

Like so many new technologies, test-tube meats and other cultured foods are still pretty expensive and produced under very strict, controlled guidelines. Each ingredient is noted and recorded, and each stage of development is observed and monitored. So even if a "test-tube burger" tastes a little dry, you know exactly how it turned into what you're looking at. It's sort of like the way that some people will only eat meat if they know where and how the animal was raised.

Even so, test-tube meat production could have risks that scientists just haven't identified yet. Can we be sure that government departments in every nation will insist on rigorous testing to make sure that humans will come to no harm from this development? And what about the conclusion that "everyone's a winner" with this type of meat production? Sure, it saves the lives of loads of cattle and helps the environment by letting forests re-blanket large areas of cattle-grazing land. But at least one study shows that large-scale test-tube meat production would use *more* energy than existing methods for obtaining meat. Might increased global warming (a big no-no) be part of the price we'd pay for this breakthrough?

EXPERIMENT
WHAT'S THAT GROWING IN MY KITCHEN?!
WARNING! ADULT SUPERVISION REQUIRED

Time Factor: **2** weeks

Growing "meat" or anything else in a confined space like a test tube calls for a growing culture. That's a substance that provides a good environment for this growing to take place. One of the most commonly used substances for this job is agar. This demonstration shows you how to prepare a similar substance for experiments.

Then you'll do some growing yourself. But you're not going to be growing anything edible—instead you'll probably give yourself a shock by seeing how germs can grow in unexpected places. Try taking one of the samples from somewhere that you always thought was "germ-free." You might be surprised!

Scientists use special jars called petri dishes to do this sort of experiment. If you have six of them, skip to Step 6. Otherwise you need to do a little preparation by sterilizing six lids and letting them cool to room temperature. Figure on that taking about 90 minutes.

YOU WILL NEED

- Oven
- 6 jar lids
- Baking sheet
- 1 beef bouillon cube
- 1 pack of unflavored gelatin
- 1 cup of water
- 1 teaspoon of sugar
- Saucepan
- Stove
- Wooden spoon
- 6 cotton swabs
- Plastic food wrap
- Magnifying glass

METHOD

(1) Have an adult preheat the oven to 350°F (177°C).

(2) Wash the lids in hot, soapy water, then rinse (but don't dry) them.

(3) Place them upside down on the baking sheet and have an adult put it in the oven.

(4) Turn the oven off after 15 minutes and let the lids cool for another hour or so.

(5) Make sure the lids are completely cool before continuing, then place the baking sheet with the lids on a table or counter.

(6) Mix the bouillon cube, gelatin, water, and sugar in a saucepan on the stove and bring the mixture to a boil, stirring constantly.

(7) Have the adult pour the mixture (your made-up "agar") into the six lids and put the baking sheet into the refrigerator for 30 minutes.

8 Think of six places that might have germs—your hands, the floor, a video game controller, the TV remote, etc.

9 Rub a swab on each of these places and then rub it on the surface of the agar in one of the lids.

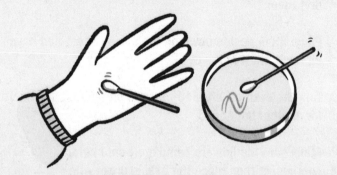

10 Cover each lid tightly with food wrap. You now have six samples for observation.

11 Transfer the baking sheet to somewhere warm where it won't be bumped.

12 Observe the growth of germs in the lids, using a magnifying glass at first, for the next two weeks.

13 Throw away the "germy" lids without unwrapping them.

"Germs" is a general term to describe a wide range of tiny organisms that are all around us. Bacteria and viruses are examples of germs. Not all germs are harmful: For example, our bodies use bacteria to help fight other germs. And you wouldn't have tasty foods like yogurt without germs.

You've provided germs with a head start by creating an environment in which they can develop and grow. The medium that you brewed up is special: It provides nutrients for just about any microorganism and doesn't play favorites—they all have a chance to thrive. So each of your six lids, with its agar base, should be a great breeding ground for germs. Have they shown up?

CHAPTER 23

"HARVESTING" WATER FROM THE AIR

To some, rain is just an inconvenience: soggy picnics, muddy shoes, and rained-out ball games. But you don't need to live in a desert to realize how much we rely on rain. Without it you would find bare shelves in the fruit and vegetable aisle at your local supermarket. Or a stretch of sun-baked mud instead of your favorite swimming hole. Or even dust storms blowing up where you used to see acres of corn growing.

The truth is, we all need fresh water for just about everything we do, from bath time to agriculture. And desert dwellers need it even more urgently. That's why cultures from all over the world have customs that are meant to bring on rain. Some are scientific (like "seeding" clouds to make them rain) and others are more religious (like rain dances).

A new technology seems to introduce magic into the mix—plucking water right from the air. It could be the answer to all those prayers and hopes . . . as long as the right people are responsible for harnessing it.

HOW LIFE IS BETTER

Ever listen to a weather forecast and hear the term "relative humidity"? Have you ever wondered what it means? Well, relative humidity is a measure of how much water is contained in the air at a particular time, place, and temperature. The higher the number, the more water is contained in the air and the more humid it feels. That's the sticky feeling when it's hard to sleep at night and days feel heavy.

A dry place like Phoenix, Arizona, would have a really low relative humidity reading— probably around 35 percent as an annual average. Extra-humid places, such as New Orleans or Miami, have more than double that number as an annual average.

What's this got to do with harvesting water from the air? Well, it's a first step to understanding that developing technology. Even a place like Phoenix, which most people consider to have a desert climate, still has water floating around in the air above it. But what about the millions of people who live in places that are even drier than Phoenix, places that don't have a regular supply of fresh water that they can use? That's where this new "harvesting" technology comes in.

Billions of people lack a regular supply of clean water for much of the year—or they have to travel long distances to fetch it. Many regions in Africa near the Sahara Desert and in central Asia face this problem. Other parts of the world could soon be in the same difficult situation—especially if climate change continues to alter landscapes and "bake" places drier. But it could be that the very thing that has dried up much of the water—the Sun—could be used to release new supplies from the air itself.

Scientists from the Massachusetts Institute of Technology (MIT) and the University of California, Berkeley, have developed a pretty exciting new way to collect water from even desert air. They use solar power to heat up super-absorbent crystals, which then suck water right from the air.

Using this basic model as a starting point, the team had the first of two big breakthroughs. The scientists focused on a type of crystal called metal-organic frameworks (MOFs), which can hold enormous amounts of water in relation to their size. A piece of MOF as small as

Humidity Versus Relative Humidity

Both of these terms refer to moisture (water) floating around in the air, and both are expressed as percentages of the air itself. The water isn't in its liquid form; instead it's in the vapor (gas) phase. That means that the moisture is invisible, but an instrument called a hygrometer can measure the humidity level.

Relative humidity is slightly different because it tells us how much water vapor the air can hold within a given temperature. How does that work? Warmer air can hold more moisture than colder air. That's because the warmer air (like any gas) expands as it gets warmer.

Time for a bit of math. If no water is added to air as it warms, then the relative humidity would go down because it was making up less of the expanded warmer air. And when things go the other way—air temperature falls—there's a temperature at which all that water vapor turns back to water (condenses). You've probably seen the result in the morning, when dew (water that had been held in the air) forms on grass because the air temperature dropped overnight.

a sugar cube has about the same internal surface area as the surface of *six football fields*. That huge surface area—packed in a tiny space—attracts and holds on to the water molecules. That's the key to MOFs' holding all that water.

Another team, called Zero Mass Water, had the next breakthrough. They developed solar panels to produce enough energy to drive the "water harvesting" process. Water vapor is absorbed by the heated crystals and then condenses into liquid water as the crystals cool.

These two advances—both of which are already being produced—might be wonderful news to anyone living in countries that desperately need reliable water supplies. Luckily, most of those countries have lots of strong sunshine, so the same sun that baked their rivers dry might now be able to help provide fresh water.

RELATED TECHNOLOGY

For many decades, scientists and engineers have tried to turn salt water into drinkable fresh water. The technology is called desalination (meaning "de-salting"). It is possible to use this process, but the technology has a number of drawbacks. The first, of course, is that it can only work in places that have an ocean coastline. Another is the enormous amount of energy needed to power desalination plants. And then there's the problem of what to do with the mountains of salt that pile up next to the factories that have extracted it from seawater. There aren't enough French fries in the world to put all that salt on!

TERRIFYINGLY AWESOME?

The super-absorbent quality of the "harvesting crystals" could almost remind us of an old joke with no answer: "How much deeper would the oceans be if sponges didn't grow there?" Could we reach a point where those crystals were so incredibly strong that they sucked up all the water in the air? Hmm . . .

But as we know, not having enough water is genuinely terrifying. Increased human water consumption and rising temperatures worldwide could make water a resource that countries fight wars over later this century. Not having this water-harvesting technology (or something as effective) could drive some countries to desperate measures to gain control of and access to rivers, lakes, springs, and other sources of fresh water.

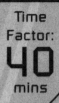

As you've just read, the scientists from MIT and Berkeley had tested and experimented with many types of material that could absorb water. Don't forget: It's the water absorbency that lies at the heart of this "harvesting" technology.

Here's a chance to retrace the scientists' steps. You're going to test four different substances to see how well they absorb water. We won't ask you to go to the next step—producing solar panels. That can wait for another experiment session!

YOU WILL NEED

- Scissors
- Disposable diaper (unused!) or cotton balls
- 4 drinking glasses
- Ruler
- Flour
- Sand
- Paper towels (several sheets scrunched up)
- Water
- Measuring cup

METHOD

1 Use the scissors to carefully cut open the diaper and pour the crystals from it into a drinking glass up to 2 inches (5 cm), measured with a ruler. (If using cotton balls, pack them tightly up to the same level.)

2 Now fill each of the other glasses to the same height: one with flour, another with sand, and the third with the scrunched-up paper towels.

3 Add water to each glass up to 4 inches (10 cm) high. (You can press the paper towel down so that it doesn't float up.)

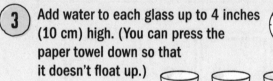

4 Wait half an hour.

5 Carefully tilt a glass over the measuring cup and pour out as much of the water as you can, leaving the material inside the glass.

6 Measure how much water is in the measuring cup, then dump out the water for the next measurement.

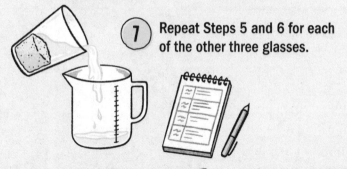

7 Repeat Steps 5 and 6 for each of the other three glasses.

DATA ANALYSIS

This is a sort of "reverse answer." Think about it. The glass that had the most water left (and filled the measuring cup the highest) had the least absorbent material inside it. Which glass produced the least water? It will be the diaper filling, with the chemical name sodium polyacrylate. Any idea why diapers might be made with this stuff? If you're too grossed out to ponder that question, think of the science behind those special crystals (MOFs) that the MIT and Berkeley scientists developed. (The cotton balls, if you used them, will also be the winners, but for a more familiar reason: Cotton is really absorbent.)

CHAPTER 24

ELECTRIC CARS

→ − +   X

Ask your grandparents whether they can remember the oil crisis of 1973. If they were around at the time, they'll be sure to tell you about the lines of cars—sometimes more than a mile long—waiting for a gas station to open. And of drivers hoping that the station wouldn't have run out by the time they reached it.

For many people, that temporary shortage of oil (and its product, gasoline) was the first glimpse of what things might be like when the Earth finally uses up all of its dirty fossil fuels. Goodbye, gasoline and diesel . . . but what then? And what can we do to prepare for that likely event?

One solution has been to develop electric automobiles. These battery-powered cars have an additional benefit: They don't pollute the air. Sounds like a winner! Except it has taken a long time to develop batteries that can take these cars long distances. So, in a way, this chapter isn't about technology that's potentially terrifying. Instead it's about a *definitely* terrifying future if we don't get going with this technology!

HOW LIFE IS BETTER

Considering that this is a book about cutting-edge, modern technology, prepare yourself for a *shock*. (Get it?) Electric cars have been around much longer than gasoline-powered vehicles. That's right. As early as the 1820s and 1830s, inventors were designing small-scale cars that could travel on tracks. Electric train engines were soon to follow. By the 1850s, inventors were developing rechargeable batteries—the central, essential element of electric vehicles.

At its heart, the technology behind today's electric automobiles is simple to understand. The vehicle has a battery that can be recharged when it runs low. Special powering stations can recharge batteries quickly, but most models now come with a charging unit that can be plugged into household outlets. It's slower, but much more convenient.

The battery powers an electric engine, which—like other automobile engines—powers the wheels to propel the car. Most owners save a ton on fuel and maintenance costs. Some figure that electric cars cost only a third as much as other cars to run.

The other benefits to the world at large are enormous. Reducing air pollution is a positive health benefit, especially in cities. And with fewer exhaust gases being pumped into the atmosphere, we can help slow the pace of global warming.

> **GLOBAL WARMING**
>
> A gradual (and worrying) increase in the overall temperature of the Earth's atmosphere caused, in part, by gases emitted by gasoline-powered vehicles.

It's this dangerous air pollution that has helped drive the "rebirth" of electric vehicles. While internal combustion engines (the sort that use gasoline or diesel) were all the rage throughout most of the 20th century, the last couple of decades have told a different story. It was becoming clear that our supplies of fuel were limited after all and would probably run out pretty soon. Even worse,

Battery Basics

Batteries are portable devices that can store and supply electrical power. They convert chemical energy into electrical energy, and it all comes down to the flow of electrons. The anode (or negative end of the battery) reacts with a chemical substance (the electrolyte) in the middle of the battery, producing electrons. The cathode (positive end) reacts with the electrolyte and *takes* electrons. An electrical current (flow of electrons) occurs when a wire connects the anode with the cathode.

the pollution thrown into the atmosphere by millions of cars and trucks was a serious threat to the planet.

Those two factors, coupled with advances in battery and electric-power technology, kick-started the reappearance of electric cars, despite widespread opposition from the "traditional" (internal-combustion) auto industry. People had already seen smaller versions, such as golf carts or airport transport vehicles, but by the 1990s, more electric passenger vehicles appeared on roads.

So where do things stand now, and what about the future? All-electric and hybrid cars make up only about 1 to 2 percent of all vehicles in the United States. Most experts agree that by 2040 that figure should rise significantly, to as much as perhaps 40 percent. Norway has almost matched that higher figure already, with electric cars making up 37 percent of all new sales, up from 6 percent in 2013. But it's clear that we need to speed up our switch to electric cars—for the future of the planet.

RELATED TECHNOLOGY

One of the main drawbacks of electric cars, at least until recently, has been their batteries. You know the feeling when a phone or laptop seems to need to be recharged every other minute? Imagine if you had that dreadful dead-battery feeling on a deserted highway in the Mojave Desert or while you are sightseeing in Alaska's snow-packed Denali National Park. Well, the good news is that researchers involved in different technologies but working on similar problems—in this case, battery life—can bounce ideas off one another. Advances in phone-battery technology can spill over into electric car battery technology, and vice versa.

Another of the most familiar related technologies lies behind "hybrid" vehicles. These automobiles and trucks combine elements of electric vehicles with more traditional gasoline-powered engines. In fact, hybrid vehicles have both types of engine—gasoline and electric (battery-powered). And the neat thing is that the battery can be recharging while the gasoline engine is running.

Hybrid vehicles are designed to use whichever engine is the more efficient at that moment. When the vehicle is traveling very slowly, for example, the electric engine

is the better, more efficient choice. Up to about 15 mph (25 kmh), which includes most city driving, hybrids use only the electric engine. Using electric rather than gasoline power means also creating less pollution in densely populated areas.

HYBRID

In biology, the offspring of two plants or animals of different species. More widely the word describes a thing made by combining two different elements.

Once the vehicle starts cruising above that speed, the gasoline engine works at its most efficient. It also powers the generator at this time, so that energy is stored in the electric engine's battery. If the vehicle needs a boost of acceleration—passing another vehicle on a highway, for example—both engines kick in.

When the vehicle brakes, the onboard computer stops sending power to the wheels but allows their spinning to power the generator. As a result, hybrid cars have much better fuel consumption than normal automobiles. Some hybrids manage 50 miles per gallon in city driving. That's more than double most gasoline-powered cars.

TERRIFYINGLY AWESOME?

It's no exaggeration to say that running out of battery power in the wilderness would be pretty terrifying. On the other hand, people run out of gas all the time, don't they? It's a matter of common sense to know the limits of your vehicle. Plus, if things continue at today's rate, electric cars will be getting better batteries, and plugging stations will become far more common.

Another risk of electric cars was once seen only as a plus: their noise, or lack of it. Think of a headphone-wearing (or blind) pedestrian crossing a busy road. They'd probably hear most gas-powered vehicles coming their way, but the silence of the electric vehicles might let people walk right in front of them.

Get ready to take your very own electric car out for a spin. You'll be creating not one but two electric vehicles, and with luck you'll be able to do some tricks with them.

"There must be a catch," you say. Well, there is. This is also one of the few experiments that calls for ingredients you probably don't already have around the house. Those ingredients are called neodymium magnets, and they're really, really powerful. You can buy them online or at any store that has a good electrical department.

You'll see below that they're usually sold according to their metric size. And if you're able to get hold of four of the smaller version, why not go the extra mile and get two larger ones? That way you'll *really* be able to get the vehicles to perform!

YOU WILL NEED

- 4 neodymium magnets (15mm diameter)
- 2 neodymium magnets (25mm diameter), optional
- 2 AA batteries
- Aluminum foil (the largest size available—often sold for cooking turkey)

METHOD

1. Spread a square sheet of foil on a hard floor or table.

2. Carefully attach a small neodymium magnet to the positive end of an AA battery.

3 Now attach another to the negative end.

4 Place the battery on the foil so that the batteries on each end look like wheels.

5 You've now created an electric vehicle that rolls without being pushed.

6 If you have a larger neodymium magnet, use it to replace one of the smaller ones on the vehicle. Now place it down and watch it drive around in circles.

7 You could even make two vehicles and have them chase each other on the foil.

DATA ANALYSIS

You probably noticed that if your "car" drove off the foil, it slowed and stopped. That's because the foil acts as a conductor (something that allows electrons to flow freely) between the two poles of the AA battery. Adding the neodymium magnets raises the stakes and creates a much more powerful magnetic field. In fact, it creates what's known as a homopolar motor. Now no one can tell you that you're too young to drive!

CHAPTER 25

POWERED EXOSKELETONS

→ − +   X

We humans can't quite match Superman by traveling "faster than a speeding bullet" or "leaping tall buildings in a single bound"—yet—but we might be getting closer. Scientists and engineers have developed shortcuts to boost speed and mobility. That's right: powered exoskeletons.

Rather than giving everyone superhuman strength, powered exoskeletons can allow people to do things faster and longer—like weld engine parts over their head in a factory—before they get tired. And don't forget improved mobility. An exoskeleton can give support to or replace weak or damaged limbs.

Winners all around then, eh? Well, like so many things, this technology could also be used by the bad guys. Imagine a gang of unstoppable bank robbers or enemy soldiers with arms that seem bulletproof!

HOW LIFE IS BETTER

Augmented mobility is the technology behind the idea of powered exoskeletons. "Augmented" is simply another way of saying "added to" or "improved." This has been the starting point of a range of technologies that also go by the name of powered exoskeletons.

But hold up—what does this word *exoskeleton* mean? The *skeleton* part you know—it's some sort of framework that's always solid. Meanwhile, that *exo-* part means "outside of" something. In nature, an exoskeleton is an external skeleton that supports and protects an animal. The solid shell around a grasshopper, lobster, or crab, for example, is an exoskeleton. Humans and other mammals, on the other hand, have an endoskeleton, which means a skeleton *inside* the body.

A "powered exoskeleton" is an additional layer on the outside of a human body that adds strength or support. It's made of molded plastic or shaped metal that either covers most of a person's body (like a modern version of knight's armor) or acts as an extension of a human limb.

The "powered" bit refers to the mechanical power of these devices, which have built-in motors that respond to voice, touch, or Wi-Fi signals. In a way, they're like machines attached to a human body, and their engines give the human wearer much more strength or endurance. An exoskeleton arm, for example, would have a powered hinge at the elbow to let the human pick up heavy objects.

Some of the most useful of these technologies, which definitely make many lives better, give people dramatically more mobility. Imagine being able to take your first independent steps—for the first time in years, or ever—thanks to a powered case attached to the side of your leg.

The really eye-catching element of this group of technologies, however, relates to adding strength. People begin to think of Iron Man, but designers are quick to

Real-Life Iron Man

People have been fascinated by the idea of "powering up" humans for decades. The notion has been the subject of tons of sci-fi novels, movies, and TV series. Seen any of the *Iron Man* movies and wondered what it would be like to have that sort of strength? Well, some real-life folks have had a chance to wield some of those superhero powers. In 2018, a British inventor demonstrated his "body-controlled jet engine power suit" in a demonstration over the streets of London. Anyone wearing this Skeletonics Exoskeleton suit is turned into an 9-foot-tall (2.75 m) robot, complete with mechanical links to transfer human movements into exoskeleton action.

point out that they're not trying to get people to lift automobiles or tanks. Instead—and many manufacturers have picked up on this—a device can be just as helpful if it reduces tiredness rather than increasing strength. Assembly-line workers at auto factories, for instance, already use arm supports that help them weld, drill, or paint equipment for long periods.

RELATED TECHNOLOGY

The part human–part machine image of powered exoskeletons links them to the study and production of robots and androids (see page 17). Indeed, many of the advances in those fields can be transferred to others, with humans taking on a few "robotic" qualities (mechanical limbs).

But powered-exoskeleton technology also overlaps with a much older technology: prosthetics, or artificial devices used to replace missing body parts. These can range from things as basic as a pirate's peg leg to complex, electronically powered devices. For instance, one of those might connect to the upper arm and transmit muscle signals electrically, causing mechanical fingers to open and shut.

Prosthetics can also cross the boundary back into augmented mobility. Some athletes who usually wear more common artificial limbs use "blades" in competition. These also attach to the residual limb (the original leg above the knee), but the base isn't a solid shoe or footlike shape—instead it's a long L-shaped blade that's very springy. With a little practice, an athlete can manage to sprint with a normal running stride while wearing a pair of the blades.

Would you consider a blade-wearer "handicapped"? Other competitors think just the opposite—that the blades give the wearers an unfair advantage! There's augmented mobility for you.

TERRIFYINGLY AWESOME?

Hmm. Giving people extra strength and mobility—it sure sounds like a good idea, until you wonder what it would be like to have a mugger or an enemy soldier with these advantages. Like so many technologies, powered exoskeletons have a nightmare side as well as a wealth of benefits. Could bank robbers forget about cracking safes and just use a powered arm to yank the safe door open? Maybe, for good measure, they've yanked some parked cars onto the road outside to slow the police chase.

Then think of how any kind of supervillain might use this sort of extra strength to break into a courthouse, town hall, or even the White House! That's pretty terrifying.

EXPERIMENT
THANKS FOR THE LIFT

Here's your chance to try out some augmented mobility yourself, with a couple of friends to become an exoskeleton—at least for a few moments. It's a fun experiment that demonstrates a simple but important principle: Just a little boost can add strength, but that same level of help would be even more useful if it gave you the chance to perform the same task over and over again.

YOU WILL NEED

- 2 heavy books (like dictionaries)
- Table or countertop
- 2 friends
- Piece of wood (roughly shelving dimensions: 1 inch by 6 inches / 2.5 cm by 15 cm) about 4 feet (1.2 m) long

METHOD

1. Lay the books carefully on the table or counter.

2. Slowly and carefully lift the pair of books up and as high as you can lift them.

3. Slowly lower them down to the surface.

4. Repeat Steps 2 and 3 until it becomes too difficult.

5. Shake your arms to loosen the muscles and wait for 10 minutes, to get fresh again.

6 Ask your friends to join you and to stand on either side of you.

7 Get them to slide the board under the books and your forearms (between your elbows and wrists), holding it firm in that position.

8 On the count of 3, lift the books again slowly, but this time with your friends pushing slowly up with the board.

9 Lower your arms (and the board) slowly, then repeat.

10 See how many times you can lift the books this time before you get too tired.

DATA ANALYSIS

Your friends, acting as the "powered exoskeleton," were augmenting your mobility by providing a bit more strength with each lift. You should have found it much easier to lift the books in Step 8 than in Step 2. And just as importantly, you should have been able to manage many more lifts. It's that bit—added stamina—that makes powered exoskeletons so useful in factory settings. Imagine welding chassis (car framework) after chassis as they slide past overhead in an automobile assembly line. After about the third car, your arms would feel like falling off. With a powered exoskeleton arm, though, you'd be able to do many more with no tiredness.

CHAPTER 26

SPACE ELEVATOR

→ − +   X

"Going up?"

Sometimes you'll hear that as you *just* make it into an elevator and a kind person has held the door open for you. You'll probably thank them and say that you're heading for the 9th, or the 27th, or even the 102nd floor (if you're in the Empire State Building).

Imagine if your answer had been "Thanks, I'm getting off at the 26 million, 400 thousandth floor." Because that's about how many floors it takes to reach 60,000 miles (100,000 km) above Earth—the height of the last stop on a proposed Space Elevator.

Okay, so it's not quite the same as a normal elevator, and no one will be holding the door open for you. It's more for cargo and large vehicles. But it's one thing to worry about getting stuck between floors back on Earth. How about waiting for a repairman in space?

The International Academy of Astronautics (IAA) sounds like a pretty serious group of scientists, doesn't it? So when those folks come up with a suggestion—in fact, it's a 350-page document—about an exciting new form of space transportation, it's worth stopping to listen. Or even to read those 350 pages.

Far from being "dry and dusty," the document describes a device that sounds like it came straight out of *Star Wars*. Their theoretical "space elevator" does pretty much what you might think it does: It takes cargo (and humans) up into space. How far up? Well, the top floor (the only floor, really) is 60,000 miles (100,000 km) up. Sure, it would take a week to reach the platform, but remember that we're talking about something that's a quarter of the way to the Moon. Human passengers would travel in a container that's a cross between a space capsule and a space station.

That top floor is a huge counterweight. It connects to a cable (called a "tether") leading back down to Earth. It's made of carbon nanotubes (cylindrical carbon molecules) that are 100 times stronger than steel and as flexible as plastic. The Earth end of the tether is linked to a huge anchor weighing 44 million pounds (20 million kg). The force of gravity (strongest at the Earth end) and the constant movement of the counterweight (at the other end) keep the tether taut and straight.

> **COUNTERWEIGHT**
>
> A weight that balances another weight.

HOW LIFE IS BETTER

So why go to all this effort to build and maintain a space elevator? The answer is simple, and it doesn't take anywhere near 350 pages to explain. It would be much easier, and less expensive, to send objects out from Earth along the tether than to send them in rockets, even reusable rockets (see page 33). The IAA report predicts that seven

20-ton payloads could make the five-day trip up the tether to the end of the line at once.

"What on Earth would you be sending up on one of these things, anyway?" you're probably wondering. The answer: Loads of stuff. Want to replace some of the equipment on the International Space Station? Send it up, and then a mini-rocket could scoot the parcel over to the ISS. You could launch heavy satellites from the elevator, too. The elevator could even be the best way to send crew members up and down.

Geostationary Orbit

An object in geostationary orbit keeps exact pace with the speed of the Earth's rotation, as long as it is rotating in the same direction. The Earth takes exactly 23 hours, 56 minutes, and 4.09 seconds to complete one spin on its axis. If a satellite orbiting the Earth in the same direction takes exactly the same time to complete its rotation, then it will remain above the same point on Earth.

The science of gravitational pull and other forces means that there is an ideal distance above the Earth's surface—22,236 miles (35,864 km)—where this sort of geostationary orbit kicks in. Satellites in geostationary orbits already do many important jobs, ranging from providing GPS technology to precise weather forecasting and communications.

Cost is a really persuasive argument in favor of a space elevator. Space launches are incredibly expensive, and scientists are trying to find ways to make them cheaper. The cost per kilogram (2.2 pounds) to send a payload by rocket up to a geostationary orbit is about $20,000. Using the space elevator, that cost could be cut to just $500 per kilogram.

Lowered costs don't just benefit governments and large corporations: If smaller countries (and companies) find that they can afford to send payloads into space, then the space elevator begins to have some of the same pluses as microsatellites (see page 25). The elevator could level the playing field between big-budget governments and the less well-off.

RELATED TECHNOLOGY

The space elevator can link to a wide range of other technologies. Earlier ideas such as the "sky hook," for example, imagined orbiting stations able to hook onto satellites and spacecraft and hoist them into a higher orbit.

Supporters of the space elevator idea point out that it could be used as a launchpad for missions farther out into space—to Mars, for example. A spacecraft launched from Earth would need only enough fuel to reach the elevator. It could add fuel at the end of the line and then be launched into orbit around the Earth, but a sort of orbit that would be more of a spiral. After a few of these spirals—building up speed with each loop around Earth—the spacecraft could then steer away from Earth at the increased speed toward Mars or even farther.

TERRIFYINGLY AWESOME?

Getting stuck in the elevator is one obvious fear that people have with this idea. Here's another: Imagine a massive cargo ship making its way in the fog or a plane flying through clouds and then—crash! It hits the cable holding the elevator up. Would the elevator just go flying off into space, like a helium balloon floating off from a parade? Or would the elevator come plummeting down?

Then there's the fact that elevator passengers would be passing through some intense radiation outside Earth, so they'd need special protection. And there's always the risk of asteroids, meteors, or "space debris" damaging the tether. This might be more than we bargained for!

EXPERIMENT
GOING UP?

Time Factor: **30** mins

It's pretty easy to picture a space elevator in your mind's eye. This experiment gives you a chance to go a little further by creating a replica (call it a "scale model" to sound more scientific) in your own home or classroom.

You'll see how the simplicity of the design has convinced many engineers and scientists that the idea is practical. Do you think it's just crazy daydreaming? Think of what many people thought in 1961, when President Kennedy promised to land an astronaut on the Moon within nine years. That must have seemed a little far-fetched, too!

YOU WILL NEED

- Chair
- String
- An adult (possibly)
- A friend
- Scissors
- Helium balloon (the floating sort)
- Poster putty
- Small metal nail or tack (about 1 inch long)
- Plastic straw
- Heavy book
- Magnet

METHOD

1. Carefully stand on a chair and hold one end of the string to the ceiling. (You might need an adult to do this if it's a high ceiling.)

2. Ask your friend to pull the string gently so that it's taut and to pinch it where it meets the floor.

216 ● THE BOOK OF TERRIFYINGLY AWESOME TECHNOLOGY

3 With your friend still pinning the string to the floor, get off the chair and cut the lower end of the string about 15 inches beyond where your friend was pinching. (You now have a length of string that's about 15 inches longer than the height of the ceiling.)

4 Tie one end of the string to the knotted end of the balloon and ask your friend to hold it.

5 Use a small piece of poster putty to stick the nail or pin to the side of the straw.

6 Slide the straw onto the free end of string and hold it while your friend lets go of the balloon (which will float to the ceiling).

7 Keep holding the straw while your friend slides the free end of the string through the open book, shuts the book again, and lays the book on the floor (to lock the string tightly in place).

8 The balloon will now be directly above the book. If it reaches the ceiling with the string taut, don't adjust.

9 If there's too much slack, slide the string a bit more through the book—or take some back if the balloon doesn't reach the ceiling.

10 The straw represents the payload, which can be raised or lowered by holding the magnet close to the nail or tack and moving up or down slowly.

You've seen the "space elevator" in action, even if it was only raising and lowering the plastic-straw "payload" up to the ceiling and back down again. Each ingredient of your experiment echoed an element of the space elevator. The string, of course, is the tether or cable that provides the transportation link. And that book on the floor is heavy, but not quite as heavy as the 44-million-pound (20 million kg) weight that would hold the elevator secure. Do you feel any more confident that the full-scale version could work, or are you having second thoughts?

AFTERWORD

Here's a true story: Back in the 1780s, a Belgian farmer was leading his cattle through dense fog back to his barn. Then, from somewhere up in the clouds, he heard a man's voice call out, "Hello there. Am I anywhere near the city of Antwerp?"

The poor farmer was terrified. A voice from above! Was it an angel? A ghost? The Devil?

The farmer quickly learned that the voice came from the pilot of a hot-air balloon, one of the very few in existence. (The first-ever balloon flight was in 1783.) The balloon had taken off in clear weather, but lost its way in the fog.

Those wacky folks back then in Europe! Nowadays we seem to be much more aware of new advances in technology. But how would you feel if you saw someone just look at his front door and have it open for him? Or if your mom was supposed to pick you up from soccer practice and the car showed up without a driver? Or if someone was taking the elevator up to the next floor—60,000 miles (100,000 km) into space?

Technology still has the power to fascinate—and at times terrify—us all. We can look deep into history or far into the future and feel a thrill that we human beings are constantly able to come up with new ways to transform our lives. We can't help it—it's part of what makes us tick.

Hmm. "Tick." Sounds technical, doesn't it? Maybe it's time for you to find out whether we humans really do tick, and then find a way to make us tick louder, or faster, or just better. And that would be pretty awesome, wouldn't it?

GLOSSARY

AIR RESISTANCE: A frictional force that acts against a moving object, often slowing it down.

AMINO ACID: A chemical building block of the human body, made of a combination of nitrogen and hydrogen.

AMPLIFY: To make larger or greater.

ANODE: The negative end of a battery.

ARTIFICIAL INTELLIGENCE: A branch of advanced computer science that develops computers or programs to "think for themselves" by making decisions.

ATMOSPHERE: The layer of gases surrounding the Earth and other planets.

AUGMENTED: Made greater or stronger.

BAR CODE: A set of black lines on a white background on goods that a computer can scan to read information such as price.

BLUEPRINT: A detailed technical plan for a construction or engineering project.

CATHODE: The positive end of a battery.

CLOUD COMPUTING: A way of storing and accessing applications and data on the internet instead of the hard disks of local servers or computers.

COLLOID: A substance that is microscopically and evenly dispersed (spread) throughout another substance.

COMPUTER CODE: A series of instructions forming a computer program, which a computer can then run.

COMPUTER VIRUS: A destructive program that can damage or disable a computer.

CULTIVATE: To provide good growing conditions for organisms.

CULTURED: Produced under artificial conditions.

DESALINATION: The removal of excess salt and other minerals from seawater to obtain drinkable fresh water.

DNA: An abbreviation of deoxyribonucleic acid, a material carrying the genetic code ("chemical building blocks") of nearly all living things.

DRONE: The more common term for unmanned aerial vehicle (UAVs).

ELECTROLYTE: A chemical substance that helps the flow of electrons to increase an electrical current, as in a battery.

ELECTROMAGNETIC SPECTRUM: The complete range of energy and light wavelengths, from radio (the longest) to gamma rays (the shortest).

ELECTRON: A negatively charged subatomic particle.

EVAPORATION: The process of turning from a liquid to a gas because of heat or pressure.

EXTRUDER: A piece of equipment that squeezes out (extrudes) soft or melted material just as we might squeeze a tube of toothpaste.

FILAMENT: A thin fiber that allows an electromagnetic current to pass through it.

FLOPPY DISK: A magnetic disk, usually protected by a hard plastic shell, used to store data.

FLUORESCENCE: The process of emitting visible light after being exposed to a source of energy such as heat or light.

FUNGUS: A member of a large group of organisms that resemble plants but cannot make their own food, using sunlight and water, as plants do.

GENE: A section of DNA that is responsible for developing the makeup of an organism—how it looks and also how it behaves.

GENETICALLY MODIFIED: Having the DNA of an organism with a desirable trait (such as resistance to disease) incorporated into another organism. As this organism breeds, it passes on the desired traits to offspring.

GENOME: The complete set of genes in every cell of a living thing.

GEOSTATIONARY ORBIT: The orbit of a satellite circling the Earth in the same direction and speed as the planet's rotation so it remains above the same point on Earth.

GERM: A general term to describe a wide range of tiny organisms such as bacteria and viruses.

GIGABYTE (GB): A measure of a computer's memory capacity. It is just over a billion bytes, or basic units of computer information.

GLOBAL POSITIONING SYSTEM (GPS): A precise system of navigation that involves connecting a device such as a smartphone with signals from orbiting satellites.

GRAVITY: The force that causes all objects in the universe to be attracted to each other.

GREENHOUSE GAS: One of the gases (some of them emitted by human-made objects such as automobiles or factories) that collect and trap heat beneath the Earth's atmosphere.

HOLOGRAM: A three-dimensional image that has been projected and captured on a two-dimensional surface.

HYPOTHESIS: A proposed explanation based on available evidence, used as a starting point for experiments.

INFRARED: Invisible radiation with a wavelength just longer than that of visible light.

INTERNATIONAL SPACE STATION (ISS): A space station orbiting the Earth, launched in 1998, and continuously staffed since 2000. The ISS is a joint project by five space agencies: NASA, Roscosmos (Russia), JAXA (Japan), ESA (Europe), and CSA (Canada).

INTERNET: A huge network connecting millions of computers around the world.

LASER: An abbreviation of Light Amplification by Stimulated Emission of Radiation, a device that produces a powerful, concentrated beam of light.

LEUKEMIA: A form of the disease cancer that affects the bones and causes the body to produce too many white blood cells.

LIDAR: A form of technology that uses pulses of light to map a driverless car's surroundings.

MEDIUM: The environment or surroundings in which something can grow.

MEGABYTE (MB): A measure of a computer's memory capacity. It is just over a million bytes, or basic units of computer information.

MICROORGANISM: A living thing that is too small to see without magnification.

MICROWAVE: A type of radio wave with a very small wavelength.

MOLD: A fungus that grows on the surface of plants or animals.

MOLECULE: The smallest amount of a substance that still has all the characteristics of that substance; a molecule can be as small as just two atoms.

NANOTECHNOLOGY: A branch of technology dealing with extremely small objects, usually measured in nanometers.

NASA: An abbreviation of the National Aeronautic and Space Administration, an agency of the US government.

OPTICS: The scientific study of light and its properties.

ORBIT: The curved path in which an object (such as a satellite) moves around another object (such as a planet).

ORGANISM: A single living thing, such as a plant, animal, or microorganism.

PAYLOAD: The cargo carried by a rocket or other vehicle.

PHOTON: A tiny particle containing energy, including light.

PHOTOVOLTAIC: Relating to the conversion of sunlight into electrical energy.

PRINTING PRESS: A machine for printing letters or pictures on paper.

PROSTHETIC: The artificial replacement of a missing body part.

PROTOTYPE: The earliest working example of new technology.

RADIATION: The sending out of energy, often in the form of moving subatomic particles. Some types of radiation, such as gamma rays, can be used medically to treat cancer and other diseases. But too much exposure to many types of radiation can change the structure of human cells, leading to illness and death.

RADIOACTIVE: Emitting radiation as the atoms of a substance break down.

ROTOR: A spinning part of an aircraft with blades or propellers to provide lift.

SATELLITE: A spacecraft sent into orbit around the Earth or another planet.

SCANNER: A device that reads and captures images and converts them into data that can be used by computers.

SPACE SHUTTLE: A partly reusable NASA spacecraft that operated from 1981 to 2011.

SPECIFICATION: A detailed description (often called "specs") of the design and materials needed to make something.

STEM CELLS: Cells in a living organism that can change into a different type of cell and then divide to produce more of the same type of cell.

TRILATERATION: A method of determining the location of one point (in the case of GPS, the receiver) if the distances between that point and three other points (with exact locations) are known.

USB STICK: A small, rectangular device that stores large amounts of data and can be transferred from one computer to another.

VIRTUAL REALITY: A computer-generated simulation of a 3-D experience, allowing a person to interact using a special helmet or gloves.

WAVELENGTH: The distance between the crests of two waves, as in the distance between the crests of sound or light waves.

WIND TURBINE: A windmill-like tower that generates electricity from the power of the wind.

WORLD WIDE WEB: A system of information on the internet that allows documents to be connected to other documents.

GENIUS AT WORK!

More Books by
SEAN CONNOLLY

Sixty-four amazing experiments that require no special training, use stuff from around the house, and demonstrate principles like Newton's Third Law of Motion.

Fifty awesome experiments that allow kids to understand 34 of the greatest scientific breakthroughs in history.

Math rocks in this ingenious marriage of middle school math with fantasy in 24 problems that challenge readers on fractions, algebra, geometry, and more.

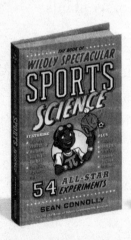

Fifty-four all-star experiments that demonstrate the science behind sports, from why a knuckleball flutters to how LeBron James seems to float through the air on a dunk.

The most infamous and dangerous disasters in the history of engineering come to life with 33 adrenaline-pumping experiments for daring young scientists.

Take an interactive tour through the periodic table of elements and discover the principles of chemistry through 24 experiments. It's elementary!

workman • workman.com